a cast of light

the story of the icpe mission

A Cast of Light: The Story of the ICPE Mission

Cover design by Stefan Attard and Sacha Attard Yeon

Image Credit: All photographs contained in this work are the property of Institute for World Evangelisation – ICPE Mission

Publishing services provided by Good & True Media
www.GoodandTrueMedia.com

ISBN: 9781505135954
Kindle ISBN: 9781505136494
ePUB ISBN: 9781505136487

Published in the United States of America by
Institute for World Evangelisation – ICPE Mission
38620 Lulay Rd
Scio, OR 97374
USA

www.icpe.org
IG: icpemission360
FB: ICPE Mission 360

Printed in India

a cast of light

the story of the icpe mission

Anna Cappello Fava
with A.G. Harmon

contents

endorsements

This book, *A Cast of Light*, needed to be written. Forty years ago, a group of people in Malta had the burning conviction that the Gospel had to be lived radically and shared freely. This book on the founding of the ICPE Mission, those committed to that mission, and their whole-hearted dedication to living and sharing the Gospel is timely and important in today's world. Thank you Anna.

—**Cardinal John Dew**, Archbishop Emeritus of Wellington, New Zealand

The ICPE missionaries are pioneers! At a time when few Catholics were even talking about evangelisation, much less doing it, the ICPE Mission began forming and sending out lay people to bring the light of Christ into some of the darkest places in the world. The Church has much to learn from this inspiring story.

—**Dr. Mary Healy**, professor of Sacred Scripture; member of the Pontifical Council for Promoting Christian Unity, the Pontifical Biblical Commission, and the Dicastery for Divine Worship and the Discipline of the Sacraments.

A Cast of Light is a must-read for any Catholic who yearns to "teach all nations" (Mt. 28:19) but has no idea where to start. It is the very personal account of the formation and travels of a growing, worldwide family of believers, told from the perspective of its mother. Like the disciples in Acts 1:14, who "devoted themselves with one accord to prayer", these courageous men and women set out from Malta to be "intentional" disciples of Jesus Christ. Her beautiful and inspiring story bears witness to the Truth that, in one's personal encounter with Jesus, the life of a Catholic evangelist is vigorous, lively, and fully engaged.

—**Robert A. Destro J.D.**, Attorney, academic, former U.S. Assistant Secretary of State for Democracy, Human Rights, and Labour; former member, Commission on Civil Rights.

A Cast of Light is more than a memoire of the founding and development of an extraordinary community. It is an invitation to take up the adventure of encountering a deeply personal, dynamic God who is alive, active in our world and in our lives, walking beside us, with us, and within us. In *A Cast of Light* there is nothing dull or formulaic. As Anna and the ICPE missionaries testify, we all have a call, and invitation to enter into the great adventure of God's mission in our world.

—**James Hanvey S.J.**, theologian, author, and retreat director; Secretary for the Service of Faith, Jesuit General Curia, Rome.

Anna Cappello Fava's beautiful chronicle of how a small group of Catholic lay missionaries from the island of Malta developed into a global force of faith, joy, service, and transformation is a balm for the soul. Anyone yearning for greater meaning and for a way to live faith to its fullest expression will find great inspiration in this delightful book. *A Cast of Light* brings the joy of the Gospel alive through a series of compelling stories about dedication to a mission of evangelisation across the globe.

—**Kerry Alys Robinson,** President and CEO, Catholic Charities, USA

The story of the ICPE Mission spans over 40 years of making Jesus known through witness, proclamation, and acts of mercy worldwide, for our faith in God shapes our vision of the world and our place within it!

—**Cardinal Peter K.A. Turkson,** Chancellor, Pontifical Academy of Sciences and the Pontifical Academy of Social Sciences

A Cast of Light illustrates how the ICPE Mission has transformed lives, inspiring many to live out their faith actively and wholeheartedly. This book is a valuable resource for those seeking to understand the role of laypeople in evangelisation and service within the Catholic Church. Within its pages, Christian readers will find inspiration and a call to step beyond the familiar boundaries of their spiritual journey. For those searching for meaning in their lives, this book offers a profound reflection on the possibility of embracing friendship with God.

—**Pino Scafuro,** Moderator, Catholic Charismatic Renewal International Service (CHARIS), Vatican City

The ICPE Mission is an amazing group of individuals serving the "least of these" (Matthew 25) in this world. They go into the world's toughest and most remote parts with hardly a thought to themselves to serve others. I hope you read this book! It's truly inspiring.

—**Tony P. Hall,** Ambassador and former U.S. Congressman

acknowledgements

This book began as a dream, but it took a few determined nudges—and the unwavering encouragement of the ICPE missionaries—to turn it into reality. For that, I am deeply grateful. My heartfelt thanks also go to all our missionaries who generously shared their vivid recollections and patiently answered my many questions, ensuring every detail was as accurate as possible. Without your support, this project would not have been possible.

A special thank you to Silvana Abela, our longtime right-hand person, and to Daniela Grillo, our secretary, whose efficiency transformed the daunting task of fact-checking into a seamless process. I am also deeply grateful to the International Council of the ICPE Mission for relieving me of other responsibilities so I could focus on this undertaking. Your trust and support are a true gift to me.

Having A.G. Harmon as my writing partner on this project was a rare privilege. A.G., I am deeply grateful for engaging your remarkable talent to help tell the story of my people and their God.

I extend my sincere thanks to Stefan Attard, a longtime ICPE member, and Sacha Attard Yeon for designing the book cover—your ability to transform a simple concept into a work of art is truly exceptional. My gratitude also goes to my dear friend, Mylène Colvin, for her meticulous proofreading, sharp eye, and constant encouragement. A warm thank you to Daniela for her careful final proofread—made even more delightful by the messages she sent as she experienced the book for the first time. Mariana Debono, your last-minute help with the Index was a true lifesaver—thank you!

To my husband, Mario—my list of thank-yous to you is endless.

To the prayer warriors, my siblings, and friends who cheered me on throughout this journey—I am profoundly grateful.

Finally, my deepest gratitude goes to all the ICPE missionaries, past and present, who bring the stories in this book to life. To those whose "yes" continues to shape the next chapters of this mission—this book is dedicated to you. After all, this is your story.

introduction

A single decision can ignite a movement.

Forty years ago, on the island of Malta, a handful of ordinary men and women made such a decision. With no grand strategy, no resources, and no guarantees—only a burning conviction that the Gospel must be lived radically and shared freely—they embarked on a journey that would transform countless lives.

From those humble beginnings, what started as a small community of Catholic lay missionaries has grown into a global family, spanning continents, cultures, and generations.

This is the story of that journey.

It traces the origins of our community—from the first spark of inspiration to the countless steps of faith that carried it forward. It introduces the men and women who laid the foundation and those who continue to build upon it, bringing the Gospel to the streets, villages, and cities across the world.

At its core, this is a story of encounters—a way of life born from a life-changing encounter with the Living God, the encounter of strangers discovered as family, and the encounter of enemies turned allies. It is a way of life sustained by prayer, the Word, and the sacraments, deepened in community, and lived out in the relentless call to bring the joy of the Gospel to the world. It is the story of missionaries who have left behind comfort for the privilege of service, of families embracing the adventure of faith, and of countless lives searching for truth and boldly acting on what they find.

Collectively, we form the Institute for World Evangelisation – ICPE Mission, and as our Mission Statement highlights, we are "an international Catholic community committed to transforming lives through the joy of the Gospel." The acronym "ICPE" reflects the Italian name *Istituto Cattolico per l'Evangelizzazione.*

Just as stories have long been the threads that weave history, identity, and purpose together, so too have they shaped our journey. The people of Israel preserved their faith by remembering God's guidance from Egypt, through the wilderness, and into the Promised Land. The Hebrew word *zakhor*, meaning "remember," carries a deep significance beyond just recollecting facts. To remember is to reflect on our past, understand our identity, and recognise our calling. This book serves as an act of that very remembrance to us as the ICPE Mission, those we serve, and those who may be inspired to journey alongside us.

More than a historical account, this book is a testimony to God's work in and through ordinary lives devoted to His purpose. I was there—I witnessed the unfolding of this journey from its inception, through both its glorious milestones and its trials. I have seen God's presence at work in the midst of our struggles, and the unwavering strength He imparts to those who place their trust in Him, carrying us through even the darkest times.

From the bustling streets of urban centres to the quiet corners of remote villages, our community has planted roots in places we never imagined, touching lives we never expected. And yet, the mission is far from over. As you turn these pages, you are invited into the unfolding story—a story still being written, a calling still echoing, a mission still waiting to be fulfilled.

1

jungles

They had heard our missionaries had a doctor with them.

The jungle was dense there, the dark green canopy shielding out the sky, filtering out the sun, so that everything beneath its fold was shaded and cloaked. Whatever light reached the forest floor was already weak, diluted even, exhausted by its long passage through limbs, and leaves, and vines.

So when the couple appeared out of the trees, there was already something unreal about them. That was owing as much to the fact that our missionary venture into the wilds of Borneo was only a few days old, as it was to the strangeness of these people's arrival, appearing as they had out of nowhere, in that dappled light. All about them were the jungle's unsettling, unearthly calls and cries, which never truly stop sounding in that hollowed-out place, within that ocean of green.

Our team of ten people had just arrived. They were all still within their own state of bewilderment, still adjusting from a series of flights from Europe to Malaysia, then a five-day, four-night trip by jeep over muddy roads, in which they were forever getting stuck, working around collapsed timber bridges and carrying only the most rudimentary of supplies. They had barely slept, as slumber comes hard in a sleeping bag, on a plank floor during an unaccustomed night. Mosquitoes were everywhere, making the nets that protected their fitful rest, the most valuable things that they had.

Besides the makeshift rug of banana leaves, upon which they ate their meagre provisions—pasta, tinned meat and vegetables, plain boiled rice—there was not a stick of furniture within the iron-roofed "long house" perched on stilts, which was to be their station. When the rains came, as they often did, water poured through the mostly open structure and flooded half the floor.

And here was this couple.

Our missionaries looked at each other, each with an identical sense of wonder.

How far had they come? How long had it taken them to find the camp? Had they travelled by canoe? On foot?

But none of that mattered when set against the purpose of their journey: the mother carried an infant, a newborn, perhaps only a few weeks old. His small body was no longer than her forearm. He was covered in open sores, red and weeping, erupting in fissures all over his tender flesh.

They had heard there was a doctor there. But they were wrong.

What did a doctor mean to such people? —desperately poor, living their whole lives in the nomadic tribes of the Malaysian jungle. The lot of them subsisted on rice as best they could; perhaps one or two families had a pig or some chickens. To such people, the idea of even the smallest convenience—water running from a pipe—light burning from a bulb—is hard to fathom. So, what could a doctor mean to them?

To this ragged couple and the isolated tribe to which they belonged, a doctor could only signify something like a phenomenon—something akin to magic. They had borne their new child from who knows where, over how many miles, through rain-soaked, mud-choked tunnels of vegetation, in search of something that must have seemed a miracle to them. And here were our missionaries, at the end of their journey, thousands of miles from home, unable to speak their language and unschooled in their ways. Not doctors; not miracle workers—willing, but inadequate.

To face inadequacy at such an early moment, when one has set out with the ambition to be of value and have influence, is a shocking and humbling thing. It is made all the worse by knowing that any feeble attempts are likely, even most probably, to be misunderstood as sufficient by those in desperate need of help. Our team alone knew, all too painfully, how ill-equipped they were.

The most they could do was provide a bath for the writhing, tortured child, cream to salve the sores that split his skin, and a fresh white towel to protect him from the incessant dampness of a place that even the sun can never truly reach. His chances were as dim as the shaded world into which he had been born.

But then, having done all they could physically do, the missionaries offered one thing more. They prayed. They lifted the suffering child up, offering his tiny body to that which lay far beyond the jungle's grim roof. They sought the help of the God who had knitted him together in his mother's womb, from whose hand he had so freshly come. Then, with prayers for his family and for God's providential care, they returned him to his mother's arms.

What this family felt about what had been done for them, who can say? The missionaries there at the time will likely never know. They only know how they themselves felt as the couple turned and disappeared into the dark damp from which they had come: an overwhelming sense of grief; that, and its awful companion, helplessness. The team had come from so far, eager to spread the great news of hope and love in the heart of this jungle, but they were now met at the very outset, with what seemed a rebuking defeat.

That day is over thirty-seven years ago now. So much has happened since. But the present, future, or even the past of the ICPE Mission, cannot be understood without recalling it and the Borneo expedition of which it was a part. It is a kind of emblem for all that has transpired, and for all that we hope is yet to come.

Although it appeared that our team did not have what the child and his family needed and that they were not what had been hoped for, without the skills, craft, and aid that was sought, the missionaries did have what had brought them there in the first place: a trust that they were part of an enterprise far greater than themselves.

Yes, they had that, and also something more. That is certain now.

Something was shared that day with those people, despite the millions of differences between the family and the ten missionaries who had come to Borneo. The family had a need—a very human need—their child was suffering miserably, and they did not have the power to eliminate it.

So, what did our people have? What did any of them have that could fill that need? And most of all, if they did have it—would they share it?

That was precisely what the Mission had come to do—to share what they had—what they had been given. It did not matter that it seemed embarrassingly inadequate in the face of the family's want. It did not matter that what was given was not even theirs—God's grace, channelled as He saw fit. What mattered was that ordinary, primal need, in a place so remote that time seems irrelevant and inconsequential there. In that need, the Mission was confirmed in the way it had been called: to reach people at their most basic level, at the ground floor of their desire, and to help them find the source of their provision. If our missionaries were to venture far beyond what was comfortable and familiar—ordinary men and women endowed with whatever talents God had deemed to bestow upon them— they were assured that what they were bringing was simply news, nothing more, nothing less—of the answer to those who seek, those who travel for so long and from so far, with a vast want that can be read in the pain of their eyes.

It is the news of friendship, of home. It is the news of solace and peace and an eternity of these things. It is the news that they are not lost after all, as they might have feared. It is the news that they do not have to search anymore.

Some days after that family and their child left the camp, our team received word. Alpheus, a fellow missionary who, along with a local man, Jason, had been one of our first ambassadors to the frontier of Malaysia, brought the report.

The child's wounds had healed. His skin was clear.

The light had made it through the forest after all. Despite all.

The news they had shared returned to them then, like an echo. It confirmed and sealed everything, convicting them of their purpose. Sharing the light that came that day in Borneo was to be the mission; we—those there in Borneo and all of us who have taken up this life—were to bear it, wherever it would lead.

Forty years later, it shines to whomever it is brought, over whatever it is shown.

This encounter on a trip to Borneo was one of our earliest ventures in what would become the ICPE Mission. Our journey began in the final quarter of the last century and now has crossed into the first quarter of this one, but what is definitional about our efforts remains the same. In many ways, that Malaysian mission outreach is a template for what we do and goes a long way towards explaining who we are to anyone who asks.

Our team spent eight weeks in that jungle. Eight weeks in which they slept in long houses and lived out of backpacks stocked with basic foods, flashlights, batteries, a change of clothes, toiletries, and only the most fundamental of medicines. Malaria and worms were the greatest plagues, though typhoid, hepatitis, yellow fever, diphtheria, and tetanus were also threats. As to malaria, nothing more effective than chloroquine existed at the time, but the malarial parasite in Borneo had grown resistant to it. One of our team fell so ill from fever and dehydration that only the extreme measure of a helicopter airlift wound up saving his life—a feat that in those conditions was itself nothing short of marvellous.

Days were spent in one of two ways, which now strikes me as something that resembles the Church in its earliest form. One-half of the group left the camp each morning and set out into the jungle to find people. A family could live at a great distance from others, and there were no settlements where people congregated in numbers—nothing like a "village" in the sense that the Western world conceives it. To make any headway at all in bringing the Good News of Jesus to the jungle tribes, first, they had to be found.

This half of our number would walk for miles into the jungle, fighting the mosquitoes, mindful of snakes and spiders, aware that you could stumble upon almost anything in that close, claustrophobic vegetation. Injuries were serious matters in so remote a place. The paths themselves were only rough markers even to the guides, as the grass and forest were always spoiling to reclaim whatever inroads men had made through them.

It was clear that the hard work of the first missionaries there, like Alpheus and Jason, had paved the way for our arrival. Yet while the tribespeople we met in Borneo—who had only a few decades earlier renounced the brutal practice of headhunting—proved to be welcoming, the possibility of rejection is something that those in this life must form a hard skin about—and early on at that. It is not easy to be rebuffed, or worse, only tolerated, and sometimes when efforts fail and pile up into a succession of failures, it can become embittering. But one must have a short memory about such things. Today's and tomorrow's defeats, which might even cascade into weeks and months, must be seen as part of the larger effort—the longer view—the objective of which may take time and persistence to achieve.

Patience is the hardest of virtues to cultivate, but it is essential to missionary work. Strangely enough, it takes courage to be patient—a heart stout enough to wait. It is always possible that something besides the planned objective might occur, some ancillary good that might be accomplished, precisely because of what had seemed only an obstacle, a delay, or a frustration. And if courage and patience are essential, trust is all the more so; it cannot be merely a word or an aspiration. It requires hard practice and much work to develop an attitude of surrender to God's providence. Courage, patience, and trust are a trinity of virtues that nurture each other in the missionary's life.

As this group cut their paths through the jungle in daily searches, the other half remained back at the main site. There, they tended to the daily needs of the mission team—cooking and washing while offering prayers for the group's efforts—like deacons in the early Church.

Having some of the team remain in place was also key to our purpose, as the site could not be abandoned in case the locals were to come by with some need or another. The missionary effort is always one in which trips, forays, and ventures are being taken, but only so that a foundation can be established. It is comprised of a great deal of movement—"toil and circumstance"—spent so that at some point, the seeds of the Gospel can be planted, take root, grow, and remain. The missionary travels so that the Church, the community of Jesus' disciples, can spring up and endure—so that others have a place to come to. We move so much in order that we might finally be able to stay put. This is just to say that those who mind the foundation are as important as those who clear a path towards it.

The people of Malaysian Borneo—as distinguished from Indonesian Borneo and the Kingdom of Brunei, the other two political divisions on the island—are historically a combination of religions: primarily Muslim, with a small percentage of Buddhists, Confucianists, and Hindus.

Christianity is second behind Islam in devotees, but second by a good-sized margin. The area to which our team travelled in 1988 had no association with any formal or recognised religion when it was picked to be one of our first outreaches as the ICPE Mission.

Had it not been for political instability in Kenya, our primary focus would not have been sending the team to Borneo. But several factors recommended it as an ideal second choice.

First, the location provided a good staging ground for non-native missionaries. The capital of the state of Sabah in Malaysia is the city of Kota Kinabalu. Leaders of the Light of Jesus Christ Covenant Community ("LJCCC"), a Catholic lay community from there, had visited us and pitched the idea of our coming into the area around the settlement of Paitan, in the Sandakan division of Sabah. This would allow for a friendly base from which European missionaries coming into the region—accustomed to working in urban areas—could acclimate themselves before setting out into the jungle. The LJCCC provided excellent support, as Alpheus and Jason, members of their community, were our guides in so many ways. The LJCCC families even hosted our team when they had completed their mission.

Second, the Catholic Church in Malaysian Borneo during the late 1980s was a vital institution deeply involved in life's spiritual, educational, and social aspects. Despite facing various challenges, it played a significant role in the local communities, thereby establishing a pipeline of support. Furthermore, other Christian denominations were working in the area, and a network of interdependence and cooperation was in place.

Third, the possibility of cutting a way into the heart of a tropical wilderness and bringing the hope and freedom of the Christian faith to a remote people—one who only a quarter century before had been quite warlike in their tribal skirmishes—had met the right time.

Our mission then was nothing short of radical in its level of commitment, a term I use quite literally. The men and women who were part of those pioneering days of ICPE Mission's history, the ones who were there at its birth, counted no costs in their commitment to this life. They quit lucrative jobs, gave up promising careers, and left expected trajectories that would have provided them with safety and security for years to come. And in place of that settled future, they chose to risk all in a great gambit—to live their lives like those two thousand years before them had lived—in the dusty towns and lonely byways of an ancient Middle Eastern world—following a first-century Jew, the Christ who had turned existence upside down.

Every choice those first ICPE missionaries made was a form of renunciation. It had to be, as to choose one thing is to deliberately turn one's back on many others. And there is always a cost to such a surrender—often quite a high price. The rational side of life counsels against it so vigorously that doubts constantly battle with convictions, however strongly the latter are felt.

For those who overcame their reservations, the ICPE missionary life in the late 1980s meant living together, starting out in a block of rented apartments in the fishing village of Marsaxlokk in Malta. They had nothing but each other and shared trust in God's guidance that they were to go somewhere, do something, and spread the Good News of Jesus Christ—a mission that made lines on a map irrelevant.

Young families with children and singles alike trusted that their daily needs would be met, just as they sought to meet those to whom they would bring word of a world transformed. The ten members of the Paitan team had recently completed the third, four-month ICPE School of Mission in Rome, previously known as the School of Evangelisation, where they pondered questions of who and what God is and our relationship to Him.

That was the nature—the makeup—of the ICPE Mission then. The expedition to Borneo was a confluence of the right people, the right time, and the right opportunity.

Weekly, up to thirty or forty tribespeople would travel three hours on foot to attend the meetings. No doubt, some of those who came did so because they'd heard that one of our crew would be there, a man they had started to speak of as the "jungle doctor"—not because of any medical training he possessed, but because he was brave enough and game enough to take on that role. He had once stitched a six-inch gash made by an ill-fated cutlass swipe. Jason, the local companion, had been cutting a path through the brush and opened the wound in his knee from misjudging the swath of his blade. Fortunately, our team member—a former policeman—had been practising "surgery" on a pair of old shoes and immediately flew into action. His job was so good that the recovering local was surprised to find that the procedure had been the first time the jungle doctor was put to the test. Therefore, his reputation preceded him whenever the call to services went out and was undoubtedly part of the draw for the crowds.

But no matter. Questions were never asked about motives; if people came, they were welcomed, regardless of the reason that prompted their journey. The life-endangering incident, frightening as it was, and though we would not have had it happen for the world, had been turned into something good. News got out about it, and it was evidence of one man's everyday efforts being called upon in the service of his brother. Even in such a thing as that, there is testimony.

Another means by which the team established camaraderie with the Malaysians was by showing them ways to improve their lives. To prevent the illnesses that constantly beset them—and could sicken or kill them so easily considering that they had no healthcare, the missionaries taught them how to sanitise and prepare their meals; how to clean their clothes and dishes; how to perform bodily hygiene and dispose of waste; and how to treat and care for wounds. Such gestures are part of building trust, an indispensable prerequisite to friendship, itself a prerequisite to community.

At the open meetings that our team held, Alpheus and Jason served as interpreters. Cheerful songs were sung, and everyone joined in clapping. One of the team would then read Scripture and deliver a message on God's love—something short and simple to begin the process. The team later broke up and prayed with individuals, so that the tribespeople too could start to understand that God is not a distant or impersonal force but knows us intimately and dwells in us through His Spirit to guide, comfort, and strengthen us.

The ICPE missionaries on this trip told of the inestimable reward of seeing the flicker of delight spark up and catch flame within the recesses of the human eye. They shared the refreshing joy of celebrating such things as Christmas with those who had just heard the astonishing news that the all-powerful God took on human flesh and lived among us to show us who He is and who we are. Gifted with a fruitcake, a bottle of whisky, and two chickens (it would have been four, but two escaped), our missionaries gathered the tribespeople and their children for a feast, carols, games, and sugary pancakes to celebrate the first Nativity beneath rough, improvised decorations. It is not difficult to imagine the gift of such an experience.

Of course, the work was and is just as hard as it is fulfilling. When trying to explain the mystery of God's love that Jesus revealed to us, despite an eager audience, finding the right words, even in your own language, does not come easy. Hoping that the meaning of whatever words you find can make it through the convolution of one tongue into another adds much more anxiety to the attempt. Moreover, the prayer services at the longhouse, amidst the stifling heat and humidity of the jungle, with people and dogs constantly coming in and out, sitting on the hard floor surrounded by backpacks and beneath makeshift clotheslines, were far from the kind of quiet, reverent affairs that stories and movies depict. The missionaries and the tribespeople were often tired, having travelled hours to get there and facing equally long journeys back. It is a wonder that progress in helping them learn of God's love and mercy was made in any way. But then one of the points to be understood about this life is that things happen despite all appearances and conditions. What seems to be happening or not happening is no indicator of what in fact is.

And what in fact was happening there—in the middle of that damp, dark jungle, surrounded by that close suffocating heat—atop rain-soaked plank floors and the cries of wild animals and the threat of disease—separated from electric light and stove-prepared food and forks and napkins and tables and chairs—swirling in a Babel of different tongues and cultures, old beliefs and primal instincts—was a beginning. It would become these people's embrace of Jesus Christ—God, made man—and of a community that lived by that truth. This had all happened a millennia before, along the sides of lakes and in the chalky mountain passes of Israel, and it was happening again in 1988 at Paitan, on the island of Borneo.

When the time on mission had come to a close, Alpheus and our missionaries reported to the bishop about the nascent Christian community in the jungle. The people there had been stirred by the news and the light that they were brought. They were open now, ready to grow in their faith. Hearing the result of that initial cultivation, the bishop was confirmed in his decision to bring more missionaries into the area to nurture what had begun.

For two years afterwards, catechists travelled in and out of the jungle, fostering the tribespeople's discovery of a living God and strengthening and enriching them. At length, a brick-and-mortar church was built, and over two hundred people walked up to its font of their own accord. They then bowed their heads to be washed with its waters and were baptised in the name of the Father, Son, and Holy Spirit.

Since that time, the Christian life in Malaysia—particularly in the jungle area around our first effort there—has flourished. Missionary orders of priests and nuns have come to the Catholic community, which can only be called established, now. Twenty-two primary schools, educating children six to ten years old, and four secondary schools, educating adolescents eleven to sixteen, have also taken root. While these ancillary, spiritual and educational developments cannot be tied directly or exclusively to the ICPE missionaries' work, they were part of a collective effort—a groundswell of Christian evangelisation—that brought that milestone to the area. As might be expected, this has also led to infrastructural developments around Paitan. The ten-member team's journey had achieved what all missionaries hope to achieve: establishing a lasting foundation for the Christian faith to grow and thrive.

That flourishing is not meant to be only spiritual. The entirety of the world order—everything that touches the human life, everything that the human life touches—the mystical and the material—the theoretical and the practical—is meant to be made new through the life, death, and resurrection of Jesus. That means that there is infinite variety and creativity in the missionary vocation. There is no limit to how Christ may be brought to the world—no contribution is too small, none too mundane.

It is hard to guess what good might, in turn, come from that early foundation. Perhaps one day, those from that place will themselves bring the Good News of hope and joy to others in a new place. The cycle may well continue. There is no telling where the light may lead. We are only assured that it does.

I might be asked about the implications of the Paitan story. If it is indeed a template or prototype for ICPE missionaries, as I say, is such a thing expected of those who are considering this life now? But the truth is that while some still give up careers and set out on expeditions to the remote places I have described, most ICPE missionaries now take a different but no less radical journey.

They are people who have recognised that they were created for more than merely to live as cultural or Sunday Catholics. Raised in a tradition and being tied to it by habit are not necessarily bad things; if they tie us somehow to Christ, then, of course, that is better than the alternative. Yet, as we are witnessing predominantly in Europe, such faith can be stultifying and depleting, contributing to a massive exodus from the Church. The ICPE missionary decides to live the Christian life intentionally—to cultivate a dynamic faith relationship with Jesus that is creative and productive of the good—in other words, to be an intentional disciple of Jesus Christ. Such a life is not static; it is vigorous. This life draws upon the Ignatian concept of *magis*, the unceasing pursuit of both a deeper engagement with God revealed in Jesus Christ, and the greater good of His children. In this way, the modern phenomenon of self-idolatry—an obsession with the superficiality of personal aggrandisement—is refuted. The dignity and integrity of the self are realised through the disciple's unwavering commitment to the way of Jesus. The result is both profound and ironic: giving up self-interest for the sake of others results in a paradox of transcendent riches—a hundredfold.

ICPE missionary disciples want to do something authentic with their lives—something that touches every dimension of the way they live. What they want wakes them up, gets them out of bed, and compels them through the day. It unites them with those from other parts of the world who speak different tongues and are formed by the hand of God in myriad ways—the African, the Islander, the Asian, the Westerner. They are not perfect, but they join with those no more perfect than they to spread the fragrance of the perfect Christ to every corner of the world. This makes them one. They are not alone, but they are the children of God who know Him and seek to share Him with those who do not.

They are players upon the world's stage, "going forth", as Pope Francis has envisaged, to a wounded world trapped in ignorance and indifference to Christ. They go forth as healers, as beggars showing other beggars where bread can be found, as those who have drunk deeply from Living Waters only to be left thirsting for more.

They share the realisation that holiness is not measured by moral perfection or the result of a planned life of asceticism, mortification and sacrifice; holiness is rather belonging to God, who, by way of the loving embrace of His crucified Son, engulfs the sinner and reclaims him—a lamb lost but found, a pearl of great price.

Their lives have turned into a celebration of divine and everlasting acceptance of a place at the eternal feast. Nothing can separate them from the love of God, revealed in Christ Jesus. Their gatherings lift praise to the One who walked out of the empty tomb and turned their dying into rising and their mourning into dancing.

They are people who know that the "jungle" today exists as much in the cities of our most urbanised civilisations as it does in the wilds of our most primitive ones. The paradox of our times is that awash in the pixilated light of a thousand technological suns, with our communications sent over a million miles being only a matter of how quickly our thumbs can type, and able to satisfy even the vaguest of whims by merely touching a computerised pad, human beings are more isolated than ever. They are more alone—more confused—and more anxious for their futures in an existence that pretends to include them but only betrays them with alienation and contempt. In twenty-five years, it is projected that almost 70% of the world's population will be urbanised, creating the cultural irony of claustrophobic crowds composed of complete strangers.

The ancient cultural institutions that bred unity and belonging have been undermined, which has led to the fragmentation—the shattering—of the individual psyche. The anaesthesia of pretence, seen in lives lived behind computer screens—on anonymous "social" media sites—or trapped within artificial distractions meant to numb despair through fleeting pleasures, but that really only worsen the condition—has led to a mental health crisis of historic proportions. This was only exacerbated by the pandemic and lockdowns of 2020, driving an already alienated humanity further into its pathologies with a cruel, merciless whip. As the late philosopher and commentator Roger Scruton surmised, even the artistic efforts of the modern age reflect this. Our twenty-first-century epics feature an individual estranged from his world and himself, seeking a place to belong but forbidden at every turn.

In short, we are rich in everything but clarity now, and the ICPE missionary disciple of today must face something much darker and forbidding than a rainforest filled with vines, much more threatening than a disease that can be fought by medicine from a bottle. Scepticism, relativism, and an increasingly hostile technological complex—witness the ascendance of artificial intelligence that, with breathtaking speed, makes whole professions redundant before a sun can rise and set—have led us into what some now call the post-human era. We watch, but we do not see; we move, but without destination; able to buy anything, there is nothing that satisfies us. In many ways, we have become no more than fuel for the relentless grind of a soul-killing machine. A missionary today faces all this, as well as the age-old enemies of false ideals about religion, an ill-formed understanding of the Church, and a history of all-too-true betrayals of purpose and trust.

But there is an answer; there is hope. We have the best pattern for what to do about the universal crisis as it comes from Jesus Himself; it was His way to form a small group—teach its members who He was and what that meant for them and the world. They were to then go out and do the same again—in small groups, learning the essentials of following Jesus, living their lives in support of each other as an expression and manifestation of divine love, and then venturing out to witness that love to others.

The early Church took shape this way, primarily in the homes of the believers and nourished by *koinonia*, cells of people who gathered for fellowship, prayer and the Eucharist. Increasingly, Christians everywhere are now pointing the Church back to its original calling: to be a gathered, united community that demonstrates the transforming love of God by celebrating together His presence in the journey of life. This is what the ICPE Mission points to. We do not follow Christ in isolation but as a people.

That is not to say that what begins in small groups produces only small results. On the contrary, the consequences of this dynamic are significant, both in objective and scale, as the following list bears witness.

In Singapore and Malaysia, ICPE communities bring together families, singles, professionals, and workers for in-depth and comprehensive formation, guiding them to live as intentional disciples of Christ in their daily lives. The ICPE community in Korea and Indonesia host retreats covering diverse themes, conducting Schools of New Evangelisation, reaching out to divorced adults, and running programmes that empower singles. In India, ICPE communities work actively with groups in their vernacular language and run online Bible courses, reaching thousands of subscribers. Their ongoing philanthropic efforts include food distribution and support of charitable causes for the elderly in hospitals and orphanages. In the Philippines, the missionaries' efforts intertwine humanitarian service with a passion for imparting the experience of God's care for the materially poor. The ICPE Mission community in Ghana has been extending crucial support in significant projects of *HopeXchange*, the humanitarian arm of the ICPE Mission, including the HopeXchange Medical Center, the Long-Distance Adoption Project, and the ICPE Mission school in Kantinkyiren. In the Americas, the ICPE Mission is present in Guatemala, where it runs another HopeXchange Medical Centre; in Colombia, by far the largest of the communities of the ICPE Mission, numbering over 2,000 individuals, member lawyers and social workers run rehabilitation programmes with prisoners, accompany prostitutes who want a different life, and work with disadvantaged children and their families; and in the United States, ICPE Missionaries run campus ministries, youth retreats, and parish programmes. In Europe, a dynamic, intergenerational community gathers regularly for prayer and Christian formation in Poland, transforming a former convent into a studio to cultivate a vibrant online faith community. The list goes on.

When I reflect on the abundance, the vitality, and the sheer beauty of the grace we've received, it feels no different from the first encounters we had many years ago in that ocean of green. I recognise the nature of the mission in it now just as I did then, much like how the face of the child can still be seen in the face of the man he has become. It is the simple transaction of one person, aware of his patronage in the family of God, and bringing that same knowledge to another—then allowing the wonder of that news to unfold in the countless ways that it will.

It is the transaction of the Paitan missionaries that day in 1988, who were brought a suffering child in great need. Such a small occurrence, but such a large moment in the eternal design—a moment of wonder and mystery. But then, it is no more wondrous than when I look back further still—to another moment, another experience, that is the true beginning of our story.

It starts in a place and time and occasion that not even a scriptwriter would have dared to suggest, with an altogether unlikely focus: a young man from Malta had wanted to be a pilot, but his eyesight wasn't good enough. He settled on being a doctor instead. And in pursuing his studies a thousand miles from home, in faraway Scotland, he stopped by an ancient church and walked about a college's medieval grounds. In one place, they were having a Mass, so he lingered a while. It was a blustery, frigid day; night would soon be falling; to his surprise, he was invited for something warm to drink.

Simply because it was cold outside, he said yes.

2

stepping out

In winter, the short Scottish day can be brutal. All the more so in a city. The wind whips and punishes those who brave it, seeking any chance to steal inside your collar or up your sleeve. The clouds are swollen and turbulent, pressing down upon those below and constantly threatening to burst. It can be too frigid to snow, but not to rain or drop a harsh frost. And in Aberdeen, on the North Sea, the cold gets inside the bones—the kind of weather that woollen and fires and teas can blunt somewhat, but only a hot bath can truly drive away.

The Scots are used to this, of course; their blood is thick from generations who have lived in their native climate. But for a visitor from the Mediterranean, it is a formidable part of the adjustment—as much as is the strong brogue and the hearty, combative spirit of the Scots. The warm waters that lap around the fishing villages of Malta seem impossibly far away.

So it was for Mario Cappello, only a few months shy of twenty. He knew no one in the city where he had come to begin his adult life. He only knew that it was freezing outside on a grey early evening in January of 1974 and that he would have to find a place to shelter while he waited. The college secretary at the University of Aberdeen, King's College, had agreed to meet him to discuss his plans to study medicine there, but the only possible time for an interview was after the man's scheduled theatre arrangements.

There were options among the places he could duck into. Old Aberdeen, north of the city proper, is a medieval town full of pubs and tea houses, and it's graced with all the expected spots that interest students and tourists. But King's College Chapel was nearest. At the northern quadrangle of the school, with its iconic tower topped with a stone crown, it stood with fortress-like permanence in the landscape. He had not yet been inside. So, to kill the time until his meeting, and to stay warm, he opened the door.

After the Protestant Reformation, medieval Scottish churches and cathedrals suffered the same stripping of the altars and violent iconoclasm that began in England. And as Scotland became the birthplace of John Knox and the Scottish Presbyterian Church, the Catholic character of almost all ecclesiastical buildings in the country has been largely erased. But that is not entirely the case with King's College Chapel. Dedicated to the Holy Trinity and the Nativity of the Virgin, it retains its fine medieval woodwork, the delicacy of its vaulted ceiling, its elaborately carved choir stalls, and the original rood screen. The antechapel still serves as a war memorial for the Scots who died in the world wars, and the distinctive smell of candles, altar cloths, and a worn stone marks the interior with a hushed reverence. All of this was at its most imposing on the dusky evening when Mario visited. He found the surrounding buildings to be equally lovely, and one was enhanced by the fact that a liturgy was being observed—an event that always adds to the importance of a sacred space when its beauty is being summoned in service of its intention.

Mario was captivated, as all tourists are. But as the service ended, he was met with a surprise. He had been noticed. Some of the young people there—likely college students, approached and asked if he would like to join their prayer meeting that was about to begin. Their friendliness and sincerity took him aback; it was disarming, unlooked for.

He glanced at his watch. His meeting was still a way off. It was likely even colder outside than it had been before he came in. Besides, they'd offered him a cup of hot chocolate. He had time.

It is no small shock to find that you're lost when you had no sense of confusion before. The landscape looks the same. For all intents and purposes, you're safe and unthreatened. You have not gone in the wrong direction; far from it. You're precisely where you've planned to be.

But just as the scent of smoke raises the hackles of a man despite no ostensible sight of fire, the feeling that you've lost your way is unnerving, especially when it won't abate. It colours the way you see things and disturbs what had always been a comfortable position.

In the shadow of King's College Chapel, wrapped within the architecture of an old faith, Mario had experienced something altogether fresh and new—at least to him: an authenticity, an earnestness, a vibrancy that was not opposed to the intellect, but was, in fact, enfleshing it.

The belief he witnessed was one that breathed and lived. It was evident that the people there possessed something that he did not. At that time, his life was lived in what he now calls a kind of "silent desperation"—a pointless, hollow set of motions. But the faces of those he beheld bore an air of serenity, as though manifesting an outward display of some internal resolution. It even had a kind of soothing impact. To his surprise, a rare sense of peace enveloped him as the singing and praying began.

But when the prayer meeting concluded and he went on to meet with the college secretary, he realised that he'd left something behind. Not a scarf or a hat. Not a glove. Not a wallet—but a way of being. He had encountered it there, in that prayer service, with those people, but now it had been replaced with this peculiar disorientation—a strong impression that something was missing. He wanted to go back.

There is a great irony in finding oneself at home so far from where you were born and raised, where everything from the language to the clothes to the music claims you as its own. But the kind of home that arrested Mario so entirely, was "home" in a different sense. It was in the sense of a state where the soul rests. It has nothing to do with geography, but everything to do with peace—ironically, a peace that is more complex than the word's standard definition.

This peace is an assuredness about a state that has been found, a certainty about its fitness—aptness—as if this is, of course, the way things were always meant to be. It is also a conviction—that in the soul's discovery, in its reclamation of its native kingdom, there is freedom from confusion and wandering and indecision. The soul can now be about its business, as it has recovered its orientation. The north and south and east and west of things are clear. Now it has a compass. Now it can move.

That was what Mario began to understand and feel in Scotland, but he could not put a name to it yet. Epiphanies sometimes break slowly. When his plans to study in Scotland did not work out for various reasons, he returned to Malta and took a job teaching high school chemistry. Still, the new yearning he'd felt in Aberdeen travelled with him as surely as if he'd packed it in his bags. It would not leave; it was there to stay. But he did not yet know what it meant or how it would change things in his life—though perhaps he was confident that it would.

He was to encounter it again when his twin brother Henry, himself, and their old friend Thomas were invited to an event at the parish centre in Balzan, an old village in the very centre of Malta. Mario was not expecting anything special that evening—certainly not the kind of experience he'd had in Scotland. But the Franciscan priest who invited the young men, Father Max Mizzi, had not asked them to come to an ordinary meeting.

What they found was a varied set of congregants of various ages, lay people, and religious backgrounds. And they were not all facing in the same direction—as is customary for an audience waiting for a speaker—but were in a circle, as friends who have gathered at a table. Some had their eyes closed, praying; others had their Bibles open on their laps, reading. At some point, they began to sing. Prayers followed, offered in a way that struck Mario as stemming from a different kind of relationship with God than he'd known—except that it was very much like what he'd seen in Scotland. The message delivered by the group leader brimmed with the same kind of sincerity and honesty he'd heard there as well. And just as in Scotland, when the prayer service was over, he felt the peace of home. Moved, he told the people there as much; he'd been lost but now had found his way.

He and his friends returned the next week, and the next, and the next.

What he was given in these meetings was different from the Catholicism he knew, for all its beauty and majesty. At that time in his life, prior to these experiences—perhaps due to his youth, when anything that is native or received is drawn into question—he'd grown fatigued with his faith, even indifferent to it. Of course, it is part of maturity to decide what you believe on your own and to examine the principles that are part of your legacy. Each person must pass a set of critical eyes over his ancestral home to ensure for himself the stability of its foundations and the beauty of its design. I was going through the same process, simultaneously.

Mario and I grew up in Malta in the late fifties and early sixties. At that time, faithful Catholic families, such as the ones from which we came, prayed the rosary and went to Mass daily. It was all part of the place's habit, not unusual at all, though it may seem so to a reader in the twenty-first century.

Malta was then alive with the legacy of its Catholicism, proud of the fact that the island played such an important role in the early Church. What other place has been blessed with the fact that the first itinerant missionary of the faith—and the author of practically half the New Testament—St. Paul and the gospel-writing physician, St. Luke, were shipwrecked upon its shores? The natives met them with hospitality, were graced with their miracles, and evangelised by their testimony. For the Maltese, the missionary life itself is part of the national heritage—a fact that could not and has not escaped our own notice.

In our youth, and still today, the villages came alive on the patronal feast days. Marching bands and fireworks displays at night were common all over the island. Special foods for the festivals include the traditional Maltese sweet "qubbajt" made of nougat, often containing almonds or other nuts, "imqaret"-deep-fried date-filled pastries, and not forgetting the famous "pastizzi"—flaky pastry filled with ricotta cheese or mushy peas.

Lent was particularly spectacular, with Good Friday the most impressive of all. In our time, everyone fasted on that day —a simple meatless meal to mark off the solemnity of what was being commemorated and to prepare us for our parts in the sacramental observance we were about to join. Not a shop or business was open, as the entire village poured into its streets, shoulder to shoulder, pressing in upon each other but also holding back to make way for the spectacle: all strained to catch sight of the processions of men in white robes, bearing platforms—"vari" in the local language—on their shoulders. Atop the elaborately decorated platforms were life-size holy figures depicting Christ's passions—His bearing of the Cross, His transfixion, and His agony as He endured it. Bands played dirges as the men passed, their gate in a military, penitent unison that seemed to make a single sonorous drumbeat on the paved stones as they passed. Attached to the marchers' feet, chains dragged behind them and scratched at the stone in a bitter melody. And among all of these "vari" were marchers dressed as biblical figures—Pilate, Abraham, the Centurion. On and on they came. It was impossible to look away.

This is all to say that the culture of Malta in our youth was infused with faith like dye colouring the water. But perhaps because it was so ingrained in us—so inextricably intertwined with who we were, who our people were, and with everything about the days, weeks, and years of our land—its impact had lost the ability to change, motivate, or inspire us.

Also, we'd both somehow formed the impression that God was distant, foreboding, and inaccessible. We were observant, following the rituals and habits of our families' faith, but in the rote, work-a-day fashion that demands no thought. What comes naturally is often done by instinct, not intention. It's no wonder that we both, independently, felt less and less tied to the spiritual side of our lives. And as the sixties and seventies gave birth to a generation of rebellion and societal flux, our languor and disillusionment found every reinforcement in the era itself. Besides, there were other things to be about: a career and self-fulfillment were the pressing focus—the practical and immediate things of the future, not the staid, ominous trappings of the past.

I now have a concept for what Mario and I most assuredly did not have in the late sixties and seventies, and what we were to find so completely in the new life that was about to come to us—him after his experiences in Scotland and Balzan, me after receiving an answer to an open-letter prayer in the form of a poem. The concept is "flourishing," and by that, I mean in the Aristotelian sense—the cultivation of a fulfilling, meaningful, and virtuous life. It is an invigorating process—a fountain, ebullient and effervescent—that transcends the empty trophies of earthly attainments. That is what both of us, independently, yearned for in our young, parallel states of confusion. And as things turned out, the realisation of our separate searches was to come by way of our paths' convergence. They had been headed in the same direction; ultimately, they met.

The poem I spoke of was written as I sat atop the rocks overlooking the harbour in the fishing village of Marsaxlokk. I was then living with my parents for the summer, and this place was a regular refuge. The brilliant blue bay that afternoon was full of "luzzus," what we call the brightly coloured boats in which the fisherman set out to sea. Behind me were the sandy-coloured shops, a church, and homes that hug the coastline, all guarded with a colonnade of palms.

If you've never seen Marsaxlokk, you must search for an image to gather what I describe. But the veritable mosaic that it paints along the blue Mediterranean Sea beggars all pictures, and even for the native, it has a power that makes you stop and stare. It could well be that the beauty of the day and that particular place conspired to make me especially reflective, as I'd come there to write. Poetry was, at that time, a means by which I could draft out the discontent I felt and probe my muddled understanding of life's point.

I remember it very well: I was listening to the waves lapping at the boats, rocking them in the water. I had heard that sound so many times, its rhythm as soothing as a hand upon a child as she falls into a summer's slumber. But that day the waves seemed to blend with the distant but distinct tolling of church bells somewhere—the round, whole, resonant sound of one solid call, followed by another, and another, and another.

The bells and the waves—each keeping the time—each marking the time—but also, as it seemed to me then—beckoning, summoning. They did this softly, in unison, and in a fashion as familiar as a song from one's childhood, forgotten for ages and then all at once recalled.

A profound nostalgia swept over me—a desire to have God in my life again—not a remote God to be feared—but a God who was as beautiful and present as the glory of the very place where I was. So I wrote that plea to Him—in that poem—that He would come to me in that way.

We often don't realise at first when God is answering us. But I can see now that He did not delay in His response. Within a few days, things began.

I can also see now that, in a subtle way, my turning had already begun, even before that day when I wrote my poem to God. Back in my school days, a group had come to lead us in prayer and conduct Bible studies. Mario, of all people, was one of the leaders. Though God would still seem distant from me, He never disappeared altogether but remained as one who lingers and waits patiently in the background.

Then, one day, after my encounter at Marsaxlokk Bay, I was drawn to a group of Charismatics singing and preaching on the streets—people who insisted we could know Jesus now as a living God, immediate and available, not as a historical divinity, abstract and aloof. A leader of this group whom I knew, a man we called "Dr. John," approached and spoke of a new Evangelisation Course. He wondered if I would be available to mind the attendees' children as it took place.

Much like Mario in Scotland, I'd been surprised with an invitation; and just like him, I found myself saying yes.

It may come as no surprise at this point that the Evangelisation Course I'd been invited to was being led by Mario, who I remembered from the prayer group at school. As the teaching sessions got underway, I undertook my own duties to organise activities for minding the children, but with an ear towards what was being said.

A great deal had transpired since Mario's night in Balzan. His was no longer a faith that was mainly memory lessons and precepts, a set of facts to which he intellectually attested but had no warmth for—as one knows how to work a math problem but is unmoved by the result. Instead, he'd found something vital. He'd begun experiencing God rather than just thinking of Him. Reading the Bible was no longer merely an intellectual exercise but a deeply spiritual and relational experience with a loving God who longed to enter into dialogue as a Father with a son, to guide and build him up:

> "I have struck you with the words of my mouth because I want love, not sacrifice ..." (Hosea 6:5-6)

> "I have come that you may have life and have it in abundance." (John 3:16)

These were not some words on an old papyrus or platitudes chiselled into the marble of a tomb. These were instructions for living a life of integrity, dignity, and vitality—messages whispered to the soul of a thing fearfully and wonderfully made. This was life. This was freedom. Mario, being a man who has never shied from either work or risk, knew that this apocalypse in his vision was not given him to sit with and reflect upon. So, he began looking for a way to start.

The land was to be tilled. The labourers might well be few, as the Scripture says. But as far as he was concerned, their ranks had just gained one man more.

As is so often the case, this revelation came to him not only by way of his own understanding but through the influence of others—those with a common fervour, a keenness that would not let them rest. As C.S. Lewis said, friendship occurs at the moment when someone turns and says with wonder: "You too? And I thought I was the only one." These included his Jesuit friends, who introduced him to Ignatian spirituality, as well as those in the Catholic Charismatic Renewal ("CCR") who had walked this path before him.

As the Church refers to it, the CCR is a "current of grace" that began in America among lay people. Recognised by the then Pontifical Council for the Laity, it draws upon Pentecostal spirituality that translates into a personal relationship with Jesus and the gifts of the Holy Spirit. The Australian Brian Smith, later to become the President of the then Catholic Fraternity of Charismatic Covenant Communities and Fellowships, had visited Malta in 1975. His powerful message had made a strong impression, and the influence of the CCR had grown steadily ever since. In time, Brian would ultimately prove a crucial guide in our lives.

Mario was called to be part of the CCR National Service Team in Malta, organising prayer meetings and conferences. Later, he would be the Director of the CCR in Malta. The CCR's spirituality also led people to form "covenant communities," committed to living a shared spiritual and communal life according to specific charisms and commitments, often formalised through a public declaration. This form would later heavily influence the shape that the ICPE Mission was to take.

In 1978, Mario was fresh from the impactful Dublin International Charismatic Conference, which had drawn approximately 20,000 people in attendance that year. He'd left that dynamic event with a charge to be a living witness for the Good News of Jesus, so he was well prepared for and receptive to Youth With a Mission ("YWAM"), a group of evangelical Christians who came to Malta that summer.

YWAM, with its roots in Pentecostalism and the Assemblies of God Church, is non-denominational but retains the same evangelical character as its founding. Mario followed them about as they preached in the streets and shared their testimonies about Jesus working in their lives. As a result, he became fast friends with members of the group and had them over for dinners at his home, hosted by his very gracious parents.

He was intrigued to learn that they had come to Malta from Lausanne, where they'd participated in a four-month School of Evangelism. Most striking was their authenticity as Christians, the love they shared among each other and extended to him—to anyone—as they spoke of Jesus. Their immediate fervour was the result of that time they'd spent in Switzerland, so if he wanted to possess what they had—and he did—there was nothing left to do but go there himself.

This was not an ambition that was met without objection. The CCR at that time—though it was ultimately to be acknowledged and affirmed by the last four Popes—was controversial. The era was so turbulent in the world and the Church, post Vatican II, that something very different from traditional Catholic expressions of the faith was met with fear and scepticism. Was this a movement that would upend the Church in a new reformation? In that context, Mario's plan to travel to Lausanne and be immersed in four months of formation from evangelical protestant teachers seemed to some, a dangerous course. He might well lose his faith. This could be the first step in his leaving the Church rather than his first step in bringing a fresh zeal to its testimony.

There was also a problem with his job. He was then working as an officer with the Malta Development Corporation. How could he expect them to keep his position open while he took a months-long leave of absence, one in which he would learn nothing to benefit the business but instead how to be a more effective Christian evangelist?

Still, he was not deterred, and his determination was quickly met with auspicious events that brought the trip to pass. With the help of his boss, a devout Catholic man who took his request to the highest levels of the corporation, he was granted leave without fear of consequence. His close circle of friends and respected Church leaders assuaged any concerns others had regarding his endangering his disposition towards Catholicism. So he arrived in Switzerland in January of 1979, almost a year after the Dublin conference had given him a charge to take up and bear.

The YWAM base was a five-story, thatched-roof hotel in Chalet-a-Gobet, a suburb of Lausanne. The place was surrounded by deep forests and the vast plain of Mauvernay, renowned for its hiking trails. Mario met his roommate, Scott, from America, and they struck up a fast friendship as they went through orientation on the facilities and the city.

What followed was something altogether new to him. There were classes, of course, and activities and prayer time, but the pattern of formation—meant to shape them in the evangelical enterprise—was not just through instruction. It was also imparted through living as a group in a communal effort. They were not to be simply a set of separate students with a common intellectual goal, but an assembly of believers learning to live together inside a system of faith—again, much like the way the early Church was formed. They were to share their lives as well as their witness. Within a week of living this way, Mario sensed God speaking to his soul in a clear, unmistakable commission:

What you experience here, bring to the Catholic Church.

One year before, he had left Dublin with the charge of being Christ's witness. Now, he understood that part of such a witness was to be brought back to his own Church.

He returned to Malta and shared his impactful experience in Lausanne with his brother Henry, who was also deeply involved in the CCR, and other close friends in the movement. Taking all that he lived in Lausanne into prayerful reflection, he sensed that the first step was to start at the small, intimate level—by building a community of lay people committed to a life of evangelisation. The model, taken from the early Church—worked as Jesus had worked—and it was being reclaimed from those ancient times and marshalled into action in the modern era through the efforts of groups like YWAM, the CCR, and others, sprouting in different parts of the world.

But there was more. Mario did not conceive this call to be ringed in by the sea surrounding Malta. It was to grow beyond its shores. That message was strong enough that in May of that same year, he wrote in his journal that in prayer, he'd had an image of himself "flattened like a bridge" between Malta and the world—a means by which the beginning here would move over whatever vast barriers seemed to forbid it and travel to other places, to make other beginnings. It had to start somewhere, and so it had to start where he was. Any journey must start where we stand. Mario stood in Malta.

He presented the vision of a community for evangelisation to the CCR leadership and other local Church leaders, who approved and blessed it. His initial step was to obtain a temporary release from his duties as Director of the CCR in Malta. Then, with the help of a young woman named Rosemary from YWAM, he set about planning that first Evangelisation Course to begin in October—the one for which I'd been asked to mind the children.

What I experienced through and with those involved in the Evangelisation Course was the answer to my poem to God. Through these new people and this new way, the resurrected Christ had walked through the walls of my defences and found me where I was.

It did not happen all at once, though. I was holding onto things that made me bitter and distrustful. They triggered an impulse to move further away from my faith rather than to look to it for an answer. But what began the day I sat at the Marsaxlokk harbour had split a crack in the carapace of my refusal. The waves and the bells had never ceased their soft, cadenced call, and in time, my resistance shattered and fell. I surrendered my trust. Nothing has been the same since.

June 1980 came around, and the next step in Mario's plan was announced. At the end of the eight-month Evangelisation Course, he rose and told us all that he was making an invitation. He asked whether anyone of us felt prompted to come together in a committed way as a community for evangelisation.

With this much—the idea of such a thing—we were all familiar, but he had more for us to consider—a bigger bargain if we agreed to undertake it. He did not mean for the proposed community to stay small, to remain a haven of comfort and consolation for those within it. He meant for the community to traverse the bridge he'd envisioned, to go out into the world and spread the Good News of Jesus—again, not just to Malta, or to Italy, or even to Europe—but to the whole world.

Such a proposition might be expected to face silence at first, as the charge is one that has to be considered. The first movements towards its acceptance started to stir within our group, I'm sure, but at the time, no one was quite ready to come up and accept the invitation. No one but me that is; perhaps no one was as ready as I.

What Mario was proposing was the path I'd wanted, and I knew it utterly. I might have been the only one in the room feeling the way that I felt—I might have been the only one asked, so complete was my receptiveness to the call. It found its echo in the verses from Isaiah 61 that I'd heard Mario preach upon, words I marked in my Bible that day:

> The Spirit of the Sovereign Lord is on me,
> because the Lord has anointed me
> to proclaim good news to the poor.
> He has sent me to bind up the brokenhearted,
> to proclaim freedom for the captives
> and release from darkness for the prisoners,
> to proclaim the year of the Lord's favour…

It was yet another way that God answered the prayer of my poem. I had wondered, "What next, God?" Here was His response, calling through the waves and the bells. This was my next.

Mario and I began to pray together, with Isaiah 61 as our guide, interceding for those we hoped would join us in this community. We set aside Thursdays as our community day, even when it was only the two of us. Patience was called for, but only three months later, two couples showed up.

Then more came. Every Thursday we met in each other's homes, worshipped God, read Scripture, and enjoyed each other's company. Communities of this type were spreading throughout Malta, and the National Core Group of the CCR granted them formal recognition.

More came yet, people of all ages and walks of life, and the original plan to meet in each other's homes on Thursday evenings had to change. The Franciscan Friars generously gave us a meeting space in Villa Lauri, a magnificent townhouse in Birkirkara that had come under the Friars' auspices. One of our fondest memories is of the monthly "Agape Meals" there, with different members helping to put together a feast meant to celebrate our togetherness in Christ. The surroundings were grand, but it was the humble strumming of a few guitar chords and sincere prayers that transformed the community gatherings into a vibrant, mini-Pentecost of the Holy Spirit.

Our most significant endeavours were the Friday outreach efforts. This was a serious undertaking, going out to find others and point them to the Light—much like the later ventures into the jungles of Paitan. We prepared for them with prayer and fasting to mark the mission's importance and to seek grace for those who would serve that evening in different capacities.

This too was rewarded. Hundreds of people from across the island started attending our "Life in the Spirit" seminars, filling the hall at Villa Lauri to hear about a life-changing encounter with the Holy Spirit. The meetings grew so full that once again we had to move, only to find the same phenomenon reoccur at our new hall on the top floor of the Catholic Institute in Floriana. Whenever we found a new, larger space, God filled it, week after week.

As Mario and I were thrown together in those early days of the mission—two young people living in a vibrant community of faith with a shared objective—it was naturally only a matter of time before the personal dimension of life would present itself. Mario wanted to take our relationship further. It was the next step, so he presented the question. As I've said, one of Mario's gifts lies not only in perceiving which course it's time to take but also in having the courage to plunge ahead and take it. Mario can make a decision.

But at the time, I wasn't so sure. I was young and enjoying being single. I'd found a great purpose in my life, and that was enough.

There was no need to complicate matters. And on top of that, I'd always preferred the kind of boyfriend who rode a Harley Davidson and could keep up with me on the dance floor. Mario was made of different stuff. There were other differences, and they all added up to make the idea impossible. Resolved, I went away on holiday with my close friend Tania and put all such considerations out of my mind.

Or so I thought. When I returned only a month later, something must've changed to bring me around and open me up to a longer view. God was helping me appreciate things in a man like Mario that I hadn't before. For some reason, I decided going on one date wouldn't be totally out of the question. It cost nothing to do that.

That was in January of 1981. What followed was a two-year courtship not unlike the kind of cosmic turmoil that occurs in an interstellar collision—at times seeming as though things are in unison and will combine in a peaceful co-existence—at other times showing signs that the whole thing will end in an incendiary implosion, or explosion, or both. But following a period in which we took a break to discern where we stood, we came back together. The stars started to settle into a rough pattern, dodging each other here and there so that the spheres aligned and hummed along in mutual peace.

We were married in January 1983 in a packed church. My mother sewed my wedding dress, and Mario's lovely sister was my bridesmaid. We had so many priest friends that the altar was filled with concelebrants—as though they were there in large numbers to make sure the match of such opposites held good and tight.

We knew we were headed into a different life even then, so our newlywed apartment was a small, sparsely furnished studio. But the place was always bustling with family and friends coming in and out. I recall it now as being redolent with the fragrance of cakes and cinnamon biscuits and with members of our young community sitting around the floor on cushions instead of sofas and armchairs.

Mario and I are as different as night and day, yet people say our differences create a remarkable synergy that makes us an exceptional team. He is more rational, analytic, and objective-driven—a gifted preacher, but also an introvert, more interested in how long the party is going to last and when it will be time to go. For him, music means classical music, period. I am more creative, intuitive, and concrete in actualising the plan—a teacher and a people-person who not only throws the party but also wouldn't mind if it never ended. For me, there is *every* music—and all the better if you can dance to it.

But together, we balance each other in an equipoise that God has made, a point and counterpoint of His design. For that, and each other, we are eternally grateful.

Such a relationship did not happen by chance; rather, it is the product of intentional, persistent, and mutual effort. Like iron sharpening iron, we've allowed each other's influence to refine, enrich, and ennoble our lives. At times, this involved confronting uncomfortable truths in ourselves and each other. But then, God often uses our partners to shape us into the version of ourselves that fulfills the design He has planned for us.

"You cannot walk on water unless you step out of the boat. It's up to you to decide to get out."

Father Elias Vella, a holy Franciscan priest and lifelong friend, told us this at the beginning of our marriage. It was when we were about to undertake our boldest step yet—both of us resigning our jobs and devoting our lives to full-time Christian ministry. No words have ever rung truer. Reckless and irresponsible—it certainly seemed; audacious it certainly was.

But had we not stepped out, we would not have paired up with two great brothers from YWAM—Bruce Clewett and Rob

Clarke—who assisted us in leading our first School of Evangelisation in Malta in January 1985.

Had we not stepped out, we would not have known the adventurous times spent setting everything up in a block of apartments in San Ġwann—one housing Mario, me, and the ten men who joined the School, all sharing a single bathroom, another for the women who joined, and the other two serving as kitchen, dining room, laundry, and a lecture hall stationed just above an animal farm. The latter circumstance made opening the windows for a breath of fresh air a completely futile enterprise. If the pipes weren't leaking in that building, they were bursting, so that we were never left so long in our studies that we were allowed to forget the hard labour that supported them—through mops and buckets and floor cloths.

But had we not stepped out, we would not have experienced our courageous community joining with us to turn a dream into reality six years on. The community prayed incessantly for this School and rolled up their sleeves to clean and furnish the living spaces from scratch. Silvio, for one, purchased second-hand angle iron beds from 'il-Pickless' of the NAAFI House, which formerly supplied services to the British Armed Forces stationed in Malta. He then painstakingly scratched the old paint from each one to give it a fresh coat. Then came the washing machines, wardrobes, and other furniture to be carried up the winding staircases, and Karmenu, Philip, Tancred, and all the rest lent their strength to ensure it was done. Bed linen and kitchenware had to be provided, and the women provided all. The community numbered less than thirty people at the time, yet entirely on faith, they brought water and trusted that it would turn into wine—which, of course, came to pass in this, the foundational effort of what would become the ICPE Mission.

Yes, Mario had meant to be a doctor but had gone to Scotland and been invited in from the cold. He came back to Malta a changed man.

I had gone to the Marsaxlokk harbour to write but was stirred by the sounds all around me. Friends had invited me to mind some children. I came out a changed woman.

Since that day, upon which our journeys crossed and joined, we've never failed to be surprised at the paths God has led us through or in the changes He has brought about—always in directions and ways we could never have predicted.

But had we not stepped out in faith, as Father Elias counselled, we could never have known the joy of walking on water—sustained all the while by Christ—the One who rebuked the wind and calmed the waves—who told us, over and over and over, that we were not to be afraid.

So we stepped out, and grace took over.

3

crossing the waters

On October 22, 1978, newly installed Pope John Paul II celebrated his inaugural Mass in Rome. As part of the day, he stood ready to deliver his speech, looking out at the sea of faces gathered in St. Peter's Square to hear from the first non-Italian Pope since the sixteenth century.

What would he say? They all must have wondered. Something extraordinary had happened in the selection of a Polish pope; surely something extraordinary would inspire his first address.

And John Paul—then young, strong, vigorous—did not disappoint. He delivered a message drawing upon the words of Jesus when He'd calmed the turbulent sea for His disciples, and when He'd urged Peter himself to walk upon the waters without succumbing to them: "Be not afraid."

As the violent twentieth century ended and the uncertain twenty-first dawned, he saw the moral dread in the hearts of the faithful and emboldened them with a divine call to courage.

Courage had been Father Elias's counsel when we'd begun our mission; courage was the direction of the new Pope in 1978; courage was the charge of those, Mario included, who returned from the CCR's Dublin International Conference that very same year to be witnesses for the Lord who had uttered those words: "Be not afraid."

I've spoken of courage, patience, and trust as a trinity of virtues that sustain any missionary. They generate each other—make each other possible—in a perpetual interflow of one to the next. So it was a particular gift that at the prospect of the millennium's turning, Mario and I would be given the opportunity to meet this apostle of courage and, best of all, to obtain his blessing upon what we were proposing to do.

It was 1986, and at the time of our meeting with the Pope, we had only the year before completed our first School of Evangelisation. We had also just pioneered the first outreach efforts in Rome and Austria and were on the eve of launching our first School outside Malta. Things were moving fast.

But in addition to those monumental first steps of the ICPE project, Catholic groups in the Charismatic Movement were coming together for what was to be the Church's largest evangelistic effort in history, *Evangelisation 2000*. Our friend, Father Tom Forrest, a Redemptorist and then Director of the International CCR, was the mastermind behind this initiative to train scores of lay evangelisers in anticipation of the year that would mark the great transition. The endeavour was to include *Lumen 2000* within its remit, which itself aimed to launch evangelistic efforts through the mass media, particularly television. The culmination of the effort would be a worldwide satellite telecast on Christmas Day, 2000.

In the last decade of the twentieth century, the whole world lived with its eyes on the coming of the third millennium. People were both excited about it and fearful of it, some expecting a dawn of hope, others sure of a coming apocalypse. As for Father Tom, he and his collaborators were ready to seize the opportunity of such a pan-global focus: "The year 2000 is the celebration of Christ's incarnation," he'd said, "the centrepiece for all creation, for all history, and all nations." It meant "nothing less than a greater presence of the Lord Jesus", and the goal of *Evangelisation 2000* was "to give Jesus Christ a 2,000th birthday gift of a world more Christian than not."

As Father Tom was a great mentor to Mario and me, a devoted patron and advisor who wholeheartedly championed the vision of the ICPE Mission, he'd included us in his inner group of collaborators, intent on bringing the plan to bear. And we and our staff were in Rome preparing for our first School there in September of 1986 when Father Tom asked us to accompany him to a meeting with Monsignor Stanislaw Dziwisz, the Pope's personal secretary, to explain the initiative of *Evangelisation 2000* and our Schools of Evangelisation. Monsignor was receptive, but came up with a better idea than that of letting him act as our intermediary:

Why couldn't we simply present the plan to the Pope himself? he asked.

Not only were we asked to do that, but we were to do it that very night. At dinner. At Castel Gandolfo, where the Pope's apostolic palace is located, high in the Alban Hills.

Somehow, one of us must have found enough composure to say "yes" to the invitation because the next thing we knew, we were in the van—Mario at the wheel, Father Tom and I alongside.

Quickly, we had to decipher a set of archaic road maps, as this was in the pre-GPS days, when getting lost was a real possibility. Then, with a rough idea of the roads to take, we made our somewhat stunned way through a lovely autumn afternoon towards the village, which is truly one of the loveliest in Italy.

Although dinner was not until eight o'clock, we arrived early enough to walk around the streets, take in the breathtaking views, and let the beauty of nature level our excitement and calm our nerves. But before long, it was time to gather a deep breath and approach the stately, pastel façade of the apostolic palace.

The Swiss guards—always a glorious sight in their Renaissance uniforms—let us in. Monsignor Dziwisz then ushered us down a warren of dim corridors and left us in a small waiting room. I had only enough time to glance about at the antique mahogany furniture when the door creaked open.

Upon meeting a man who would be partly responsible for the fall of communism in Eastern Europe, who had chosen Mission Sunday to deliver his first papal address about a dynamic, missionary, and universally engaged Church, and whose long papacy had spanned the Cold War, the rise of secularism, the clergy abuse crisis, and significant cultural shifts—you might be forgiven for expecting someone altogether otherworldly. It's an intimidating moment, that of waiting for an individual who would one day be declared a saint.

The Pope was indeed a man who faced down his adversaries, be they human or circumstantial, and stood his ground. That was obvious to all who saw him; all that was reported in that line was true.

But the impression John Paul made upon Mario and me that evening included not only those factors but also the feeling that we were among a humble and welcoming host. With us, he seemed, above all, to be a simple Christian—first and foremost—a man fulfilling his vow to be a servant of the servants of God. He wore no zuchetto, no cincture for his cassock, and his hair had been smoothed hastily. It even seemed that he'd just slipped on his shoes and come downstairs in a rush, the way you greet a family member who's dropped by to say hello. All of this put us at ease, which was said to be his way—and I can confirm that it was.

Despite the surroundings, the comfort of the atmosphere he created carried on to the dinner table. The Pope, Monsignor Dziwisz, and the Pope's other secretary, Monsignor Mocombo, were our hosts, and we were served the typical Italian meal that was said to be the weekly fare: stracciatella soup as a starter, veal with vegetables and roast potatoes as the main course. Fresh raspberries, which John Paul was pleased to say had come from the Vatican gardens, were served for dessert.

As we ate, he listened to Father Tom explain the hopes for *Evangelisation 2000*. I remember the Pope tapping his fork gently on the table as he contemplated what was being said about training a host of Catholic laity to make the new millennium more Christian than the last. He was sincerely and intently listening.

When such momentous occasions happen, as at the dinner that evening, it's difficult to appreciate everything that transpires in real time. There's an overload of sights, sounds, and comments. But after it was over when the three of us drove out to nearby Lake Albano to walk about its shores and reflect upon the encounter we'd just had, something occurred to us.

In addition to explaining *Evangelisation 2000* and winning the Pope's approval, Father Tom shared the story of our first School of Evangelisation in Malta. John Paul wanted to know more. So we elaborated on how we'd taken our zeal for sharing the Gospel onto the streets, into the schools, behind the prison walls—anywhere that would open the door—and through testimony, song, and dance offered people a new way to encounter Jesus. We also explained how at the end of our school's formation period—what we call the three-month "lecture phase"—we'd travelled to Rome for what we call the one-month "Outreach Phase," the fruitful application of the lectures. The group had performed a well-rehearsed and costumed pantomime on the salvation story entitled "*He is Alive*"—a captivating crowd magnet—and followed it with a short preaching, testimony, spontaneous conversations and prayers among the gathered crowds in Piazza San Pietro, Piazza di Spagna and Piazza Navona.

The Pope smiled, bright-eyed at our story, and then said: "Don't be surprised if you see me joining you on the streets of Rome one day."

It was the same affirmation of a new evangelisation that he'd called for a few years before, in Haiti, at an address to the Latin bishops: "Evangelisation will gain its full energy if it is a commitment, not to re-evangelise, but to a new evangelisation—new in its ardour, methods, and expression."

He'd encouraged and expected something novel from those who pioneer at the front lines of the mission of the Church to bring

Jesus to the world. Walking about the shores of Lake Albano that autumn evening, we fully realised what had just transpired at Castel Gandolfo.

We had come there seeking the Church's understanding and blessing of our humble attempts to breathe fresh life into its missionary heart. We had left there with the heart of the Church, breathing fresh, missionary life into us.

The first School of Evangelisation, of which we'd spoken to the Pope that night, had been the natural fruit of a long gestation. It was the result of a holy seed planted in Mario's surprising encounter in Aberdeen, Scotland back in 1974, watered on the YWAM school in Lausanne in 1979, and through the years of tending and husbandry by a growing flock of believers with similar calls, it came to bear in January of 1985. But if we'd ever needed the courage I've spoken of, we needed it then, in the early days when we were preparing to launch that School.

The San Ġwann apartments were in place—our local community had done yeoman's work to help set them up with furniture and necessities. And a strategy for how to form the new evangelisers was determined—a systematic progression building on our relationship with God, leading to our relationship with the Church, then finally moving to our relationship with the world. In the pre-internet era, promoting the School demanded relentless effort. We assembled and mailed brochure packets to a global network of CCR leaders, inviting applications supported by two confidential references. In a remarkable blessing, an international courier dispatched them for us free of charge.

It is a distinctively unsettling set of feelings one has—a peculiar vulnerability—when you put every bit of your energy into an initiative. At the same time, a gnawing concern lingers—what if nothing comes of it? We were proposing something completely new for the Catholic laity.

Anxiety is not something that stops haunting you just because you're doing what you believe is God's will. It is a relentless foe that must always be fought, bringing us back to trust and patience. They indeed sustained us in those days. In fact, the School was the result of our meditating upon II Chronicles 1-2, in which Solomon asked God not for riches or long life, but for wisdom. God had favoured the humble request, and Solomon built His temple. With that scripture as our model, all we could do was ask for God's wisdom, summon the courage to open the doors, and then trust and wait.

Joy, gratitude—and, I must admit, relief—came by way of twenty young people from eight different countries answering our call. They came from New Zealand, Germany, Austria, Holland, Ireland, America, Switzerland, and Malta—all of them enthusiastic, eager to learn, perseverant, despite endless water leaks and electricity cuts and cramped quarters. Our mornings were spent together in Mass, prayer and lectures, followed by afternoons spent on everyday chores, and then evenings made up of small groups, staff meetings and closing sessions. There were plenty of organised activities on the weekends, and the friendships we formed were easy and long-lasting. They endure to this day.

But Mario's plan—the vision he'd had when the first community was formed—was to reach beyond Malta—to stop at nothing short of the whole world. So within a month of starting the School, Mario and one of our community members, Noel, travelled to where we'd felt led to open our second School—in the very heart of the Church—Rome.

Patience was again in order, however, as well as trust and courage. With the first School in Malta up and running, Mario couldn't stay away for long trying to locate a place to house the second School. His mind was unavoidably divided—half in Malta, where he ought to be, half in Rome, where he had to be—had to be, that is if the Mission was to follow the original plan of crossing the waters and reaching the four corners of the world with the Good News.

To make things more trying, it was an unusually cold and wintry February for Rome. He and Noel had to brave sharp weather as they searched for a locale, and they were met with only well wishes and sad regrets. Refusal followed refusal.

Then it began to snow.

Not just a powdering of snow, as might be expected in Rome's mild climate, but a heavy snow. It covered the Colosseum, the Spanish Steps, and St. Peter's Square—the whole of the city was blanketed in what made for a rare and beautiful scene of the eternal city, clothed in white. And Mario and Noel would've considered it a privilege to see such a sight were it not for the fact that they were on a bus, headed to an appointment at the Dominican Sisters of St Rose of Lima in Via di Val Cannuta—one of their last hopes for the school's location. To make matters worse, the bus driver announced that the city had declared a state of emergency. Bus service was suspended. They would have to get out and walk.

Making the appointment on time seemed all but doomed, and Mario had little heart for Noel's suggestion that they pray for divine intervention—for the weather to clear and the sun to come out. But he couldn't very well be the leader of the Mission and exhibit such a display of doubt, so he asked Noel to start praying.

All he can say now is that the weather did clear that afternoon; the bus service did resume; they did indeed make the appointment at the convent; the nuns did in fact give their permission to house the School in Rome.

Within the remarkable snow globe of a Roman February in 1985, things were set in place. The Mission would cross the waters by the autumn of the following year by way of its second School of Evangelisation—-the first in Rome.

Back in Malta, while all of this was happening, we undertook new ventures with the School staff and our local community. It was a time when we were feeling out the scope and shape of the Mission, to hoist the sails and allow the Holy Spirit to blow us wherever we were to go.

One example is the birth of the Youth Ministry. We'd conceived of a short weekend retreat for around 50 young people at the Mount St. Joseph Retreat House in Malta. But in the end, we had to borrow military beds and allow for sleeping bags on the floor to accommodate the 250 young people who actually showed up. We tested the waters again with a more challenging outdoor gathering in the remote Zurrieq valley of southern Malta; again, we were overwhelmed by the number who came. The Youth Ministry eventually evolved into a vibrant weekly worshipping of God, with 400 young people on average attending the events.

After the first School term ended, we also took time to travel back to Rome and Linz, Austria, on mission trips. These were taken in July 1985 and were comprised of our ICPE missionaries, local community members, and Youth Ministry members—all intending to share the joy of the Gospel but with another objective in mind as well. Such trips were a means of tightening and strengthening communal bonds.

Then, in the autumn of 1986, we launched the second School of Evangelisation in Rome. The planning for this return was aided by the gift of our first computer—a generous contribution from the parents of a young American volunteer—which helped us break into the technological age. If the first School got our feet under us and enabled us to stand, take shape, and prove our mettle, the second School established us in the Catholic world. Cardinal Tomko, the then Prefect for the Congregation for the Evangelisation of Peoples, visited us with other Church dignitaries, marking a great step forward in the Church's recognition of our Mission.

As the lecture phase of the Roman School drew to a close, just before our planned outreach in Malta, we extended a bold invitation to the students. Regardless of their talents or skills, were they ready to take on the challenge to become Vision Carriers—champions of the Gospel—ready to take on the world for Christ?

Thousands of years before, Isaiah answered God's call with a bold reply: "Here I am, Lord. Send me." In response to our call, twelve young men and women from six different countries—Germany, Holland, New Zealand, Mexico, Korea, and Malta—agreed to be sent that day. We had never felt more convinced of our stepping out to take this path.

As I said, our Outreach Phase for the Roman School was to occur in Malta, so we all packed up and headed south by train. Just before our departure, Pope John Paul himself had seen us off with a warm private audience for the participants.

It was the middle of December 1986, so winter was in earnest. At that time, you could get to Malta by ferry from Catania, in Sicily. It was a seven to eight-hour trip, depending on the ferry line and the weather conditions. But as though to remind us that we would be tested and tried in our future lives together, a set of storms and harsh winds hit Catania as soon as we arrived. The ferry company cancelled our trip, and in fact, all the lines suspended service. That left us on the dock with tons of baggage, no money, and nowhere to stay.

St. Paul was shipwrecked onto Malta, where he hadn't meant to go; we couldn't find a ship to get us there, where we most certainly did mean to go.

But even this worked to the good, as we came together and navigated our way through the test as a group—practice for the demanding experiences that make up any life, including, and perhaps especially, that of the missionary. Despite the freezing temperatures, two big American young men in the group volunteered to guard our bags, which we'd sequestered in an empty shipping container. The rest of us set out to find a place to stay for the night—pre-Christmas exiles in search of a room at the inn.

With little cash and credit cards seldom used at the time, we found nothing except the sacristy of a nearby parish. The parish priest let us huddle inside the cold, marble interior, and we found ourselves congregating around the votive candles as much for warmth as for consolation. Nevertheless, we settled in. Someone even located a coffee bar still open that was selling paninis, and we feasted on them like they were the divided loaves and fish.

It took us three more days in the same half-starved, half-frozen conditions to get back to Malta, and Christmas was never as bright and warm as it was that December. Few of the new missionaries had experienced Nativity celebrations to the extent that we enjoy them in Malta as a matter of course: Nativity cribs everywhere; Christmas plays and carol-singing; Christmas cake and mince-pies; and the solemnity of a midnight Mass, with the Nativity Story proclaimed by a child. All these things made up the pageantry of that season then, and thankfully still do, to some extent.

In the following spring, the twelve "Vision Carriers" of the ICPE Mission moved into rented apartments in Marsaxlokk, the fishing village where I'd heard God calling me back to Him years before. Then more apartments were rented so that members of our local community could live close by the twelve missionaries and form a more extensive, consolidated community. Men's and women's residences were established in the fashion of a residential college, and we designated a makeshift lecture hall and chapel. Our beloved Father Karel, a Mill Hill missionary from Holland, became our resident ICPE missionary priest.

It is easy to make too much of first things; they carry with them an understandable nostalgia. But that is not the case when we look back at this first ICPE missionary community in Marsaxlokk. It became the lodestar for the ICPE way of life that would be lived in the years to come. In talking with some of those original twelve missionaries stationed in Marsaxlokk, I've heard them recall why that experience was such a watershed moment. So many of them relish the time spent deepening their knowledge of the Word, growing in Christian character, learning how to express their faith through testimony, and encountering the close-knit, life-affirming interdependence of Christian community life.

But one thing that stands out the most is their relation to the unheard-of freedom they felt—a release from needing to control every aspect of their lives—from the stress of an alienating self-obsession. By abandoning life's deadening calculus—the constant inventory of material wants and glories—they allowed God to provide for their needs and guide them on their way—a way travelled by others with whom they shared their daily bread.

For the ICPE missionaries, that has become life's pattern: they are no longer alone, bound, and aimless, but together, free, and on a mission from and for the Saviour of the world.

When you grow up on an island, you develop an "island mentality." Every other place seems incredibly far away. Even though you know better, foreign lands take on a mystical, fantastic quality—as though marked off by dire warnings and fierce pictograms on a medieval map. If your whole world is only 316 square kilometres (120 square miles) large, distance has a very peculiar meaning.

Mario has said that his own father would worry about him whenever he travelled "all the way" to the other side of Malta at night. So he couldn't help but have some of the same reservations about long distances himself—an unfortunate predisposition to have if your calling is to be a missionary. Nevertheless, he summoned all of his fortitude in 1987 to go halfway around the globe. Word of what we were doing had reached New Zealand—another set of islands—through a participant from our first School in Malta.

It seemed four couples had learned from Michelle—this former participant—about her experience at our School. Along with two Marist priests, they decided to write and enquire about how we'd establish a training ground for Catholic lay evangelists. Shortly thereafter, an invitation came from New Zealand, supported by the Bishop's Conference. They wanted us to establish a presence of the ICPE Mission in Wellington, the nation's capital.

Joe, a fellow Maltese missionary, joined Mario there and helped the New Zealanders lay out a plan to pioneer the first ICPE School of Evangelisation in 1988. Since our second School in Rome was to take place in May of 1988, a good number of the group from Wellington decided to participate, in order to observe and learn the ropes firsthand.

By then, we had witnessed a significant number of developments: an established local community, our first School of Evangelisation in Malta, our second School in Rome, a Youth Ministry, multiple trips of missionary outreach, and plans for our third and fourth Schools—one back in Rome, the other in the opposite hemisphere—New Zealand.

While all this was happening in different parts of the world, other communities similar to the local community in Malta that gave birth to the ICPE Mission in 1985, were sprouting up in different countries. They had a similar vision in scope and mission to that of the ICPE Mission, but each community was rooted and expressed this vision and mission within its local context. Together with the local community in Malta and the ICPE Mission, these other communities formed one broad, international spiritual reality founded on covenant spirituality. The leadership team of this diverse yet unified global network of communities was united in purpose, spirit, vision, and resolve.

All of this occurred within nine years of Mario's calling to bring what he had experienced in Lausanne to the Catholic Church. We felt God's hand in our work, guiding us all the while.

Mario had boarded that flight to New Zealand with an "island mentality," but he says now that he lost it somewhere over the vast ocean below. As he'd watched the progress of his flight tracked on a screen in the plane's cabin—marking silently the crossing of country after country—he felt inspired to pray for each of the nations in turn. And as he prayed, God spoke to his heart, as though telling the native Maltese—for whom twenty kilometres had always seemed a journey—that in sending him to the other side of the world to do His work, He was giving him the grace of knowing that any other such mission would be that much nearer home.

Since then, he says, nowhere has seemed too far when God has asked him to go there.

The second ICPE School in Rome—our third altogether—took place from late spring to late summer of 1988 at the Dominican Sisters Convent in Via Cassia. By that time, we'd established a presence in the Catholic world.

It was also undeniable that there was a need and a desire among the laity for this kind of transformative formation in the Christian life and that it was not limited to only one corner of the world. That was verified by the fact that thirty-three students from sixteen different countries attended the second Roman School, and they came from all points on the map: Malaysia, New Zealand, India, South Korea, Indonesia, Singapore, Uganda, Kenya, Mexico, the Netherlands, West Germany, England, Ireland, Austria, Italy, and Malta. And our support among Church leaders was just as widespread. That summer of 1988, we were blessed with a multitude of guest speakers, including Cardinal Francis Arinze of Nigeria, Cardinal Josef Tomko of Czechoslovakia, and Archbishop Jose Sanchez of the Philippines. The capstone of the second Roman School was an August 21 invitation from Cardinal Dziwisz, who had brought about our dinner with John Paul II two years before. He invited the students back to Castel Gandolfo for a Mass, in which they sang and played music, followed by a private audience with the Pope in the palace courtyard.

Participants in that School recall gaining a better understanding of their relationship with God, the sacramental life, and evangelisation through the school's lecture phase and experiencing a sense of reconciliation, healing, and freedom in their life story. The focus extended beyond mere instruction to true transformation. With each iteration, the schools' dual mandate—offering Catholics a life-changing encounter with Christ and equipping them to share the joy of the Gospel—became increasingly distinctive.

From late August to late September 1988, the Outreach Phase of the Roman School took place in West Germany at Augsburg, West Berlin, Ulm, and Cologne. There, the participants shared their new-found joy and hope in Jesus across various settings, including hospitals, prisons, nursing homes, schools, and parish youth groups.

They also posed the provocative, eternal question in these venues—"Why are we here?"; "What if God is real?"—which engaged the crowds right where they were, in the public arena of the market square. The effect in Germany was of a special caste—bringing young people into the Church and bringing lapsed or lukewarm Catholics back to it. An avowed atheist in his final year of legal studies was typical. Brought into conversations with the team, he was drawn into reflection, confessed, and reconciled to the Church of his youth.

We also formed a fellowship centre at St. Peter's Church in Augsburg, which became an ideal place for meetings and for sending people with whom we'd interacted on the streets for further formation and follow-up. The relationship with St. Peter's continued when we sent a small team of ICPE missionaries back to Augsburg in November to conduct leadership training and faith formation.

As soon as we'd ended the Outreach Phase of the second Roman School, it was time to turn to our first ICPE School in New Zealand—our fourth School overall and the furthest extent to which our missionary ventures had reached. In late November of 1988, we inaugurated the School within the historic Redemptorist Monastery of St. Gerard, an impressive landmark built in 1908. It has long stood as a defining feature of the Wellington Bay skyline.

The undertaking there presented a different kind of challenge because, as the New Zealand clergy explained, the country was swiftly morphing into a "post-Christian" nation in many ways. The hope was that the School would play a catalytic role in reviving the nation's Catholic faith—one part of a larger movement to inspire the island's laity, priests, and religious with a renewed ardour capable of shifting its spiritual trajectory.

Sixty students and staff, our largest group from nine different countries, attended the School. They came from Malta, Germany, Austria, England, Malaysia, Korea, Holland, Ireland and New Zealand. And the group was comprised of a diverse array from all walks of life—among them students, housewives, and businesspeople. While we undertook our characteristic work on the streets and in parishes and hospitals, we were invited for the first time to a government division, New Zealand's House of Parliament. Furthermore, Bishop Basil Meeking invited us to Christchurch and opened many doors for us throughout the islands, broadening our missionary opportunities. Our outreach at St. Gerard's swelled the congregants of the Sunday Masses from around 20 to around 250 by way of animating the liturgy and inviting the Congregation to morning tea after Mass. When the School finished its tenure in March of 1989, the original four families and other supporters who had brought us there could follow up our efforts by taking people through Faith Formation Courses.

By this time—only four years had passed since the beginning of the first ICPE School of Evangelisation in Malta—we had to take a step back and look to consolidating our training efforts for the missionaries who had joined us. We also felt a need to streamline our organisation to enhance our missionary impact and strengthen our community network.

This became the project of a seven-month intensive Leadership Formation Programme (LTP) in Malta, consisting of full-day courses for participants who were accommodated in households and rented apartments across the island. Cardinal Francis Arinze travelled from the Vatican to officially inaugurate the course on May 23, 1989.

In conjunction with this significant step in consolidating our leadership training, members of the LTP launched the initial Staff Formation Course (SFC) for young working adults in the local community. The participants received teachings on character formation, fundamental theology, and biblical knowledge. This interaction between the ICPE missionaries and the local community made for a healthy goodwill exchange. A total of 75 LTP and SFC participants from Switzerland, the UK, Korea, Singapore, Malaysia, Austria, Germany, Holland, Mexico, New Zealand, India, Kenya, and Malta made up our cohort. Reaching the objectives of the LTP reaped enormous benefits for the ICPE Mission as we were about to enter an even more rapid period of growth and expansion.

We had been provided for in ways that far exceeded our expectations. But one thing was still missing. It had to do with the most fundamental of needs.

Inevitably, missionaries must learn to travel light, taking only essentials and making do with what we can find. Months at a time, we may be on the move and, therefore, must live with only what we can carry. Improvising is another skill that must be added to the repertoire. All of this develops a discipline that has both practical and spiritual benefits. The liberty of a life free from material pursuit is something celebrated by poets; the itinerant evangelist knows the truth of it—of the room that is cleared in the soul for a burgeoning of faith when it is uncluttered and unbound.

But even missionaries need a home base, a place to which they can return and live in kinship with those who share this common call.

Mario and I had been living in rented apartments, and from time to time, we and others in our community welcomed visitors from America, New Zealand, or other places into our spare bedrooms who wanted to join the Youth Ministry or learn more about missionary life. But there was no central location that we could call home, no spot that was the outward-looking face of the ICPE Mission.

Then, in 1990, a friend in Malta who knew of our desire made available to the ICPE Mission an old villa in the heart of the farming region. It was called "San Martin," a set of buildings within a compound that could house us all and provide the central location for our presence in the world. It would be our physical space, housing us, but also the outward symbol of our charism.

Mario and I moved into one of the smaller buildings of the compound and our missionaries moved into the other spaces, all for once under one set of roofs in Malta—where it had all begun only a few years before. Undoubtedly, we were a curious new neighbour to the surrounding farmers, but soon they became warm and accepting supporters.

Everyone, including Mario and I, moved into the different buildings within the compound, all of us now under one roof in Malta—where it had all begun just a few years before.

Then God's grace towards us proved itself even more abundant. At practically the same time as we were led to San Martin, Karl, a German friend of ours who had been on the staff at our first School, found us a property in Germany. Located in the

Black Forest, it had previously served as a sanitorium for tuberculosis patients. The Church in Germany upgraded the building and then offered it to us free of charge and on an unlimited basis, allowing us to establish the ICPE Mission Centre in Allerheiligen in the very heart of Europe. For eighteen years, it was a sanctuary where individuals from different parts of the world found spiritual renewal, nourishment, and a profound sense of community.

Within the space of one year, friends helped us find two properties—a home for our missionaries' comfort and growth as a community, and a Mission Centre for our vision's expansion. We were also given a consequent moment for reflection, understanding, and resolution since, whenever such great favour is shown as we experienced, one must take stock of what it all means.

We had spent five years on a steep uphill climb to fulfill a clear objective—that of providing a way for those who had experienced God's transformation in their lives, to bring the same to others across the world. With willing hearts but little else, certainly no funds, His benevolence had guided the establishment of a financially autonomous Catholic missionary organisation to begin the new millennium. We had closed out that first period by reconstituting our operation to strengthen and streamline it while remaining mindful not to let our vision, imagination and creativity be hampered in the process. If the Spirit led us, we wanted to be as spry and nimble as we were when first called—ready to go, packing light, up at dawn and off.

It had taken courage, trust, and patience to stare down both fears and setbacks—to make it happen because it was our conviction that God wanted it to happen. We were not afraid, as He had told us we were not to be, and we took Him at His Word.

After all, He was doing something within the Church and giving us more than enough by way of signs and circumstances to show that the ICPE Mission was very much a part of what He was up to. We were forging ahead.

4

diaspora

On some level, we instinctively know that only on the rarest of occasions does anything come easily. Obstacles stand in the way of nearly every enterprise. However settled the purpose or pure the quest, resistance will meet it apace. The pleas and jeremiads of the Israelites, wandering in the desert for so long, provide the pattern of what a journey of faith means. It can often be mystifying, no less to the person of faith than to the person without it. After what at times seemed a reversal of her hard-fought efforts to achieve some great good, St. Teresa of Avila famously asked God why. His answer was that His friends must expect such things, to which she replied with characteristic wit, "Then it's no wonder You have so few of them."

Of course, Teresa, though disappointed, was not defeated. She soldiered on. But perhaps she did so with a more battle-scarred understanding of what would be required of her. What she faced might well look like a wall too high and wide and thick to breach; what she faced might well be the sea. Her call was to face it all nevertheless; she had to trust that the difficulty of the undertaking was not reflective of either the worth of the cause or the certainty of its achievement. Friction of some sort, great or small, of long duration or short, is part of the journey of faith. Still, the pilgrim must press ahead.

By May 1990, we had seen so many of our pioneering efforts come to fruition, bolstered by those who stood with us on the frontlines—the local community, the Schools in Malta, Rome, and New

Zealand, the mission trip to Paitan, and the Youth Ministry—all of which were incredibly blessed and affirmed our purpose. Then, when the doorway to Europe was flung open for us in Germany, we took the plunge to establish an ICPE Mission Centre there.

As I've said, Allerheiligen stands in the beautiful Black Forest region, famous for its waterfalls, hiking trails, and the ruins of a twelfth-century monastery. The nearby towns of Oppenau and Offenburg provide tourists with amenities, accommodations, and transportation links. The three buildings from which we were staging our efforts were not only adjacent to the ruins of the historic monastery but also close to a baroque garden with fountains. Our retreat was peaceful, picturesque, and remote. Best of all, though we had not sought a retreat atmosphere *per se*, there was nothing to interrupt the Centre's purpose of prayer, study, reflection, and the intense experience of communal living.

Nine of our missionaries had agreed to move to Allerheiligen from an array of countries: Michael and his wife Patricia from there in Germany; Derek from Malaysia; Consuelo from Mexico; Sacha from Holland; Kirsten from New Zealand; Rob from Great Britain; as well as Mario—another Mario, not my husband—and Patricia from Malta. We were busy establishing the Centre when a substantial problem arose—one that ultimately threatened the sustainability of the entire undertaking. Five of the group were not from the European Economic Community, meaning that the 90-day tourist visas they'd arrived under were about to expire; under the Immigration Office's rules, they would have to leave Germany and reapply from their home countries. While we were able to forestall that worst-case scenario—they were allowed to go to Malta for two months instead—their return was conditional upon each obtaining a financial guarantee from a German national and proof of medical insurance. After a tense period of looking for a way to provide for this need, our rescue was secured. Through the outstanding efforts of Caritas Mainz, a regional branch of the Caritas Catholic charity in Germany, the guarantees and insurance were obtained, and the visas were extended until December 1990.

That was not the end of our troubles, however. The next School of Evangelisation was to start in November, and the German Immigration Office again said that visas for participants from non-ECC countries would have to be issued by the German embassies in the countries from which the applicants came. This could take two months, and the participants would consequently miss the start of the School's tenure. Approval issued by fax from the home embassies was disallowed. But again, after great effort and by obtaining intercessory help from various groups—the Catholic Office of Germany, the Governor of the State, and the Interior Affairs Department—the process was expedited. All but one of the twenty-two applicants were allowed to attend the School for its duration, and it seemed things were once again on the right path.

But the circumstances of that one individual out of all the participants created a problem that began to test our relationship with the Immigration Office. The applicant from Kenya had entered the country without medical insurance, which was illegal and would result in his deportation.

At length, storming heaven with prayer, we were able to locate the required medical insurance. And through what amounted to an altogether inexplicable clerical error, the Kenyan was allowed to stay for the entire duration of the School. There was a grand celebration of thanksgiving at the successful completion of the Lecture Phase of the School in March of 1991, as it seemed we had been seen through to the end of another problem.

However, we were only to learn that our visa woes were just beginning. We had given the School participants the option to stay on for another year of discernment and formation, thereby joining our community life at Allerheiligen. Nineteen of them agreed, but ten of that group were from non-ECC countries—a fact which is abundantly clear by now, amounted to a thorn in our side.

There was a peculiar twist in this new iteration of the same old trouble. We were unsure whether the participants' current visas would be extended or instead result in us having to start all over again. If the latter were the case, would they all have to go back to their respective countries and apply from there? Further, the more extended residential stay would precipitate the Immigration Office changing their status from "students" to "teachers", which would be an additionally complicated matter under the process at that time. The immigration standing of our participants was turning into a relentless and recurring obstacle created by the very fact that we were an organisation made up of people from all over the world. Our greatest blessing brought about our foremost complication, procedurally at least.

Worse, the Immigration Office was noticeably irked when we brought them the matter this time. We'd already won several extensions, permissions, and workarounds. Now we were back again. They were beginning to suspect us of trying to take advantage of them with ulterior motives for each new request made and with special pleading proffered at every turn.

One more extension was granted to us—until June of 1991—but that was to be it. The trouble was that the deadline came and went with no answer as to the status of the applications. And we had no power to press the issue, given the strained relationship with the Immigration Office. This put us on the horns of yet another dilemma.

The School participants were supposed to start the Outreach Phase of their formation abroad; if they left Germany, would they be permitted back into the country given their expired status? Plus, the Office would know that they had been outside the border during the deliberation process. We were already in disfavour with them; this could seem like presumptuousness on our part, or worse yet, that we'd adopted a scofflaw attitude.

But plans had already been made for outreaches in Ireland and England and for the International Charismatic Conference on World

Evangelisation to be held in Brighton, England. The implementation of all that the participants—and our School staff—had worked for in the School would be frustrated if we did not take the risk.

What had started with the best of intentions and highest hopes for a new, growing community—in an ideal place—with international participation and widespread support—was in danger of falling to pieces. The calling of the Mission was to be a worldwide community—not serving Malta alone but reaching out to every nation. Mario's vision was to set out across the sea, not to be confined by it.

But in those early days, this administrative/bureaucratic question was an existential threat to the very nature of what he'd understood that call to be and do. What was facing us in our first Mission Centre outside Malta was a test case for what might face us anywhere we went, so that the answer there would likely portend our answer everywhere concerning our status and our ability to stay in a place for any length of time. The leadership team prayed for wisdom and guidance in a matter that seemed to have no clear path to resolution.

In the end, we put the question to the participants, apprising them of the whole scenario: things could go well—the granting of the visas, followed by their approved return to Germany and our new community; or they could go badly—deportation with no guarantee of reentry, or at the very least, no reentry for the foreseeable future. The decision was left to the choice of each, with time given for prayer and reflection.

Down to the last person, they all decided to go on the outreach—on faith—together. Although they appreciated the risks, they were willing to take them in an effort to complete what they'd felt called to do. Of course, we all held our breath the entire time they were on the outreach, nervous about their passports and visas drawing attention at customs both going and coming. In England, there were indeed questions about the expiring visas. And there were some conspicuous stamps and endorsements in all the most visible places that could well have attracted the eye of German customs officials. Still, they made it through without being stopped, a blessing that resulted in great rejoicing and relief, especially considering the meaningful contacts in the Christian world that were made on the trip to England and Ireland. It was a very productive one for the Mission.

The coast was not clear, however. The Immigration Office had not yet made its decision on the residence permits. The next School of Evangelisation was to begin in August of 1991; the chronic theme of any new start was anxiety over immigration status, making communicating a set of caveats part of each plan. We had to alert the participants in the upcoming School of the unsettled nature of any status they would have in Germany while things were in a state of flux. The Immigration Office had also transferred jurisdiction over our matter from a local office to a more centralised one, changing the administrative players involved and delaying any action that might have been taken. The new people were unacquainted with our case, and we were always subject to different eyes drawing an unfavourable impression of our facts.

Mario and I felt a great deal of pressure at the time, no small part of which was our fear as to what this might mean to the plan to establish the presence of the ICPE Mission in Germany. The darkest day of all during this stretch occurred while we were entertaining my parents on a visit from Malta. We were all on a walk around nearby Lake Mummelsee, which should have been a chance to escape the concerns for a while. But the negotiations between the Immigration Office and our people at the Mission Centre were taking place simultaneously. Mario had to interrupt the walk with periodic dashes to a phone booth to check on matters. And on one of these calls, he returned with the sombre news that we were to expect a letter any day that required those with expired residence permits to leave the country. There was nothing to do then but brace for the worst.

So we waited. And waited. But the letter never came.

For some reason we have as yet to find out, the Office never acted on their decision at all. In fact, two men soon took over at the Office, and they were quite sympathetic to our case and wanted to help us work out a relationship that would regularise and normalise our status in Germany so that it would not be put in peril each time a new administrator took over. It seemed that one of the main sticking points at the Immigration Office was their confusion about how we could support ourselves as ICPE missionaries—working as we did but without making money. At this point in our history, a major Dutch donor was supporting our organisation. Then, as individual missionaries and families, we were able to provide for ourselves through the generous contributions of friends who supported our call. That uncertainty and the uncertainty related to the distinction between "students" and "teachers" so central to their administrative scheme did not fit how we ran our Schools and Centres. Through a great deal of work by our German community member and man on the ground there—Michael—we were able to have the process streamlined in our favour. The procedure became so efficient that the overwhelming success of the Allerheiligen Mission Centre—with its Schools, seminars, and outreaches—was thereafter a model of routine performance.

That turmoil lasted for well over a year before it was resolved. Then, through the heroic efforts of friends, the unflagging commitment of our community, and the unquestionable intervention from on high, what had been a constant source of recurring trials was transformed into a smooth road, leading to one season of blessings after another. It didn't start out that way in the beginning, but beginnings do not always foretell endings.

While the difficulties caused by the visa process were a great deal of trouble in 1990-91, they in no way dampened the spirits of the nascent Allerheiligen community. With the ICPE Malta Mission Centre settling into its work in San Martin—running Schools of Evangelisation and preparing to send ten missionaries to Ghana for a two-month outreach in early 1991, the new venture in Germany was quickening into what would become a model of the communal spirituality that is so emblematic of the ICPE Mission.

The inauguration of the ICPE Germany Mission Centre was held in December of 1990; Mario and I moved there from San Martin soon after. In that location, in the very heart of Europe, the growth of the entire enterprise was unfolding. It was, in fact, to become the Formation Centre for the ICPE missionaries. The success of the first School of Evangelisation there further confirmed our impression that the Mission Centre in Allerheiligen would be the motherhouse of our Institute. Thirty-six participants attended the Allerheiligen School, which ran concurrently with our second School in Malta, and eighteen staff members supported Joe—the School leader— who led it. Out of the Allerheiligen School, twenty participants stayed on for a year of formation to become ICPE missionaries.

The German Mission Centre also became the location for leadership formation. It was at Allerheiligen that we held our first ICPE International Leaders' Conference in 1993 and the ones to follow. It was also in the heart of the Black Forest that we concluded the drafting of the "Norms and Orientations of the ICPE Mission." This document sets out the guidelines and organisational structure of our way of life as the ICPE Mission.

Moreover, what made Allerheiligen pivotal to the ICPE Mission's history was the communal life lived there. It was a time in which couples, families with children, single people—all joined in a life led together, a shared journey that engaged the entire calendar of the Christian and human life—its Christmas liturgy and Easter Triduum, its baptisms and birthdays, its weddings and anniversaries—even, sadly, its deaths. We were one in our joy; we were one in our grief.

Amidst the deep, mystical hollows, among a colonnade of ancient trees and the rush of white cataracts, we experienced what it was like to live as one body—the Body of Christ on this earth—as close as if we shared the same skin and breathed in the push and pull of one force. It is a unique grace, this profound integration of lives so that they all become one life—a paradox of individuals, with their unique personalities, somehow retaining their distinctiveness but nevertheless contributing to the beauty of one existence—like the features of a face, parts of a whole, each contributing to the totality of its beauty. Anyone could join us who would answer this call—from any continent, any present circumstance, any past history.

Our stories were even one story—a commonality of memory that all family members define themselves within.

We went through two significant windstorms at Allerheiligen together, tucked away in that far-off valley: Storm Vivian, which brought hurricane-force winds, and Storm Wiebke, occurring shortly after Vivian, which was equally powerful with cataclysmic winds and record rains. With an elevation of approximately 700 metres (2,297 feet) above sea level, snow detail was a regular part of our lives at Allerheiligen. We always had a morning shift to clear the paths between the chapel, residences, and lecture hall, shovelling away piles of snow and spreading the walks with salt. If the downfall was especially intense, we also needed an afternoon shift. To keep our cars as mobile as possible, we parked them in a lot up a short hill close to the main road, which was as far as the snow plough came. But sometimes, when we'd been shopping or had children with us, it was more convenient to park close to the residences.

We paid for that convenience on one particular occasion. One morning, we awoke to a dreaded sight: a massive amount of snow had fallen during the night. The cars, parked close to the houses, were buried in mounds of fresh, soft snow. But living together as we were, we shared both benefits and challenges, so the job was everyone's, not just someone's. The whole community swung into action.

Every coat, hat, glove, and pair of boots was commandeered for the hard job of digging out the cars, and those who weren't shovelling ran a relay getting dry things for those who were to replace all the wet gear. Hot tea with the occasional shot of schnapps kept us from freezing, and we were met with cheers of victory from the audience of mothers and children watching from windows, as each car was freed from the snow caves.

We also went through a baby deciding to come into the world in the middle of a heavy snowfall before the plough had cleared the path to our place. Tony, the expectant father who was driving the car, couldn't get it up the hill. The labour pains kept coming, faster and harder, yet the snow and ice stopped the parents-to-be in their tracks. That's when the brothers of our community came together in the early dawn hours—slipping and sliding, freezing in the process—to clear the path just enough to push the car up onto a road that the plough had already reached. The trip to the hospital after that was as fast as it could be, and we welcomed a new baby girl among our family there at Allerheiligen.

Our bond was strengthened further through the various outreaches staged from Allerheiligen. One took us to Russia and Romania at the end of 1991, and those on it became known as the "Joshua Team." They were taking the Spirit of the Lord with them, just as the Israelites had borne the Ark of the Covenant to Jericho and marched it around the walls. At the beginning of the last decade of the twentieth century, it was a time for the wall to come down, mainly in Eastern Europe.

The large group set out in two vans—the "Orange Van" and "The White Lady"—on a five-day and five-night trip, driving into the dark epicentre of totalitarian rule, with the Good News that frees every soul. In Moscow weather, the team preached and performed on the streets, at a university, and in a parish and school. Members of the team slept six to a room, with one of the brothers staying in the icebox of a van to guard the amplification system.

In sub-zero Romania, despite stops and starts and a confusion of plans, the bundled-up team went to orphanages and homes for persons with disabilities and gave a presentation in the solitary existing Catholic church that was there, with the men sitting on one side and the women on the other. The nearly empty supermarket stocked little food, so the missionaries lived mostly on takeaway pizza. Indeed, pizza would prove a modern-day manna for our missionaries, keeping body and soul together as they journeyed.

But none of these conditions or barriers were insurmountable; none of them made the team turn the van around and head for home, consoling themselves with a noble attempt that failed. Instead, they pushed on and did whatever they could, joyful at the accomplishments made—however small the flame of faith enkindled in the vast tundra of unbelief, disbelief, and doubt that had darkened Eastern Europe for so long.

In time, very soon, in fact, all of us at Allerheiligen realised that we were ready to go out into the world and share what we were experiencing there. A *diaspora* started to unfold, with mission teams sent to various countries on various continents to recreate what we were living at Allerheiligen in other countries. An abundance of grace poured as a libation, as thick as if it came from a jar.

But it was always Allerheiligen to which they would return for staff conferences, leadership formation, and simply to come home again to the soul of a community that was growing in number, depth, and meaning. Allerheiligen means "All Saints" in German—a collection of souls touched and saved by the Word. From Allerheiligen, so much of what we have been given to do really all began—in this hope to gather in a larger eternal family—saints, all.

What was true of our life in Allerheiligen was also true of all our ICPE Mission Centres that developed around the world and the local communities that shared the same call. Understanding what took place in Germany is key to understanding who we are and what we stand for.

In addition to the Centres in San Martin, Malta and Allerheiligen, Germany, we were—in time—to establish ICPE Mission Centres in Wellington, New Zealand in 1993, Manila, Philippines, and Seoul, South Korea in 1998, all serving Asia and South Pacific; Maslonskie, Poland in 1998, serving Eastern Europe, and Bangalore, India in 1999 serving the vast Indian sub-continent. The Centre in Maslonskie—with its motto of "We Dream. We Do"—was a particularly innovative, high-tech community that ran outreaches in Eastern Europe and large Polish communities in Chicago and Richmond, Virginia in the late nineties. Our ICPE Mission Centre in Oregon, U.S.A., was established in 2009.

ICPE Mission Centres were, for years, vibrant hubs of communion and mission in which our ICPE full-time missionaries lived. Life revolved around community living, prayer, faith formation and evangelisation. In their outreach, the communities in Mission Centres engaged not only those who have never heard of Jesus but also those who wanted to rediscover their Catholic faith. Their primary resource was the "Schools of Evangelisation" (now called Schools of Mission). We held Schools of Mission in Allerheiligen every year throughout the nineties and did the same in most other Mission Centres around the world. In addition, other schools and formation modules ran in different Mission Centres and at various times of the year—such as the School of Humanitarian Work and Christian Formation, which was a central feature of ICPE Mission Philippines, officially recognised by the Archdiocese of Manila in 1997; the International School of Intercession at Allerheiligen in 2000; the Pastoral Counselling School, begun in 1993 at Allerheiligen; the annual International School of Theatrical Arts, started in Allerheiligen in the summer of 1998; the School of New Evangelisation and Youth Alpha; Mission Possible that brought relief and assistance through teams travelling to disadvantaged areas around the world, such as an outreach to Badoza, Spain, devastated by catastrophic floods in the late nineties; Woman-to-Woman, started in Allerheiligen in April 2000, a ministry that empowers women to live out their feminine genius; a Concert Tour outreach to Belgium and Germany in 1996; and Set Free, bringing healing and wholeness through a psycho-spiritual approach.

The ICPE Mission also created resources to introduce the spirituality and lifestyle to those wishing to explore the adventure of joining our communities in one of our Mission Centres. These included modules we commonly refer to as the Come and See programme and the FMS, which stands for the Year of Formation in the ICPE Missionary Spirituality.

Mission Centres operated under the direct authority of the local ordinary and served both the parish where they were located and the diocese through parish missions, RCIA programmes, Lenten retreats, confirmation classes, and the like.

The way of life we lived in the Mission Centres was not only what sustained us, but also what attracted others—a group of Christians leading a unified life—yes, like those who first followed Jesus lived it, but most importantly, Christians living it in the present day, as enactors, rather than reenactors of the salvation story.

We wanted then and want now for others to "Come and See," as Jesus asked of those whom He called to be His disciples. We wanted then and want now for others to behold people attempting to live a life in the Spirit—to fathom the shocking news of its possibility for the immediate condition—not as part of an antique convention replayed without heart or understanding but as a blood-and-bone way of existence, lived on the ground where we all stand, within the air in which we all move and have our being: Christianity not as a pure idea, but as an engaged experience—a shared experience—the glory of the God-made child belonging to the God-made family—no less himself because he is part of a greater whole, but more himself because of the greater whole of which he is a part.

Key to that understanding is what we mean by "community life" and "covenant spirituality."

The Christian life is inherently social and communitarian. It does not unfold in isolation but within the fabric of community. While Christians remain distinct individuals, they are never merely private or autonomous; they are always communal. Our spirituality, like our very identity, is shaped by relationships, with community serving as its bedrock. In stark contrast to the individualistic, isolationist model of the twenty-first century, which encourages self-sufficiency and limits relationships to those that serve personal goals—whether carnal or material—God created us to be part of one family under His Fatherhood. We were made to belong. Christ came to remove us from our isolation, to help us rediscover that we are not—and never were—the orphans we often feel ourselves to be. Community life makes this rediscovery possible.

Fraternal love is integral to the Christian life. Benedict XVI describes it as "the true test of the authenticity of our faith." We can surmise that the true impact of evangelistic efforts hinges on Christians living in deep communion with one another. Vatican II rightly calls this brotherhood and sisterhood in the Lord "sacramental"—a communion of missionary disciples who, together, become the living epiphany of Christ. John's Gospel makes it clear: the world will recognise us as Jesus' disciples only when our unity becomes a radiant testimony of love—a unity forged in washing one another's feet, in walking the extra mile, in forgiving seventy times seven—a unity that demands we remove the plank from our own eye before pointing out another's speck, that we leave our gift at the altar to first seek reconciliation, that we consider others above ourselves. This is the love that reveals Christ to the world.

The covenant spirituality of the ICPE Mission is a relationship based upon a gift, the creative act of God's love. The communal lifestyle, as lived out by the members of the ICPE Mission, is intrinsic to God's call to become His people and accept the divine invitation made on Mt. Sinai: "I will be your God, and you shall be my people." Baptism, the sacrament through which every person enters this covenant, plays a pivotal role here. This, in fact, is what happens in Baptism—we are immersed into the life of Christ, united with Him and joined together as His Body, the People of God.

Today, as adults, the desire and privilege of the members of the ICPE Mission is to live their Baptism—their covenant with the Lord—in its fullest dimension with brothers and sisters who share the same call as ICPE missionary disciples. This conscious decision is renewed during the annual Covenant Celebration held in every ICPE Mission Community worldwide on Mission Sunday. The periodical commitment then leads to a life covenant commitment within the ICPE Mission, following a formation and discernment process.

Such Covenant Celebrations held in the ICPE Mission communities would be empty rituals unless they were rooted and understood in the light of the New Covenant. ICPE missionary disciples assimilate covenant spirituality insofar as they allow the Holy Spirit to transcribe the commandment of love of God and love of neighbour carved on tablets of stone, onto their hearts of flesh. Though covenant is celebrated annually, its spirit is lived daily—strengthening the fragile relationship, restoring the broken bond, and safeguarding the tie that endures. Covenant spirituality shapes how we relate and respond, forming us in faithfulness, self-giving love, and responsibility. It therefore is a path to becoming not only better members of a Christian community but better family members, co-workers and citizens engaged in building a world that reflects God's purpose and love.

Finally, ICPE missionary disciples can be known through certain characteristics of our spirituality. Three of these might be seen as consequences—the outward reflections, expressions, and fruits—of the communal life we lead: a spirit of joy, a spirit of hospitality, and a spirit of celebration.

ICPE missionaries are joyful witnesses to the Good News. We aim to nurture this joy even in the midst of suffering, anchored in faith and trust in the object of our joy: God revealed in Christ. In both good times and bad, we aim to cultivate a spirit of gratitude rooted in the awareness that all has been given to us freely in Christ. All is grace, all is gift. This gratitude sharpens our sensitivity to the gifts of God around us and the beauty and goodness of the world, enabling us to express our thanksgiving and praise to God and others freely. Gratitude, in turn, becomes the wellspring of our joy. As Ben Jonson said in his Cary-Morison Ode: "In small proportions we just beauties see; And in short measures, life may perfect be." Indeed, true beauty and perfection in life can exist in small or seemingly insignificant forms.

For the members of the ICPE Mission, hospitality is an extension of the Eucharistic liturgy, in which Christ, under the species of bread and wine, invites and welcomes us to our salvific banquet, washing our feet and strengthening and comforting us through the Word. We listen to the world's needs, particularly where we live, and strive to show active hospitality through kindness, attentiveness, humility, and a readiness to make a stranger a friend. We try to make the old saying—"He never met a stranger"—something that defines us all.

As members of the ICPE Mission, we live our celebrations—and we have many—as prophetic events. When we are not celebrating, we are preparing for a celebration—big or small—on the many human and religious occasions that mark our journey. What will unfold when Christ returns in glory is already stirring among us—not in its fullness, but as a living foretaste of the joy to come.

Through our lives together as Christians and our service to the world, we desire to bear witness to a faith marked by immediacy—present, not distant or abstract—and authenticity—sincere, not superficial or pretentious—a faith that arrives with every dawn and carries us through every night.

During that important span of years, 1990-91, there was an outpouring of productivity through ministries and outreaches throughout the world—the realisation of Mario's vision of our taking the Spirit-filled charism of the ICPE Mission across the seas.

For a year, a roving mission team traversed New Zealand, exploring and acquainting themselves with what the aboriginal natives call the "Land of the Long White Cloud." Our ministry there would become one of our oldest and most deeply rooted.

A team of ICPE missionaries and members of the local community in Malta travelled to Bern, Switzerland for an Ecumenical Congress entitled *Jesus—Hope for Europe.* Three thousand people attended, with a welcome, though surprising influx of participants from the Czech Republic and Hungary. Sharing quarters with them in the nuclear shelters under the Wankdorf Football Stadium, our ICPE missionaries learned firsthand about the experiences of people in Eastern European countries during that cataclysmic time that resulted in the fall of the Berlin Wall and the end of the Cold War. The conference was a milestone in the European Christian community's efforts to engage with contemporary issues and promote a message of hope and reconciliation in a changing Europe.

In March of 1990, eight ICPE missionaries left Malta for Nigeria on a two-month mission, running the first ICPE School of Evangelisation in the continent of Africa. The team came from India, Germany, the Netherlands, New Zealand and Malta and helped train and form 30 young priests,150 seminarians, leaders of the National Charismatic Renewal from Kenya, Nigeria, and Ghana, and key lay leaders from 7 different Nigerian dioceses. Four years later, another team from the Mission Centre in Malta ran outreach missions to Malaysia, Singapore, the Philippines, Indonesia, Hong Kong, and Thailand. At the same time, in 1997, ICPE Mission Malta conducted a three-week outreach to Gibraltar.

A great deal of work grew out of our involvement in Ghana during the decade of the nineties, including mission trips, Schools of Mission and Leadership Training, until in 1998, two native Ghanaians, Dominic and Kwaku, became our first Coordinators of the ICPE Mission community in Kumasi.

At Allerheiligen, we staged significant outreaches to Augsburg, Germany, the Czech Republic, Warsaw, and Lublin, Poland. Our first outreach to America, in Oregon, was staged from there in 1994. And of course, it was from there that we launched the Joshua Trip to Moscow and Romania. We also held our first ICPE Staff Conference in Allerheiligen, revolving around a theme that by now can be seen as foundational to the ICPE Mission: "Community."

Those early years of the Mission's development were very much an example of the wheat and the tares growing up together: much to be thankful for, much to endure. Our obstacles were not always the expected ones.

All missionaries can count on cold and lukewarm hearts, secular adversaries, and a culture opposed to everything they propose. They can count on freezing weather, boiling temperatures, record-setting storms, cramped quarters, sickness, disease, and the strain of long-distance travel with its attendant dangers. They can even count on the everyday anxieties of providing for themselves and those to whom they minister. Those things meet them face-to-face.

What is more challenging to count on but must nevertheless be faced is what comes out of nowhere—the mundane, the banal, the time-consuming—such as bureaucratic challenges and revolving door administrators, official misunderstandings and paperwork threats. The turbulent sea and the fortress walls that stand in the way do not always present themselves under their regular guises but are just as difficult to engage and overcome.

Jericho was impregnable. The hearts of the Israelites must have fallen at the very sight of it. But just as Joshua knew, we must also know that it is not the size of the wall, nor its age, that can defeat us. It is the fear that we are not up to the task—that forces more powerful will defeat us—that we will not be seen through.

But we must not fear that there is no way because we can't see the way.

The first step in defeating that fear is to lift the burden onto our shoulders, as the Israelites carried the Ark, then fill our lungs and blow the trumpets of the Lord. The first step is the scandal of believing the improbable, even the impossible: that with God, Jericho can indeed fall.

5

first things first

"Are you Catholic?"

Mario turned at the question, then smiled at the questioner.

It was the late nineties, and he had just spoken—at the Vatican's invitation—to a group attending a conference on addressing the crisis of young people in the Church. Poorly catechised and increasingly secular, young Catholics were either leaving the Church or becoming lukewarm about it. Around 450 conferees from around the world—clerics and laypeople alike, gathered in Rome at Domus Mariae, a beautiful Conference Centre and guesthouse that the Vatican often used for such meetings. Clearly, the topic was a major concern. The future of the Church depended upon the answers to such a question. The health of any institution, secular or not, can be gauged by those at the youngest end of the spectrum—both in terms of the numbers involved and in the depth of their conviction. Equally clear was the proposition on the table: the need for new ways to bring the joy of knowing Christ to our own youth.

Mario's invitation was due to our development of the Schools of Evangelisation, as they were then known, and ICPE Mission Centres, which were well-established by that time. They had received not only the support of John Paul II but also that of many influential figures in the Church hierarchy. The question being asked at the Domus Mariae conference was, for all intents and purposes, "How can young Catholics be evangelised?" Mario would be able to explain the methods and ministries that we had found so fruitful in that regard ourselves. Our schools had a demonstrable track record of appealing to young people and adults alike.

As was customary, part of the conference was conducted through an open-exchange platform where speakers had the opportunity to approach the microphone and address the crowd. When it was Mario's turn, he emphasised the importance of young people encountering Christ personally and being equipped with the skills to propose Him to others. He stressed that a genuine encounter—or re-encounter—with Jesus, is essential. Through such an encounter, one that ignites our souls with His love, a living faith is awakened—one that can be passed on to others. We witnessed this truth firsthand in our own lives and the lives of the participants in our Schools and programmes.

Mario's remarks were warmly accepted but did not stir up much discussion or comment from the crowd. After all, he was only one of many speakers in a long day of speakers. He had attended many such conferences over the years, for that matter, and the one at Domus Mariae would have simply numbered among those without any experience to make it stand out, were it not for the question he received afterwards.

He'd been on his way to get some coffee and something to eat when he felt a hand placed on his shoulder:

"Are you Catholic?"

A bishop stood there, attempting to mask his confusion with a smile. Mario's smile was all too knowing.

He wasn't exactly surprised, as he'd been asked such a thing—directly and indirectly—subtly and not so subtly—many times before. But in this context, it was particularly unusual. That the Bishop could imagine the Holy See would invite a non-Catholic to a conference on how to engage young people with the Church again, was beyond perplexing. Still, it only reinforced what we already knew: many Catholics did not accept or were not entirely comfortable with the idea of "evangelisation" as such.

No matter its role in the New Testament chronicling the birth and spread of Christianity, its history within these two millennia, or the Church's trumpet call for a New Evangelisation—many were deeply confused about evangelising and, in consequence, about us. It was not always clear why.

Had not Paul VI issued a landmark document, *Evangelii Nuntiandi* ("Evangelisation in the Modern World"), in 1975, drawing together the teachings of Vatican II and describing evangelisation as the Church's deepest identity and mission, stating that "She (the Church) exists to evangelise"?

Had not John Paul II's encyclical *Redemptoris Missio* ("The Mission of the Redeemer") promulgated in 1990, emphasised the importance of the New Evangelisation aimed at reinvigorating the faith among lapsed Catholics and at engaging the contemporary culture? Had this theme not proved a focal point in the Church's teachings, pastoral plans, and language?

Still, even in the late nineties, all too many saw "spreading the Gospel" as something done by missionary monastics, not by lay people. St. Francis Xavier, the North American Martyrs of France, and the Jesuits who braved the South American jungles were the Catholic exemplars. The traditional vocation of such heroes of evangelistic commitment somehow obscured people's openness to the need for the new evangelisation—a business of all believers—of which we were a part. In fact, the very use of the term "evangelisation" was thought to ring with a Protestant tenor, not a Catholic one.

All Mario could do was smile at the Bishop, offer a few words, politely excuse himself, and look for a stronger cup of espresso than he'd set out in search of. It was not the time or place to explain all of this in the middle of a crowded Roman coffee bar. But it was dispiriting.

In truth, this perception had been around a long time, practically since we'd commenced our work. As I've mentioned, Mario himself had been questioned about his association with YWAM at the beginning of his call. It was all born from a deep-seated worry that he would leave the Church altogether if he went to Switzerland and was taught by Evangelical Protestants. He had no small work to do in convincing people that he was bringing something good, consistent, and traditional back to the Church—evangelistic zeal—not something threatening to Church doctrine. It was not demystifying of the Almighty Christ to proclaim the expansiveness of His Love, he had to explain.

But while Mario successfully reassured his doubters, similar obstacles resurfaced in other ways on a consistent basis—from Catholics who couldn't understand what we were about, as well as from Protestants. On the one hand, Catholics wondered why, if we believed what we did, we wanted to *do* things in such a non-traditional way; on the other hand, Protestants wondered why, if we wanted to do things in such a way, we *believed* the things as we did. Even at Allerheiligen, it took us years to overcome the scepticism of the local Catholic community, who questioned our *bona fides* and even debated whether we were some sort of sect. We then had a guest speaker for an entire week at one of our Schools, a woman who'd witnessed our prayer life and communal commitment, who complained of our orthodoxy simply because we scheduled daily Mass at the end of the workday, rather than at the beginning.

The doubts and assumptions about our method also manifest at the recruitment level. Granted, the families of the young men and women drawn to our Schools of Evangelisation had no model by which to understand the life we proposed. What were all these people from different countries doing—living under one roof for several months, studying the Bible, and learning how to spread the Gospel? That was the job of nuns, monks, and priests. In that way of thinking, the options for those called to a missionary life were only two: either *become* religious or leave such things *to* the religious. Anything else smacked of Protestantism, which raised the old and by now all-too-familiar misgivings about where this might lead and what we were truly up to with this project.

In addition, we had worked closely with YWAM in the beginning, which had Pentecostal origins. YWAM had done nothing but provide us with unflagging help as we got the first two Schools of Evangelisation off the ground; as such, they rank among our oldest supporters and deserve great credit for their assistance. However, schools with the unique module the ICPE Mission was providing were only taking place in the Protestant world at that time, and those that conducted them were from traditions wholly unlike those in the Catholic world. This latent distrust was not only difficult to address from an apologetic standpoint, but it frustrated our efforts to raise the financial support we needed for the growing schools, Mission Centres, and outreaches—which were spreading across five continents at that time. In some ways, we were the victims of the Schools' success in that our enterprise was taking off, but the backing it took to sustain it was hampered by doubts about what our success would mean to the Church.

There are also cultural reasons that have always stood in the way of missionary efforts. Modern Catholics are often absorbed with the inner problems of the Church, which tax it as an institution; this accounts for an interior concern with "Catholic problems" that leaves little time for, and even less responsibility to, spread the Gospel. And then some Catholics feel inadequate to the task, as their own ignorance of and doubts about the faith seem insurmountable.

Moreover, a set of dysfunctional conceptions plague society as a whole, let alone the modern Catholic: the idea that religion, like politics, is purely a private matter, which makes it embarrassing to speak of such "personal things"; an outsized concern for "tolerance," which has become the supreme secular virtue; the conviction that all religion is relative and should not be foisted upon another; and the fear of the cost that will undoubtedly be exacted from being so open about Christianity in what is now a post-Christian world.

All these obstacles had to be dealt with in various ways, but some were built into more than mere resistance. Some manifested in outright hostility.

In the Spring of 1986, Fr. Tom Forrest, who played a central role in *Evangelisation 2000*, invited Mario and me to a conference in Dallas, Texas. The meeting was held in *Lumen 2000*, the Catholic Global Television Evangelisation Association, which was part of the larger global effort aimed at the new millennium. The main leaders in Catholic media and *Evangelisation 2000* were gathered in anticipation of the first-ever six-language direct satellite broadcast to occur in July 1987. The broadcast was to be accompanied by the release of an affordable 24-inch portable receiving satellite disc to facilitate global evangelisation through television.

As the founders and leaders of the ICPE Mission, fresh from conducting our second School of Evangelisation in Rome, Mario and I were honoured to be part of the group. It was an exciting opportunity to be involved in a new avenue for both literarily and figuratively transmitting the Gospel around the globe. Our contribution could be more than merely acting as by-standing supporters; we had practical experience in this area, having worked in TV evangelisation on the local station in Malta.

But when we arrived at the conference, I felt from the outset that something was wrong. Our welcome was not open and friendly at all; instead, it was rather frosty, with strange looks and furtive glances. Mario explained my misgivings away, putting them down to jet lag, and I did my best to shrug them off. Still, my sense of things persisted. Something was not right, and it wasn't long before my intuition proved well-founded.

It turned out that prior to our arrival, a French delegate had been actively lobbying the Conference leaders—in particular, Piet and Trudy, a Dutch couple who were the conference sponsors—to have us disinvited. He'd concluded that we were not orthodox Catholics and had been conducting a phone-call campaign against us for days.

There was talk that we would not only be excluded from the event but also publicly denounced by an international newsletter of the CCR. Fire was suddenly coming from all directions.

We were blessed to have a champion there with us at that time, Fr. Tom himself. His international profile in the Church was very high, and the depth of respect in which he was held was equally high. No one knew us better than he did, and no one could explain us better than he could. His endorsement of our newly launched Schools of Evangelisation— the first of their kind under Catholic auspices— was unequivocal. But he did not let his *imprimatur* alone stem the attack being waged upon us. He publicly reprimanded the French delegate who had spearheaded the exclusionary campaign, then worked in a series of side meetings not only to set the record straight as to our orthodoxy and approach but also to put an abrupt end to the newsletter denunciation that was planned.

In the end, we survived that attempt to derail our mission. We even gained some ground in our wider acceptance among the leaders of the conference. Piet and Trudy, the devoutly Catholic sponsors, were intrigued by what they'd learned of our efforts and subsequently invited us to their holiday park in Holland to learn more. While we enjoyed their gracious hospitality, the most important thing to come out of that trip was a long-lasting friendship and the crucial support that ensued. Until they passed away, Piet and Trudy were financially and spiritually among our most valued collaborators and supporters. They adopted the ICPE Mission and its outreaches, included them in their philanthropic efforts, and in this way enabled us to spread our projects across the continents. I firmly believe that what the enemy means for evil, God can turn it for our good and His glory.

As might be apparent by now, the challenges we faced wound up strengthening our resolve. Patience was necessary, as it took a great deal of time for us to prove ourselves to those who resisted our charism for a myriad of reasons. Over time, any doubts about our intentions were proven unfounded. As the facts established, we were uncompromising in our commitment to the Catholic faith, what was new was our way of bringing that faith to the world. That new way was one promoted by the Church itself, a grace which underscored the entirety of our work.

At length, the impact of the four-month-long ICPE Schools of Evangelisation became evident as the number of those participating in them grew in tandem with accounts of lives touched by the Holy Spirit working wonders in and through them. The training and formation of lay Catholics as evangelisers became less and less peculiar in the Church, and even more and more intriguing. There followed an overwhelming number of requests from dioceses worldwide for our work—so much so that the demand exceeded our capacity to meet it. It was a good problem to have. Throughout and despite the obstacles, our purpose—to conduct Schools where participants are invited into a life-transforming relationship with Jesus Christ and equipped to share His love, truth, and beauty with others—grew ever clearer.

This history of the ICPE School of Mission, both its grace-filled beginnings and growth remarked upon in earlier chapters together with the difficult stretches elaborated upon in this one, paints the background necessary for a bird's-eye view of the School's composition, where content and method are closely interconnected.

The ICPE Mission serves the Church by creating avenues for Catholics to encounter Christ personally, shaping them into intentional disciples of Jesus and empowering them to be credible witnesses wherever life's journey leads them. The Schools are the flagship endeavour among our efforts to implement this goal.

The ICPE School is divided into two distinct phases: the first three months, known as the "Lecture Phase," and the final month, called the "Outreach Phase."

Participants benefit from several dynamics we employ during the Lecture Phase; these include around 180 hours of teaching by qualified ICPE missionaries and experts in the field. Lectures address, among others, the nature of the Trinitarian God, the deconstruction and reconstruction of ideas of God as distant and remote rather than personal and caring, Sin and Salvation, prayer and the Sacraments, the meaning of worship and liturgy, Christian anthropology, Church history and doctrine, the substance and practice of evangelising, and modern obstacles that face Christianity and the apologetics needed to address them. The lectures impart a wealth of knowledge, yet the emphasis here is not merely on receiving accumulated truth but on integrating that truth into one's life. To support this process of application and transformation, each participant is paired with a seasoned staff member and joins a small group, ensuring personalised accompaniment and meaningful engagement in a supportive and nurturing community environment.

During this process, participants wrestle with Truth. They ask questions and embrace the discomfort accompanying the clash between one's beliefs and objective reality. This search for Truth is active and transcends their own limitations and inner biases. It is a difficult, if nevertheless essential process. But as the writer Flannery O'Connor said, "The truth doesn't change according to your ability to stomach it."

The initial part of the School's Lecture Phase is meant to evangelise—or re-evangelise—those who come to be evangelisers. During this phase, special attention is paid to our relationship with God. The *kerygma,* the core message of the Christian Gospel—Christ's death, resurrection, and the call to repentance and faith in Him—is allowed to permeate and dwell among the participants and to work its transformative power upon them.

Participants are also invited to a fresh *metanoia*, a repentance that renews the mind and heart and changes attitudes, values, and behaviour. The Gospel of John describes this transformation as being "born again." Old ways are left behind, and the action of the Holy Spirit begins a new life in Christ, breaking the power of sin.

At its core, sin is about relationships or the rupture of relationships. Sin primarily touches our relationships with ourselves, others, and our world. It unravels the potential for flourishing that could have been there had we not succumbed to arrogance, greed, rage, resentment, contempt, fear, and neglect. Sin is always a failure to love—a choice that shatters the bonds that hold us together and dims the light of what we are capable of becoming.

We all must confront the fact that in sin, we are leaving God of our own accord and thereby alienating ourselves from ourselves. We lose our identity, purpose, and source when we leave our Father behind, just like the prodigal son. From such self-involved licenses, we become less free, not more. We are all at once detached, afloat, aimless. Cut off in this way, wandering further and further away from what would sustain us, if we would let it, we cannot help but dissipate and die.

In his famous work *Confessions*, St. Augustine reflects on how he was "outside of himself in his search for God." God had remained with him; he had not remained with God. Like the father in the parable, God waits for us to discover and embrace this truth. God, like the father, is on the front porch, as it were—looking for us to come over the hill, back within the realm of His sight and care.

This is the most personal of all journeys—looking within the self to find what has beckoned us away from the source of our being in a siren's call, bent on our destruction. Honesty and courage are the gifts that must assist those who dare to delve into the depths of the soul, and honesty and courage are the gifts that must assist those who resolve to take a new path. As God is our origin and destiny, the place from which we start and the place to which we seek to return, every person must undertake this hard task. The Good News is that God is with us all the way home.

In addition to the foundational phase of the School devoted chiefly to the vertical relationship with God, there is another phase or dimension; this dimension concerns the horizontal relationship with others, the wider Church, and the world at large. In this way, the School covers the entire spectrum of the evangelisation process, beginning with the compelling proclamation of the Good News of Jesus Christ, the formation in the Catholic faith that fosters a mature understanding and appreciation of the community of followers of Jesus, and the discovery of one's talents to answer the call to join in the mission of Christ in the Church and the world.

Sacred Scripture holds a central place in our Schools, just as it does in ICPE communities around the world. We strive to form the participants—as we strive to be disciples with the Word of God inscribed on the tablets of our hearts. Participants at the Schools—and on all our formation programmes—are never without their Bibles, as the Word is the living God, Christ Himself, the Second Person of the Trinity, who exists in an eternal communion of Father, Son, and Holy Spirit. As such, the Word is more than a compendium of history; it is God with us, drawing us into it and driving us forward to share its news. Furthermore, participants are given time for personal prayer and meditation on the Word of God daily, forming habits that they will take with them whether on missions or at home. In truth, the personal encounter with Christ changes the very way that the Bible is read, in that what was once only an intellectual exercise becomes a relational experience; what was once mere text is infused with keen and innate relevance; what was once abstract becomes intimate; what was once the history of God speaking to the problems of others becomes God speaking to the very soul that comes to the Word for answers.

Another fundamental aspect of the ICPE Schools of Mission is that which is fundamentally characteristic of all ICPE Mission endeavours—community. Living in and as a community throughout the term feeds the fledgling evangelistic soul. This transformation occurs through the community experience at the School that embodies the spirit of *koinonia*. *Koinonia* is the deep fellowship among believers stemming from their shared relationship with God in Christ. It is a profound spiritual and intimate bond with each other and with the Lord Jesus; as such, it is a reflection of the life of the Trinity. This communal life at the ICPE School is nurtured in personal and communal prayer; it involves learning how to provide and attend to each other, share work duties and responsibilities, and delegate and undertake as gifts, strengths, and opportunities dictate. *Koinonia* is then celebrated through festive *Agape* meals, International Evenings, Skit Nights and countless fun activities like sledging down snow-covered hills in Allerheiligen on large garbage bags, making habitual ice-cream pit stops in the middle of the night while returning from outreach in three vans in Rome, and exploring hiking tracks on free days in New Zealand, such as the City to Sea Walkway or Brooklyn Wind Turbine to Red Rocks. Several of the participants testify to such community life as a first experience. This comes as no surprise when Pope Francis himself has stated that our parishes have not yet sufficed as "environments of living communion and participation, and to mak(ing) them completely mission-oriented". The immersive experience of the Church's broader reality that participants encounter at ICPE Schools often inspires them to return to their dioceses and offer their talents and service, helping to cultivate vibrant faith communities at the local level.

As the Lecture Phase progresses, the transformation in the lives of the participants becomes observable; in some, it can be more subtle but always, we witness lives being grounded in humble, sincere authenticity.

The end of the Lecture Phase involves practical preparation for the Outreach phase. This is when creativity is unleashed, and participants are accompanied to seek ways—through their talents—to propose Jesus, whom they have discovered as someone knowable who can change their lives.

Pope Paul VI said that "the man who has been evangelised becomes himself an evangeliser"; the sign of genuine acceptance of the Gospel is the willingness and motivation to share it with others. And so, enlivened with the spirit of service, participants travel to different locations for the Outreach Phase of the School. There they share the Gospel message through various ways and in diverse circumstances. Engaging the world where they find it—everywhere from a church to a street corner, from a school to a nightclub, from a jungle in deepest Borneo to the reaches of an American cityscape, the evangelists invite others into the fellowship they enjoy and proclaim.

At this point, evangelisation is not so much an effort as it is an outpouring—an unveiling of the internal grace the missionary possesses freely and undeserved as a gift of God. It is a feast too great, one that must be bestowed on others to be enjoyed. Again, the participants find themselves evangelising while continuously being evangelised. This, too, reflects the eternal confluence of the Trinity—always alive, in motion—a love enjoying even as it is being enjoyed.

On their return from the Outreach Phase, participants are guided in making intentional, concrete decisions to continue growing in their Christian journey through a time on retreat. They are encouraged to follow the guidance of the Spirit in discerning how they are called to contribute to shaping the world in a way that aligns more closely with the Creator's original design. As they start making their way home, participants have described their time at the ICPE School as life-changing, particularly in how it challenges and reshapes their understanding of God, themselves, and their mission in life. Others have spoken about how the School equipped them with practical tools for living out their faith more fully and confidently.

Wherever they go, they are now fitted for their mission. Jesus sent His disciples out with only a pair of sandals, a tunic, a cloak, and a staff, but He had prepared them internally with a storehouse of riches. He has never stopped providing for those who follow; He only asks that they do.

The above explanation of the Schools of Mission would be incomplete without expounding at length upon a part of the School constituting the whole enterprise—the personal encounter with Christ. This is nothing less than meeting Jesus Himself, the finite creature's encounter with the infinite Son of God. Without that experience, the School of Mission—any Adult Formation in the Catholic Church, for that matter—would amount to a course in biblical studies or theology, good and worthy as far as it goes, but a wholly human undertaking. In March of 2023, Pope Francis remarked, "You can study all the theology you want… and [nevertheless] become [an] atheist or worldly. Studying is important but doesn't generate a new life of grace." The encounter with Jesus through the power of the Holy Spirit is essential for a transformed life of discipleship. It is all the more necessary for the life of a *missionary* disciple.

Two things must be held in tension when speaking of God as "personal" and of a relationship with him as a "personal relationship." First, God is understood as interacting with people in a manner similar to the ways that humans interact with one another. He seeks us out as we seek others out; He desires us to seek him as others desire that of us. Human relationships thrive on interaction, and the closest bonds—such as the familial relationship of God as Father and we as His children—require ongoing, intimate communication. The health and strength of any connection, as well as its warmth and vitality, depend upon a decided effort to sustain it—one that is worth any effort because it is fuelled by love. A personal God listens to our prayers, guides our actions, comforts and supports us, as a loving Father does. We, as His children, go to Him in prayer—asking both for his guidance and his pardon, his sustenance and his protection—as well as to enjoy His presence, thank and adore Him.

Second, this personal relationship does not deny or compromise God's transcendent nature, which is beyond human comprehension or understanding. God is all-powerful, all-knowing, and all-present, but God is also immanent; God is present and active within the world and human experience. We are the temple of the Holy Spirit, as St. Paul tells us, and He is as near as our blood, as active and present in our lives as the senses with which we engage His world. If sin is the alienation of the self from the source of its being—God—salvation can be seen as the reintegration of the self with that source. Sacred history is rife with the intimacy of God's contact. It shows Him as both approachable and desirous of being approached, accessible and giving access to Himself through prayer, Scripture, and the sacraments.

Believers can and do experience a sense of God's presence in their everyday lives. The Schools of Mission—and all our endeavours as the ICPE Mission—seek to enable that experience's acute manifestation in a life-changing way, fully aware that only the Spirit of God can work this transformation. Only he can "make all things new." Only He can inspire the soul with the breath of life. Only He can enflame the heart with an inextinguishable blaze, whose light and warmth must be brought to others. Once He is known, it is impossible, non-sensical, to hoard or hide the missionary fire.

Pope Benedict XVI spoke of the Christian life as an encounter with the Lord that results in the Christian following him forever after. All plans change; a lifelong journey begins. Jesus called the fishermen from their nets and the tax collectors from their tables. They rose and followed. He stopped Paul in his tracks, and for the rest of his life, Paul ran the course. Nothing was the same afterwards.

These meetings and others in the Bible are our first examples of the Christianising event, the "face-to-face" convergence of the Saviour with His people. Certainly, they are the most dramatic examples and the most intimate. Many saints in Church history have been blessed with the same. But the personal, life-changing encounter with Christ is meant for everyone who sets out to find God. It is the inheritance of any that would claim it. It all begins with a moment—bright and loud, or dark and silent—when everything is set in motion.

It is where the journey truly starts, as it is no less than the nativity, where Jesus and the believer's soul begin a shared existence in a Bethlehem of the new. The first disciples were called to follow, but part of that following is remaining with Him. Day and night, together and always. Thereby, existence is reconfigured. The life in the flesh that one has always lived becomes the life of faith in the Son of God, as Paul writes in Galatians. And the journey begins.

In his work, particularly in his book *Divine Renovation: From a Maintenance to a Missional Parish,* Fr. James Mallon, highlights the critical issue that many Catholics are sacramentalised but not evangelised, echoing the broader concern in the Church today. Many in our parishes may have received the sacraments but are unsure of what they mean when they say they believe in Jesus, what He is and means to them, and what following Him amounts to in their lives. The ICPE Schools of Mission seek to be one of the tried-and-tested tools in changing all that by enabling, empowering, and equipping Catholics to become intentional missionary disciples of the Good News of Jesus, not merely "accidental" or "cultural" Catholics. As the new evangelisation is aimed at witnessing to those who have not heard of Christ and those whose faith has gone cold or has never flourished, the ICPE Schools of Mission play a key role.

Furthermore, to the average Catholic, instruction on how one is to go about evangelising might seem superfluous.

If a Catholic on the street were polled, the likely definition of evangelisation would be, "You just tell the person you're talking to what you believe, and maybe why you believe it, and then why they should too. "

That would all be very well until they were asked to do it. To actually do it. Like anything else in human experience, what is observed looks easy when performed by masters. But things become very different when confronted with an opportunity to replicate it. Then the person is met with the multitude of things that hinder evangelistic witness: reticence and embarrassment; a lack of basic knowledge of the faith, Church history, Church structure and dynamics; no training in apologetics and no sense of how great the task is when addressing an often hostile, aggressive, secularised, and accusatory world; sets of individual doubts and fears, as well as ill-formed concepts of God and the Church; and most of all, no personal relationship with Christ that bears witness to that being spoken of, that fires a persistence to proclaim it no matter the conditions or circumstances. How to make Christ known and how to invite someone into a community of those who know him is not self-evident or instinctive. In fact, in modern times, it is even counter-intuitive; it goes against everything the culture holds and nearly every environment in which people are raised.

Yet, Pope Francis has again called for the Church to be proactive in encouraging all Catholics to take an active role in sharing the joy of the Gospel. He asserts that every Christian becomes a missionary to the extent that he or she has encountered the love of God in

Christ Jesus. So we no longer say that we are 'disciples' and 'missionaries' but rather that we are always 'missionary disciples'.

Practically speaking, educated parishioners may be able to repeat the tenets of their faith. But they cannot share a joy they do not possess. They cannot convince others of an experience that they have never had. They cannot expect others to follow a path they do not know, nor invite them to a feast they have not partaken in—not while they are still hungry.

To the best of our abilities, the ICPE Mission pledges always to extend the great feast's offering. We will reach out to the rich and the poor, the old and the young, the schooled and the unschooled. And there they will grow to understand, as we do, the great paradox—that we are both guests and servants at the Lord's table, beneficiaries of His splendour even as we wait upon those who have just arrived—those who have responded to His eternal invitation to come to His banquet, then taste and see...

Educating the world as to exactly who and what we are, has been a large part of the founding years of the ICPE Mission, as we have indeed been an unusual bridge by which Catholics cross into missionary dynamism. Our way has been the source of bewilderment from all sides, manifesting in the question Mario was asked that day in Rome: *Are you Catholic?*

This is all understandable in one way, and in another way, it is even definitional. We have indeed taken some tools and evangelistic methods of our "separated brethren," as John Paul called Protestant Christians, and brought them with renewed vigour back into the orthodox Catholic world. Many of these riches have always been a part of it, so we are only reclaiming a part of our heritage. The power, the zeal, the uncompromising devotion to the Word of God by which our separated brethren approach the "God-haunted" world, as the fiercely Catholic Flannery O'Connor called it—and as her fiction depicted it—is breathtaking and admirable. It is also dramatically effective and of the most significant importance in this day and age.

For a world O'Connor called "hard of hearing and dim of sight," she drew outsized pictures of the searcher's encounter with the Holy Spirit. These took the form of stunning, overwhelming, even violent episodes of grace: a silly grandmother who, just before she is killed, finally realises the universality of our human connectedness and suffering—"Why, you're one of my babies" she tells the bandit who holds her at gunpoint—"You're one of my own children"; a self-righteous farmwoman who yearns for and is given a vision of all humanity, of every race and nationality—those who have always lived decent, committed lives such as she, as well as those who have found God only at the last second—marching into Heaven together, without honours or distinctions, shouting in unison, "Hallelujah"; the boy prophet Tarwater, who has run from his call as far as he can go, and in the end takes up his destiny to preach the Word in a burnt out, unreceptive world, setting his face towards the town "where the children of God lay sleeping."

O'Connor said that she wrote of these backwoods people who loved God in such a turbulent, wild way because they were—whether they knew it or not—much like Catholics who for centuries have "burned with a consuming zeal," as St. Catherine of Siena did, or who have found the beloved God in St. John of the Cross' awed and trembling "Dark Night of the Soul."

In her profound "Collected Letters," O'Connor wrote of how much she actually shared with the rural believers who surrounded her farm in Georgia: "We differ in what the *Church* is and what it means, but not in who *God* is, or what we owe him." It is this fundamental similarity, this common thirst of all believers for God that comes from encountering Him, and then inevitably sharing

Him—as He is a fountain that overflows—that our Schools of Mission have hoped to foster.

In truth, the formation that flows from our time together is meant to fit the new evangelisers for that which has called them—for that which they have all come to do—rise, go forth, and awaken the children of God who lay sleeping.

6

to see jesus

In principio erat Verbum…

The Book of Kells, the Gospels illuminated by the monks of St. Columba around 800 A.D., begins the Gospel of St. John with the incipit of these words. They are gloriously rendered in a musical kaleidoscope of colours—gold, blue, red, green, silver, rust—a geometry of filigree, interlace, and knots that render the legacy of all light, Christ the King—the Word Himself enthroned amongst the very text that brings Him to the world.

In the beginning, was the Word…

The monks delighted in the power of conveying script by way of image—in the playful, epigrammatic expression of the Word in pictures, just as every rock, river, tree, creature, man, woman and child that make up our wild universe of chemistry is both that and also that which goes by a name. All are both *res* and the *verba*, as the Romans would have it—the thing and the way it is called. God made the world and then He gave his first children a way to entitle it.

The brothers on those cold, storm-ridden isles at the outskirts of civilisation, hoarding and protecting the treasure of the faith from Viking raiders and hostile elements—knew, as the Catholic world has always known, that God is an artist. He made the lilies of the field so lovely that they put Solomon in all his glory to shame. The monks also understood that when Word and image unite, their power is not merely additive but exponential—a force that shapes souls and endures through time.

Startling as it may seem, the monks were adapting the old message to a new means for its conveyance. They were, in their own way, innovators. Countless men and women have been moved by their images in the centuries since they changed the form in which the Bible was memorialised. The words had been made of light; the Word was light.

Catholicism has flooded the world with more extraordinary art, in all forms, than any other single source—from the plastic arts to the narrative to the performing, and from verse to prose. In so doing, it has been a credit both to the arts and the faith alike. During the historic iconoclasm controversies, the Western Catholic Church championed the holiness of the created world, including its imaginative expressions that honoured their Author. God fashioned the world in His image and said that it was good.

It is no wonder then, that the missionary world has employed all of the arts in its hopes of reaching the human soul. In Robert Bolt's powerful film, *The Mission*, a Jesuit priest sent to South America, soaked by jungle rains and raging river water, makes his exhausted way to a rock among the shallows. There he pulls out an oboe, playing it softly and sweetly to attract the native people from the trees, where they have been watching.

The song, the image, and the play of words upon words are all ways by which we reach what is most human in each other. In a common paraphrase of St. Augustine, "When we sing, we pray twice." Indeed. For the Word that is beyond all time chose to enter time to become one of us. And in so doing, he further ennobled all that was made.

And the Word was made flesh and dwelt among us.

That indwelling—the presence of the Holy within the space where we live and in the form by which we exist—is witnessed in the Scriptures. The story that the Scriptures tell of that indwelling is the news that the evangelist seeks to share. And that tale has been declared artistically in countless ways and through every media—Michaelangelo's Sistine Chapel, Bach's Oratorios, the Modernist verse of T.S. Eliot. For the Christian, it is the cosmic event that gives meaning to the universe. It is the point of the whole story.

In the year 2000—the turning of the new millennium that had been anticipated for at least a decade before the clock struck midnight in 1999—the Church held its World Youth Day. The event had been initiated in 1985 by John Paul II to bring together Catholic youth from around the globe for a weeklong invigoration of their faith. The year 2000 was also the Great Jubilee Year, a special 52 weeks in which people could address their shortcomings, be reconciled, and start anew. This union of factors made the time intensely special, so John Paul hosted the young people at their gathering in the heart of the Church, Rome. And as the motto for the celebration, the Pope chose the beginning of St. John's gospel:

> The Word was made flesh and dwelt among us.

He chose the phrase because it encapsulates the uniqueness of Christianity: it alone among the faiths holds as its central tenet that God enrobed Himself with flesh and entered our world as its Saviour. As St. Paul spoke of it and as the Church Fathers understood it, this *kenosis* amounted to Jesus setting aside His own will in obedience and submission to that of His Father. Over the six sweltering days of that August summer, approximately two million people from 157 countries were re-evangelised with that transformational message of John the Evangelist.

The conditions in Rome were often challenging. Besides the heat, many had to camp out on the lawns and brave the difficulty and slowness of services provided to such an overwhelming number. Still, the energy was powerful and sustained. Somehow, language proves no real barrier to those who are young and high in spirits. They knew why they were there and for Whom they were there, regardless of the words they used to express such things. A confusion of tongues has never been an obstacle to those who reach out in fellowship to each other and who recognise each other in kinship. They frolic together all the same.

On the grounds of Tor Vergata University in Rome, the site of many of the events, John Paul challenged the youth to be "sentinels of the morning." Clearly a modern hero to them all, he asked that they take their youthful exuberance, spontaneity, and devotion, and bear it forward, carrying the light of Christ into the world so that it would shine from every corner. The week's ending was thereby framed in missionary terms. Those who had come were asked not to simply return to where they had come from, and what they were doing before, but to strike out with an evangelistic fervour freshly sprung among them there in Rome at the dawn of another thousand years.

And as part of that celebration, on screens playing throughout the campus, was an image—a set of images, in fact, in the ever-wondrous form of the moving picture. Flickering across 40 monitors all about the grounds was a film depicting the life of Jesus, the wonder of God-made-man. The movie had been written and directed in a fashion that would best allow the story's dissemination to those in the world who might not be able to receive it in any other way. Copies of the film were also provided in the bags of materials given to each of the pilgrims.

Here was the story of the Word expressed in dramatic form, marshalled by light, colour, and music in service of the shared message. It was a new instrument for a new day—just as the illuminated manuscript must have seemed to the monks on those cold, desolate isles at the very dawn of the faith.

Through many years of effort and partnership, it was our great privilege to bring it to Rome in August 2000, the year of the Great Jubilee.

In the early 1980s, Mario and I met Paul Eshleman and his wife, Kathy, at a Catholic Charismatic Renewal conference in Rome where he was a guest. Paul was the President of Inspirational Films, Inc., who owned the rights to what is now commonly known as the Jesus Film. He was also a leader in Campus Crusade for Christ, an evangelical association for university students now known as Cru, and the founder of the Jesus Film Project. The latter aims to use visual media to spread the Christian message, ensuring people from various linguistic and cultural backgrounds can experience the story of Jesus.

Over the following years, Paul became our close friend, and we worked on many significant collaborations together. However, the Jesus Film was Paul's primary focus at the time, and he was pouring every ounce of effort he had into making it known when our paths first crossed.

The film had been produced in 1979 and was sponsored by Campus Crusade. Shot on location in Israel, it used the Gospel of St. Luke as its source and was directed by British directors John Krish and Peter Sykes. Five years of research and preparation went into the filming. It engaged a sizeable technical crew and featured 45 actors and actresses of various nationalities. For a time, the movie had a theatrical release in America under the flagship of Warner Brothers. Even so, its life after that run is where its effect has proved most enduring. The film's simple, forthright, faithful-to-the-Gospel storytelling had convinced Paul to gain the rights. He saw it as a work highly conducive to evangelistic efforts and especially useful for the parts of the world where literacy could not be expected.

Many years passed after that first meeting in the eighties, years in which we were busy establishing the ICPE Schools and Mission Centres and conducting outreaches and ministries around the world. Through the unwavering dedication, exceptional talent, and steadfast resilience of our ICPE missionaries and leaders, the ICPE charism had flourished. This growth had also been made possible with the invaluable support and blessing of the Catholic hierarchy. The call Mario had felt so many years before, to revive and enliven an evangelistic spirit within the Church and to provide formal training for Catholic missionaries, had borne much fruit; as the results showed, it had also evidently filled a very real need. Moreover, we were blessed to occupy a unique place, being committed Catholics, while providing a bridge to, and an ecumenical common ground with, like-minded Evangelicals.

So when Mario and I again ran into Paul and Kathy in Rome—this time only a few years before the millennium—the ICPE Mission was well established. The project that would prove to be one of our most important collaborations with another Christian denomination greatly benefited from that fact.

It seemed that Paul, typically enthusiastic and full of cheer, had met with a defeat; his downcast demeanour showed it had been a substantial one. He'd travelled to Rome from America, hoping to meet with some Vatican officials. The plan was to gain their approval to use the Jesus Film in the Catholic world as a tool for evangelisation—the same kind of partnership he had sought with other religious groups in the past. The meeting had not gone well, however, and his request was denied. He then related all the details to us; the reason for the decision became clear, at least to Mario.

Although Paul had come to the meeting in good faith, showing incredible generosity and sincerity in offering to work with the Church, there was a background that could not be overcome. Paul's intentions were never to proselytise Catholics. Yet, at that time, a significant number of evangelical organisations did indeed exclude Catholics from the Christian fold. Catholics were seen by many in their number as missionary territory, errant travellers whose misguided devotions, conceptions, and checkered history had to be corrected. As such, the Church was wary of partnering with any evangelical institution, especially those without a track record to show their intentions were not bent on converting old-faith holdouts.

Mario related this to Paul, who came to understand the reason for the Vatican's reservations. Furthermore, as one who had gained credibility with the Church after twenty years of service—and who himself had faced doubts concerning his intentions, even from fellow Catholics—Mario could offer another way for Paul to consider.

He asked if the film company would give Catholics the rights to distribute the movie themselves—namely, us. Paul's answer was an immediate and unqualified "Yes." In that, he showed himself to be a true disciple and evangelist, one who did not care who did the work of God or who got the credit, as long as the job was done.

Urgency was the order of the day since the year 2000 was imminent. We knew the film had to be within the Church's worldwide effort to inspire the faithful with fresh evangelistic zeal. The opportunity had met the occasion. But that meant we had to formalise a deal between Inspirational Films, Inc.—Paul's organisation that owned the film rights—and the ICPE Mission. Only then could we begin the enormous task of working with the Vatican for its support and participation, finding the means to dub the film into major world languages for its use, and meeting with World Youth Day and Jubilee Year planners as they prepared to greet the descent of millions of people—young and old alike—upon Rome.

First, the agreement had to be forged. To that end, the ICPE Mission established Millennium Films International as one of its initiatives. This new venture would facilitate creative evangelisation in the Catholic world, but in particular, it would provide Catholics with the use of the Jesus Film in those efforts. The division would provide a legal structure for those who wished to support the film's use and would also provide tools and experience for Catholic groups who wanted to know how to employ it in their work. Mario then flew to San Clemente, California in April of 1999 to sign the distribution rights agreement with Paul, President of Inspirational Films.

With the rights in hand, the subsequent phases of the job included a diplomatic dimension, as well as a technical one. The distribution agreement allowed us to package the film so that it conformed to Catholic doctrine, which we knew would be a requirement for Vatican approval. A new preface had to be added to the footage to accomplish that. The result was to be a Catholic Jubilee version that began with the opening of the Jubilee Door at the Vatican by Pope John Paul II. An explanatory prologue and a summative epilogue would also be added. The epilogue was to include an invitation for those watching the film to commit their lives to Jesus.

Scriptwriters and a video company were engaged for the introduction and conclusion of the new edition. Further, the packaging for the video contained the endorsements of Cardinal Alfonso Lopez Trujillo, then President of the Pontifical Council for the Family, Cardinal Josef Tomko, then Prefect of the Congregation for the Evangelisation of Peoples, Archbishop Angelo Comastri, President of the National Committee for the Great Jubilee 2000 in Italy, and Pope John Paul himself, who invoked "God's blessing upon this initiative" and imparted an Apostolic Blessing on the work. Those approvals provided a dimension of authenticity and assurance for those who wanted to use it in their missionary efforts.

The technical side of things involved dubbing the film. If it were to be utilised throughout the world, much of the un-evangelised territory—especially in developing countries—would likely be illiterate. Translation in the form of script chyrons, or translation boxes, would be useless; such people would have to be able to hear the story spoken in their own languages to understand it. Fourteen languages were the goal, and our formidable ICPE missionary, Silvana, who had served as our right-hand person since the beginning of the Mission, was the natural choice to lead this daunting task. Studios were hired, voice actors engaged, and a dubbing crew from Paul's Jesus Film Project came to help.

English was the easiest to convert into a Catholic edition, as the original movie had been filmed in English. Italian also proved a relatively straightforward process. During a press conference, Mario and the then Archbishop Sepe, the General Secretary of the Great Jubilee 2000 activities, presented the Italian edition, with the Archbishop highlighting the significance of evangelisation during the Holy Year. This official launch of the Jubilee Edition of the Jesus Film within the Catholic Church occurred in Vatican Radio's Marconi Room. With those two editions completed, plans for French, Spanish, Portuguese, Tagalog, and Mandarin were developed so that the film could be viewed throughout North and South America, in French and English-speaking Africa, the Philippines, and China, among others.

We also met in early January 2000 for a pivotal and strategic gathering with representatives from each continent to discuss national plans for using the film in various locations. Among those present were main leaders from the ICPE Mission who were at the forefront of the Jesus Film initiative—Silvana, Angelica, Jacek, Henry (Mario's brother), Joachim, Fritz and Noel—alongside key figures from other Catholic organisations. This meeting defined all that was to come, as it was made up of partners from around the globe. They all contributed their considered judgment and skills to launch a new means of worldwide evangelisation through the Jesus Film.

The plans for Italy and Poland were typical. The plans for Italy began at a conference in Rimini, where 40,000 copies of the film were distributed. To take advantage of the fact that World Youth Day and Jubilee Year pilgrims would bring an estimated 25 million people to Rome, the strategy was to use our CCR contacts, the Italian diocesan pastoral centres, and various youth ministries as vehicles for spreading news about the film. We also incorporated newspaper and television advertising.

In Poland, the strategy established by our innovative ICPE Mission community was to reach the cumulative 38 million Poles at home and around the world by showing the film and providing follow-up materials for Lenten school retreats and screenings in large Polish-speaking parts of North America. At the Toronto premiere of the film, 2050 people attended. In fact, in May of 2000, the Jubilee Catholic edition of the movie won the Gran Prix at the Catholic International Film Festival held in Warsaw. Millennium Films was awarded first prize in the multimedia category for its DVD of the movie and the Polish website dedicated to it. Other efforts included a promotional video featuring Cardinal Tomko, Fr. Tom Forrest, and other Church leaders and a magazine-format publication of St. Luke's Gospel with full-colour graphics. A second magazine publication of the Gospel was prepared for children. The magazine formats for adults and children would be a regular feature for the different language versions we created.

When the Jubilee Year kicked off in earnest, Archbishop Sepe, the General Secretary of the Great Jubilee 2000 activities, made sure that the film was part of every conceivable evangelistic engagement. It was, in fact, the only evangelistic tool made available to every pilgrim who came to the city. Videos were hauled into St. Peter's Square by the truckload and distributed by volunteers. Every bishop who attended the Jubilee of Bishops held at Paul VI Hall that year was given a copy, and many took boxfuls back home with them. During the different Jubilees that year, such as the one for diplomats, Cardinals, bishops, and priests, Pope John Paul handed copies of the film to 175 Cardinals, 124 Papal Nuncios, and 8000 Bishops and priests. Sharing the Jesus Film became a Roman phenomenon that year. To use the language of our times, it "went viral"—so that the repercussions were felt worldwide when the different versions spread throughout the continents.

Yet, one frontier was still to be crossed: China.

The East as a whole is well-known for resisting missionary efforts.

Shusako Endo's *Silence* is one illustration of many that set out the case, and there are martyrs whose deaths give more tragic testament to the faith than their accomplishments in making headway.

Opposition grew even more pronounced when China became a communist country. Entrance to the land was dramatically curtailed for foreigners, let alone evangelistic endeavours. Penetrating the Chinese Iron Curtain became an enormous problem.

Prior to the takeover by the Chinese Communist Party (CCP) in 1949, the Church had reached a certain level of rapprochement with the government. The problems had been cultural in basis, and there was an uneasy but sustained co-existence of Confucianism and other customary ways with the doctrines of the Church. Ancestry worship was always a sticking point, but the Church was working hard to find a context for honouring patrimony—a practice central to Asian cultures—within the Christian framework. But after the cultural revolution and the fall of the Chinese mainland to communist forces, persecution of all Christian denominations intensified. Expulsions and executions were common. All the progress that had been made was lost.

Once the intensity of the outright persecution phase lessened, the CCP established the Catholic Patriotic Association, a move to co-opt Catholicism within the established communist system. But that body rejected Rome's appointment of bishops, required a disavowal of the Pope's supremacy over Church matters, and forced underground what has always been seen as the orthodox Chinese Catholic Church. While at this writing there has been some halting progress in the recognition of Chinese bishops by the Holy See—a point of contention, not only among Chinese Catholics but also within the Church at large—in the years before the millennium, the obstacles to evangelism in China were more entrenched. Getting the film any type of recognition there would be a major task and would require some kind of diplomatic breakthrough. It was also one of Paul Eshleman's most fervent desires.

The key to the success with the Chinese lay in an initiative already underway on another front. As part of the millennium celebration, which for Catholics included the Jubilee Year observance and the World Youth Day components, Paul's Jesus Film Project decided to mark the 2000th anniversary of Jesus' birth in a unique fashion. They would ask cultural figures to comment on who Jesus was.

International celebrities and leaders from the worlds of politics, sports, media, and entertainment were given an opportunity to provide quotes, and many of them even came through with striking and profound video clips. Since this was an established and ongoing effort, the ICPE Mission decided that the Jesus Film Project could approach Chinese authorities for something in the same vein—a comment about an undeniably important world figure, Jesus Christ, whose birthday was about to be celebrated. It was a brilliant strategy, as everything was contextualised in a way that made providing a comment more palatable to the Chinese government.

Since we had contacts with China, our part was to extend the invitation. The ICPE Mission approached the Chinese Bureau of Religious Affairs and asked that they consider providing a quote that would go alongside other remarks from many international sources. We explained that there was a long list of contributors and hoped that China would join them. To our great delight, the Bureau said yes. They sent the following:

"Jesus said: 'I am the Way, the Truth, and the Life.' This film will help you to know Jesus, to live in him, to accept him, to witness to him and to spread further the work of evangelisation in China in this new millennium."

Flabbergasted and encouraged, we decided to take another risk. We expressed our gratitude for the quote, then ventured to ask whether the Chinese would permit us to print the screenplay of the Jesus Film. The ICPE Mission community in the Philippines, embarked to maximise the good relationships in China for the greatest impact of the Gospel—they planned to produce the Mandarin and Cantonese versions in an original compact package. Of course, the screenplay was itself effectively the Gospel of St. Luke. Once again, the government said yes. Therefore, getting the Holy Scripture into China—one of Paul Eshleman's greatest prayers and one of ours as well—was realised.

We received countless letters testifying to the Jesus Film's effect in various countries, including missives from Nigeria, Kenya, South Africa, Germany, Holland, Italy, Lithuania, England, and the Philippines. One French priest told of how extensively the film and supporting materials were used: as a gift for children in catechism class, which became a means to evangelise their families, some of whom had become tepid in their faith; as a means to evangelise on the street in Christmas markets; as a teaching tool for various diocesan schools at all levels; and even as a part of wedding and baptismal preparation.

Undoubtedly, some of the most gratifying testimonials came from China—gratifying because of the many inroads made with the story of Jesus by Chinese Catholics who had to undergo significant effort and sacrifice. Providing them with the means to do what only they could while taking risks that they could never truly gauge from one day to the next, was a privilege for all involved.

Some Chinese testimonials spoke of how little the viewers had known of Jesus before the film, coming as they had from a Buddhist tradition. They had learned for the first time of both His resurrection and what it meant to them personally. Some said they now saw what the Word meant; it was one thing to have heard it or read it, but another entirely to see it dramatised. A former member of Mao Zedong's Red Guard spoke of how, in Jesus Christ, he had found meaning in the tears and suffering that the Chinese people had endured for over 5000 years.

Those who were already Christians found the film and its accompanying materials to be an indispensable tool for catechising new believers. They were something easily shared with the poor, the sick, the elderly, and particularly those in remote locations, high in the mountains. Sharing the faith with such people, who had little time for study or prolonged explanations, and perhaps no ability to fathom—or often even read—a text, required the precise tool that the film proved to be. The letters from China attested to the fact that the move made the Gospel "portable" and conducive to immediate assimilation. Those who, for various reasons, found themselves among the world's downtrodden, learned that they were part of a worldwide family of believers. Further, as we teach in our Schools, the evangelists "on the ground" in China were themselves re-evangelised by the film. It reinvigorated their work, providing an infusion of fresh blood and inspiration for what they were about.

The words of a young woman from Sichuan represent the effect the film had in China. She spoke of the fact that she had not been a Catholic for long, only having been baptised the previous Easter. What she had been taught in catechism class had seemed vague and distant. It had undoubtedly begun to fade. Of course, her experience was not unlike that of many converts. The seed of faith was initially received with joy, but as it had fallen on rocky ground, it had not flourished. But then she saw the film:

"It seems to me that I was able to go back to the time of Jesus in my own flesh," she said, "and this gave me a better understanding of him. I am moved because Jesus seems to be within easy reach now. I can touch him now."

For the evangelist, no words can be sweeter to hear than those.

The next large-scale deployment of the film for evangelistic purposes occurred in South America. From September 8th through the 10th of the Jubilee Year, the Latin American Eucharistic Congress was held in Cordoba, Argentina. Approximately 200,000 people attended the series of events. The group included 90 bishops, 2,000 priests, and 1,500 eucharistic ministers, and it was covered by representatives from 75 distinct television, radio, and print media organisations. The scale of the event was enormous, and there was no venue large enough to accommodate all the attendees at one time. So the Congress opened and closed with outdoor events, then conducted the rest of the sessions in 253 locations, mostly parish centres. This made the distribution of the Jesus Film and the accompanying materials a huge logistical task.

The Millennium Films' Continental Director for Latin America worked with the Bishops Eucharistic Congress Committee from the outset to coordinate the film's incorporation within the agenda. Millennium Films was made a co-sponsor of the event and then worked closely with volunteers from the Congress. Representatives from Millennium Films visited as many of the local parish centres as possible, where the small-group meetings took place. There they introduced the movie, invited the attendees to a viewing, distributed the materials, and explained the various ways that all of these things could be used.

To ease the logistics involved in distribution, 60,000 packages containing the film and supporting matter were distributed at registration. Since the demand exceeded the supply, the Cordoba registrants were given information on how to receive the packages later. Multiple screenings of the film took place during the Congress, including outdoor venues to increase the number who could attend.

There were many consequences of this well-staged event. Every part of Argentina was represented, so the evangelistic tools went to those from the big cities and also to those from the smallest villages, where weekly masses were infrequent due to the lack of a priest. Fruit was also born outside the Congress, as people throughout the city—police officers, hotel patrons, business owners—grew curious about the film, which they were seeing everywhere. Only ten days after the conclusion of the Congress, we received a flood of enquiries about the film. Catechists ranked as the overwhelming majority of interested parties, as they could see how readily the film and supporting materials could be used in their work.

Given all this effort—coinciding in both hemispheres—it will come as no surprise that the scale of the organisational plan and the human resources to pull it off made the Jesus Film ministry one of our largest undertakings. It also took substantial financial resources to finance the execution of that scheme, but the Jesus Film Project underwrote the whole venture. Bill Bright of Campus Crusade and, of course, Paul Eshleman were behind our every effort, and their letters—both those addressed to us and those sent on our behalf to their constituencies—were no small part of the great consequences that ensued. The project has also proved one of the most gratifying, in that it was a joint, ecumenical venture fulfilling a fervent desire across denominational boundaries. The goal was to bring the story of Jesus, faithful to the Gospel of St. Luke, to as many people around the world as possible. What we shared in this hope was greater than anything that divided us.

The impact of the Jesus Film at the turn of the millennium must be understood in the context of the culture at the time. The world was then in a monumental transition. It was the beginning of what has proven to be an increasingly complex tension within modern society.

On the one hand, in the year 2000, Europe and North America slipped further into a marked secularism. The Judeo-Christian religion and the societal values that supported it were no longer held in high esteem. As time wore on, they would be viewed by contemporary culture in an altogether negative light. In their place, for those still seeking to fulfill the "religious impulse" so native to humankind, either weakened and "desacralised" strains of Christian doctrine emerged; alternative—particularly Eastern—religions were adopted, or heterodox, New Age spiritualities came to the fore. For the first time, it became normal for most of the population to have no religious affiliation at all, not even a traditional one, giving rise to the "nones"—a designation for those who claim no religious patrimony when asked.

On the other hand, there was a resurgence in fundamentalist Islamic practice. The rise was a response to increasing globalism worldwide and what was seen as an insistent, intrusive modernism at odds with the adherent's cultural identity. The impact of this phenomenon had significant implications for religious tolerance and world peace.

In the midst of all this, Pope John Paul II continued to play his world-changing role as a religious leader, a voice for human rights, and a tireless advocate for inter-religious dialogue and peace. And as a response to the emerging cultural realities at the dawn of the new millennium—both positive and negative—John Paul issued his call for a "new evangelisation." He urged the Church to renew its mission with vigour and relevance to a world in dramatic flux that could change—even violently—from one minute to the next.

For the ICPE Mission, the introduction of the Jesus Film and the consequent response it received meant something quite distinctive. The film and its accompanying materials were not just new practical tools for evangelisation; they signalled a need for the ICPE Mission to evolve.

We had to stay relevant in a rapidly changing society, embracing innovation without compromising our core values. At the same time, we had to forge bold new ways to engage the challenges of the new millennium.

There was nothing new to be said about the eternal Truth or humankind's desire for it. Those are constants. But how that Truth was shared had to rise to the day—be spry, quick, responsive to the modern world, and willing to work with whomever necessary to win the goal.

The film testified to the fact that people were increasingly less interested in formal programmes and more drawn to authentic, immediate connections.

Some might suggest that there are better, more complex, or more profound movies about Christ that could be used to evangelise. They might point out that films must be constantly revised to keep up with changing tastes and technology. However valid those arguments may be, in the words of St. Thomas More, one cannot make "the perfect the enemy of the good." The rights to use other films are not and would not be offered with such incredible generosity and freedom for the evangelistic effort as were the rights to the Jesus Film. There are thousands of business and financial reasons why missionaries cannot simply appropriate Mel Gibson's "The Passion of the Christ," Franco Zeffirelli's "Jesus of Nazareth," and so many other outstanding artistic accomplishments.

In contrast, those who first gained the rights to the Jesus Film and have partnered with us all along, understand the objective of its use to be evangelisation. The purpose is to bring the salvation narrative to others in clear, understandable terms that act as a common denominator for viewers of many different lands and languages. The Jesus Film has met and exceeded all expectations in that regard.

Our partners dubbed the film into seventeen languages: English, French, German, Italian, Polish, Portuguese, Spanish, Cantonese, Mandarin, Arabic, Tagalog, Bahasa Indonesian, Ukrainian, Maltese, Japanese, Korean, and Hindi. The undertaking on the part of the Jesus Film Project has never stopped, and it is said to be the most translated film in history. The Guinness Book of World Records designated it as such, numbering the languages at 1,977 as of May 2022. And the project is still in process.

With our partners, we have helped bring the Jesus Film—according to the Jesus Film Project's estimate—to a record 7.3 billion people. This number is based on calculations from the project's research firm and covers known viewings from 1979 to 2015. That makes it one of the most watched films in history.

In sum, all this underscores the need for a nimble, fluid evangelism that constantly adapts to the culture. New times create new obstacles, and we must have new tools to overcome them. Like any other enterprise—secular or spiritual—if the missionary effort does not adjust to the world, it will be left in a world that was, with no way to fulfil its calling.

Therefore, we must always be looking for ways to "illuminate the manuscript" as it were, so that Christ shines in all of his glory—so that He can be seen with fresh eyes by those who, for the first time in their lives, have opened them to Him.

7

journey to rome

> And suddenly, from heaven, there came a sound like the rush of a violent wind, and it filled the entire house where they were sitting. Divided tongues, as of fire, appeared among them, and a tongue rested on each of them. All of them were filled with the Holy Spirit . . . (Acts 2:24)

The firefighters of Rome must rise early on Pentecost, even if no alarm has rallied them from their rest. They don their boots, gear, and helmets even if no house is ablaze nor building threatened with flames. No black billow of smoke need cloud the air in a dark summons, calling them to meet their ancient task—to rush without question into a hell of heat and pain to save and salvage the lives of others. They prepare themselves anyway.

Because the purpose for their readiness is altogether different on this Pentecost Sunday. On this day, their destination is not the scene of an engulfed dwelling but is instead the world's oldest known communal building still in use—the second-century Pantheon. Originally built by the Roman emperors as a temple to honour their gods, known and unknown, the colossal space was consecrated as "The Church of St. Mary and the Martyrs" in the seventh century.

Once they arrive, the firefighters scale its massive dome all the way to the summit. Then they perch themselves around its *oculus*—a circular opening in the apex, through which the sun and rain may fall from the sky onto the marble floor below.

But on this day, it is more than sun or rain that falls through the oculus. This day, the firefighters carry on a tradition nearly as old as the structure itself—that of showering thousands of rose petals in a continuous cascade upon the Pentecost worshippers, 43 metres below. Children dance in the carpet that covers the marble floor, lifting the bounty and casting it about in sprays of red bliss as the choir sings *Veni Creator Spiritus*.

Like the tongues of fire that rested upon the apostles and the Blessed Virgin, the petals ennoble the space, the day, and all upon whom they fall. They also ennoble those who rise so early to climb the massive dome and—counter to their age-old calling to quench the fire and flames—let slip from the heavens a gentle crimson inferno symbolising the Holy Spirit's blaze of gifts.

The gifts of the Spirit are like the petals falling gently from the sky at Pentecost—a cascade of God's abundant grace. Besides, He provides special, unique, and particular gifts, or charisms, as He wills them—to the "daughters who prophesy," the "sons who see visions," the "old who dream dreams."

There is no predicting or understanding why particular charisms are given to each individual as they are. We only know that all who are baptised receive their share of grace and that once bestowed, the gifts should inflame the recipient with a zeal for their exercise.

Above all, such gifts cannot be hoarded; they must be unwrapped and poured out—just as those on whom the Spirit first fell, though gathered in one place, were commissioned to the many. They were to be extravagant with their blessings.

For nineteen years, we lived in Allerheiligen, Germany—nineteen years in which Allerheiligen was the home of the ICPE Mission as the motherhouse of everything we did. It was where we planned and where we taught, the place from which we staged our outreaches and to which we returned for restoration. It was where our community grew organically, thrived, and flourished. Friendships became lifelong bonds there, just as couples were wed, children were born, and griefs were shared. The community at Allerheiligen was a veritable tapestry of cultures, people from a wide array of countries, who shared their various traditions—foods, celebrations, costumes, stories—in a pageantry that was as laughter-filled as it was replete with hard work and intense prayer. That it was the nerve centre of our operation—the place where the labours of training, teaching, formation, and implementing the direction of the Mission were constantly underway—never overshadowed the spiritual aspect of its character. Real people lived a real life there, came to know and love God more deeply, and welcomed all who accepted the invitation to do the same.

Coming from temperate, sea-washed Malta, I remember my first fascination with the four distinct seasons within the Black Forest—autumns in a riot of red, orange and yellow leaves—winters of crisp, silent snows that might last until Easter—delicate springs dressed in a shy green as life blossomed and earth awoke—and summers, though brief, long enough to relish Sunday afternoons on the lawn having tea parties under a close sun. The hiking trails, the waterfall, the old abbey ruins—all of these things call back to me from time to time, and Mario and I are grateful for having been given the time that we had in such a wondrous place.

But then the Spirit beckoned us on. It was time to go. Mario's prayer journal from July of 1997 records the first inkling that we were to pull up stakes and set out for the destination towards which all indications were pointing—Rome. He had been discussing the possibility of our relocation with the then Secretary of the Pontifical Council for the Laity, Archbishop Rylko, who confirmed what we already suspected. The move would mean more than a change of locale; it was a resettling of our Mission within the very heart of the Church itself.

Even though our certainty about the move was beyond question—a step not only logical but consistent with our call—it was not an easy undertaking. Leaving the Allerheiligen community was bittersweet, as it had been our home for so long. Financially, our budget for the move was anything but robust. Adding to the challenge, the transition was set to take place at the cusp of the millennium, just before the veritable geyser of events that I've described in previous chapters. With a tight agenda of commitments tied to our international activities, we knew we had to be in Rome by September of 1998.

To make things even more interesting, we had only one solid week to scout out locations that would serve—in January, of all times; so many of our milestones seem to have happened in January.

Finding real estate in Rome is certainly one of the toughest logistical trials under any circumstances, as Mario and Noel learned when they were trying to find a place for our first School there. And just like back then, nearly every place that we checked was taken or insufficient. The Jubilee Year of 2000 was expected to pack Rome with pilgrims, so others had already snatched up all conceivable locales in anticipation of it.

Then, as has often been proved in the history of the ICPE Mission, the solution to our problem fell to the goodwill of friends. Father Alois, a priest friend in Allerheiligen, knew of a vacant property on the grounds of a religious compound owned by the School Sisters of Notre Dame (SSND). They were practically our last hope, so we raced to meet with Sister Mary Anne, who administrated the congregation's affairs.

The nun was very open to us as a new lay organisation, but it turned out that the sisters were in the middle of a transition period. Only their General Council could respond to our request, and they weren't set to meet for a few months. We had to live in suspense during the interim, hoping against hope for good news, while at the same time running our affairs and planning our move—in other words, preparing for relocation without any assurance that there was a place to go.

Finally, Mario called Sister Mary Anne in March to find out where things stood. With boxes being packed and new directives in place, he received what we had been praying for—an address to give to the movers.

The Allerheiligen ICPE community swung into action. The entire International Office—documents, equipment, and essential paraphernalia—was dismantled and packed up. At the same time, Mario and I had to conduct triage as we sifted through our small apartment to see what we could take and what we would have to leave behind. Our new home was to be a small house that the nuns had used for a kindergarten at one time—the "ICPE Mission Embassy in Rome," as our friends later would refer to it. While our office moved from place to place on the SSND compound, we eventually stopped working out of boxes and settled into a permanent location a short drive away from our home. It served as the International Office of the ICPE Mission serving as the organisational backbone of the global community, and ensuring that the spiritual mission is supported with practical resources, effective communication, and coordination. As such, it was also where we administrated our involvement in the Jesus Film Project, both its reproduction and distribution, where we began the initial work on what would become our Medical Centre in Ghana, and where we helped coordinate the many events that were part of *Evangelisation 2000* and its aftermath.

I recall it was a warm summer day in June when we left the Black Forest and Allerheiligen, setting out for the city to which all roads are said to lead. We had reached a landmark, closing in on the Jubilee Year of the millennium and nearly twenty years since the call had first come to us in Malta—at our own Pentecost full of "rushing wind and tongues of flame."

Much had been accomplished; much was left to do.

After attending the International Catholic Charismatic Leaders' Conference in 1998, Mario continued to solidify our relationships with the different dicasteries within the Vatican. This process was much easier than it had been, as we were now in Rome. The connections made through those efforts, the proliferation of our Mission Centres and Schools of Mission, our deep involvement in the Jesus Film Project, and our part in the *Evangelisation 2000* events all led to one of the most significant events in our Mission's history. In 2002, we were granted the pontifical recognition of the ICPE Mission as an International Association of Christ's Faithful with Pontifical Right.

The importance of this development cannot be understated, as its implications are many. The pontifical recognition formally reflects how the Church perceives and understands an association so designated. It also clarifies the association's position within the Church, placing it under the direct supervision of the Holy See. It acknowledges the lived history of the group—its birth, development, maturation and mission, thereby resulting in an endorsement of its statutes. Finally, it guarantees the association's authenticity and maturity for those bishops considering welcoming it in their diocese. In short, pontifical recognition signifies that the association has demonstrated its commitment to be in full communion with the Church. With this official endorsement, the association is formally declared to be an integral part of the Church and its mission of bringing Christ to the world.

The procedure to obtain pontifical recognition for the ICPE Mission required us to present several letters of recommendation from diocesan bishops in the different locales where we had worked. Those bishops had to speak of how our ministry, in its various aspects, had contributed to and furthered the diocese's work. Some of the letters we were privy to were quite touching, highlighting the fruits of our mission work. We made sure to pass these letters on to our missionaries so that they could be re-energised and reconfirmed by a testament as to how their commitment had resonated with so many.

It was March of 2002 when we learned the news. Twelve women coming from all over the globe were in Malta for the ICPE Women Leaders' Conference. We had begun our work on the World Day of Prayer, March 1, and were in the midst of the weeklong meeting when Mario arrived from Rome. Through an official letter, Archbishop Rylko had just communicated to him that the ICPE Mission had been granted pontifical recognition. A formal announcement was soon dispatched to all our ICPE missionaries and families worldwide, but it wouldn't have been at all surprising to hear that they'd first learned of the news through the sonic boom of joy that sounded from twelve women in Malta that day.

With obvious significance for us, the official declaration of our status was declared on May 19, 2002—Pentecost Sunday. Preparations began immediately for the ceremony commemorating the bestowal, which was to take place at the headquarters of the Pontifical Council for the Laity (PCL) the following month. The PCL is located in the Palazzo San Calisto within Vatican City. In 2016, it was merged into the Dicastery for Laity, Family, and Life as part of the Roman Curia.

While the Mission's work necessarily had to continue as we planned the event, the arrangements were a major mission in themselves. There was coordination with the PCL regarding the ceremony's date and time, the programme's sequence, the choice of prayers and scripture reading to be included, and various other details.

Of course, the logistics for our guests' travel itinerary to and from Rome—a total of four days, from June 16-June 19—their transportation from the airport and about the city, and the accommodations for their stay was another complicated task. We'd invited thirty guests from nine different countries for the occasion, ranging from the International Council of the ICPE Mission to the ICPE Leaders of Communities and Ministries, to those who had collaborated and enabled our initiatives over the years. We also needed to plan a Mass of Thanksgiving, with Father Karel as the main celebrant which required permission and coordination from Santa Maria Maggiore, a celebratory dinner to end the day's festivities in Torrimpietra, and some post-event functions for the day following.

Dressed in our best attire, we all arrived early for the ceremony and made our way to the meeting hall. The formality of the affair, accented by all the flowers and the festive mood, caused Archbishop Rylko to remark "This looks like a wedding!"—which he went on to note that it very much was.

"The ICPE Mission is getting married to the Church today," he said. "Your charism will now belong to the Church."

The ceremony began with a prayer, first pronouncing the eternal nature of Christ and acknowledging that all time and history belong to Him forever. We asked the Lord to make us witnesses of his love—a love so great that He divested Himself of His glory to live among us and die for our salvation. We petitioned Christ to enkindle us with His Spirit and to recommit us to a life corresponding to our baptismal covenant. And finally, we asked the Blessed Mother to accompany us on the journey yet to come and to help us grow in love for her Son at the dawn of another millennium.

Esther, who was at that time Secretary to the International Council, read the Gospel from Luke (4:17-21);

> ... and the scroll of the prophet Isaiah was given to him. He unrolled the scroll and found the place where it was written:

> "The Spirit of the Lord is upon me because he has anointed me to bring good news to the poor. He has sent me to proclaim release to the captives and recovery of sight to the blind, to let the oppressed go free, to proclaim the year of the Lord's favour." And he rolled up the scroll, returned it to the attendant, and sat down. The eyes of all in the synagogue were fixed on him. Then he began to say to them, "Today, this scripture has been fulfilled in your hearing."

The Gospel passage was the theme of the remarks made by Cardinal J.F. Stafford, the President of the PCL. He said:

> In the synagogue of Nazareth, Jesus inaugurated his mission of proclaiming the Good News. In making his own the text of Isaiah, a new era was begun by Christ: it is now the 'year of grace'—the time of mercy, the time of salvation. In history, the Church continues this Mission of Jesus. By receiving the anointing of the sacrament of Confirmation, each of us has been marked with the sign of the Holy Spirit. Every person sealed by the Holy Spirit now carries the spiritual aroma of the holy muron, the sacred chrism, and brings the sweet scent of the seven-fold gifts of the Holy Spirit into the many market-places of the world in Christ.
>
> At the very end of the Great Jubilee 2000, the Holy Father John Paul II wrote in the Apostolic Letter *Novo millennio ineunte:* "Over the years, I have often repeated the summons to the new evangelisation... to insist that full-strength we must rekindle in ourselves the impetus of the beginnings and allow ourselves to be filled with the ardour of the apostolic preaching which followed Pentecost."
>
> I know very well how much you cherish these words of the Holy Father. We implore the Holy Spirit to help you achieve this goal. It is very significant that the decree of recognition of the ICPE Mission fell on Pentecost Sunday this year.

> I pray that you will always have Mary's loving intercession in your generous service to the Church. May rejoicing in the Lord always be your strength!

Mario and I made our own remarks as part of receiving the Decree of Recognition. We explained that when we began our work in 1985, we simply desired to respond to God's call for radical discipleship—something unyielding, pure, and strong. On that Pentecost Sunday of our pontifical recognition, we recalled Pope John Paul II's address to the ecclesial movements and communities on Pentecost of 1994, when he said that movements like ours illustrated that "faith is not abstract talk nor vague religious sentiment, but a new life in Christ instilled by the Holy Spirit."

We expressed our desire for a deeper knowledge of God and growth in charity in order to be true salt of the world. In a post-modern society, in which truth exists only in the plural, we recognise an ever-growing need to present Jesus Christ as God's solution for humanity's ultimate search for meaning in relevant language and concepts. We then noted our endeavours to meet that need: providing Christian formation that encouraged and enabled lay people to make the Gospel incarnate in every sphere of life; using contemporary terminology and concepts to share Christ with the younger generations; presenting Christian spirituality as the prophetic answer to the concrete life situations of our times; exploring ways to present the Gospel as an invitation rather than an imposition; communicating the Good News through evangelistic concerts, contemporary songwriting, the theatrical arts, and mass media; and developing projects and relief ministries for the poor and the underprivileged.

We ended by acknowledging that as the third millennium dawned, the world faced a paradox: the rejection of absolute meaning and truth in the pursuit of material prosperity while simultaneously desiring meaning and an interior life. We had the opportunity to provide it with an answer in the form of a person, Jesus Christ. So we submitted our fiat—just as Mary had submitted her own—in the hope that through the new evangelisation, God would use the ordinary to accomplish the extraordinary.

At the end of the celebration, we thanked Cardinal Stafford and presented him with our Mission's logo etched onto a crystal surface. We explained its significance: a globe representing the world, with the Cross of Christ at its centre. The day ended with pictures and a lovely reception in a Baroque meeting hall at the Palazzo San Calisto itself. Having so many missionaries and leaders there and friends and supporters present was one of those culminating experiences that validate so much in the life of any organisation or individual. Rituals and celebrations, we have found, do not lie outside or above history—but are instead shining moments within it. They are instants *in* time that bring together all encounters *of* time—the past acknowledged in the present for the benefit of the future.

On that Pentecost Sunday of 2002, we were surrounded by those who had brought the humble work of God—the ICPE Mission—thus far and were now placed within the very heart of the Church that would see us down the road yet to come.

The first Pentecost changed things. Frightened, flawed people who had almost to the person abandoned their Master at the moment of His great crisis were assembled—ashamed of their weakness at his trial, amazed by His forgiveness of their abandonment, ignorant of what was to come in the days ahead. They were together in the way that shattered people who have survived a great storm huddle together, not so much a coherent group as a set of stunned survivors. But in an instant of God's consuming providence, they were newborns. They were made His Church. In a roar, in a flash, they belonged to Him and each other and possessed the confidence, faith, and wisdom necessary to strike out and spread the Good News of Jesus Christ.

As I've said, our own Pentecost began in Malta. There, unremarkable people decided that they would take God at His word. They invited Him to rush upon them like the wind, fall upon them like the flame, and make them love Him, serve Him, and become Him in the way those called to be His Church become His hands, feet, eyes, and tongue, ministering to His children so that they may do likewise.

When we received pontifical recognition in 2002, we were approaching our twenty-year anniversary, and the significant moment drew us out in clear relief for others to see. We matured, we grew, and we were entirely understandable for what we were and are—for what we did and do. This recognition not only clarified our role for those to whom we were still an enigma but also served as a charge for us to remain faithful to what the Church affirmed and blessed.

The ICPE Mission is the fruit of what some refer to as a New Pentecost bestowed on the Church through the Second Vatican Council. Many lay movements and ecclesial communities also were born or flourished at that time, among them Communion and Liberation, Focolare, the Neocatechumenal Way, Cursillos de Cristianidad, the Charismatic Renewal, the Regnum Christi movement of the Legionaries of Christ, and Nuovi Orizzonti. The history of each is varied, as different as might be expected in a world of individual inspiration. And just as not all are called to do the same thing, they are not all called in the same way. God being infinite, the expression of His will is infinite.

Yet, there are some commonalities among the lay movements that arose from the spring of Vatican II. Their characteristics are roughed out by Charles Whitehead, in his work, *The Role of Ecclesial Movements and New Communities in the Life of the Church.* All have "a charismatic founder, a particular charism, some form of ecclesial reality or expression, a predominantly lay membership, a radical commitment to the Gospel, a form of teaching or training closely linked to its charism, and a specific focus or commitment to bringing its emphasis or understanding into the life of the Church."

Recent popes have been strongly supporting these communities. John Paul II championed the new movements as part of a springtime within the Church. He and Benedict XVI saw them as instruments of renewal that testified to an essential vitality, signs of the Holy Spirit in response to the tenor of the times. Francis has continued this papal endorsement, while also calling for a greater discernment in how they are integrated into the wider Church itself. As we approach the second quarter of the twenty-first century, the lay initiatives that flourished in the years following the Second Vatican Council are well-established. Their engagement, energy, and dynamic witness are valued. However, it has not always been so.

In the years following Vatican II, there was a great deal of anxiety over the changes in the Church. Orthodox Catholics feared that the Church and Christ Himself were in danger of being "demystified." The beauty of the Latin Mass and the long history of Church ritual was mourned by many; they argued that the transition from these things was all too abrupt. The changes were feared to herald more profound concerns about whether Church doctrine would be "contextualised" and diluted, which was then happening in mainline Protestant churches. Many Catholics in good faith feared that all of this amounted to a confusion of the tumultuous times that comprised the 1960s and 70s with whatever necessary recalibrations the Church needed to make to address that era. "Protestantisation" of the Church was a source of deep concern for them—and the tradition from which "evangelicalism" had arisen seemed a Trojan Horse meant to undermine Catholicism in a clandestine manner. In short, what faced us as the leaders of a new group meant to "evangelise" and "spread the Good News of the Gospel" had a context that was large, complicated, and prone to misinterpretation.

In addition, some critics argued that these movements fostered a clannishness—an exclusivity that ran parallel to the Church and promoted clericalism in either the clergy, the laity, or both. There have indeed been clashes between the Church hierarchy and some groups over the liturgy, ecclesial power, and doctrinal interpretation. It must be said that some movements have faced scandals of natures that are sadly common to all individual and institutional failings but admittedly even more scandalous when in the Christian context. These issues have damaged the credibility of the movements and led to internal crises, often requiring external intervention by Church authorities.

This all serves as a sobering and cautionary reminder to any lay movement, even those who have been granted pontifical recognition—that a movement's full understanding of what it is and what it does and a vigilant dedication to maintaining the standards of its constitution, are key to sustaining the confidence with which it has been favoured. We appreciate—and as part of our practice, take time often to reiterate—that the ICPE Mission received not only a gift through the Decree of Recognition but also a solemn responsibility. Through the grace of the Holy Spirit, and carrying our imperfections, we accept this responsibility that comes with being confirmed in our call to be at the service of bringing new vitality in and through the Church, to bring forth new wine in new wineskins.

If that is the responsibility of our Mission, so must we be ever mindful of our gifts—those unique, peculiar gifts the Church affirmed as our charisms of *worship* and *evangelisation.* They are how the Spirit helps us respond to the needs of the Church and our times. These distinct aspects—or our Mission's nature—animate us and give us character. They are how we are recognisable—how we are "known." They are what we are.

This "biography" of our Mission seeks to preserve our history for the benefit of the Mission itself and those it serves. Yet, even if it were lost—even if there were no record of the philosophy and logic behind our calling—I believe that who we are would radiate through how we live and what we do, for the Spirit moves relentlessly through our charisms of worship and evangelisation, embodied in the living testimony of the ICPE missionary disciples across the world.

We receive our charisms in humility and nurture them in the furnace of prayer, where they can be strengthened, purified, and made fruitful. We are called to offer our entire being to God in every moment, which is our spiritual worship. A life of worship not only shapes us but also transforms us, deepening our relationship with God as Creator, Saviour, and merciful Lord. This dynamism of love fuels our passion as ICPE missionaries to spread the Gospel of joy and peace. We strive to be authentic disciples and credible witnesses, creatively revealing the beauty of the Gospel as the response to the challenges of our times.

While it is true that every baptised Christian is called to worship God and point the world to Christ, the charisms of a lay movement highlight particular aspects of the Christian life *consciously lived* by its members. They stir a complacent culture and challenge the Church to remember essential elements of the Gospel that may be neglected. If we are faithful to our calling, we become a visible sign of grace, a witness of what God can do—how He can transform the deficient into the competent, the reluctant into the heroic—how He can make a Peter out of a Simon, a Saul the Persecutor into a Paul the Evangelist.

The ICPE missionary disciple seeks to live as a witness to God's active presence in various walks of life today: as married couples, those discerning marriage, those who are single, those who live consecrated lives, and finally, as ICPE seminarians and missionary priests. The predominant model is that of married couples with families who, guided by the light of the Gospel, navigate modern complexities like parenting, financial stability, and work-life balance. Striving to reflect God's love, they serve others, especially disadvantaged families. Many couples in the community are involved in family ministry, supporting other couples—from marriage preparation through difficult times—to strengthen the bonds of faith and love within Christian homes.

ICPE missionaries also live unmarried lives, a state that the Church often has—however, unwittingly—left in a limbo of mixed messages. Christian singles are sometimes made to feel they lead incomplete, unfulfilled lives—something to pity or be dismayed about. In our ICPE communities, we seek to create an environment that validates every stage of life, including single parents, widows and widowers, and childless couples—everyone belongs.

Among us are also ICPE missionaries who courageously choose to live consecrated lives, embracing private commitments to poverty, chastity, and obedience. Their lifestyle may appear countercultural or even radical. Yet, it powerfully witnesses to the profound joy, freedom, and fulfillment that can be found beyond societal norms, firmly rooted in Gospel values.

The essence of diversity in states of life is rooted in the vocations that emerge from the community. This shared way of life provides fertile ground for these vocations to sprout and flourish, enabling members to thrive and enrich the community in their unique ways. As Henri Nouwen beautifully states, "Living together in community means recognising the different paths we walk and celebrating the unique gifts that each of us brings to the table."

The most recent dimension of ICPE life has been that of the ICPE missionary priest. The turn of the millennium was enormously eventful for us, and among the new developments was the serious attention given to the idea of having priests as part of our community, ordained men who shared our spirituality and would become integrally involved in our endeavours. We had, in fact, stated that openness in our Norms and Orientations written in 2003.

The identifier "missionary" in the title our community priests are given—*ICPE missionary priest,* makes it explicit that anyone who responds to the call of the ministerial priesthood is fundamentally a "missionary" of the Good News. The then theology professor Cardinal

Joseph Ratzinger, later Benedict XVI, made the point explicitly in 1970, "If the priestly being is precisely a being who is sent, then to be a priest necessarily means to be for others…and if, moreover, the concept of mission, of being sent, is the key to understanding his ministry, he (the priest) is essentially a "missionary" of the Good News".

The ICPE missionary priest shares a common identity with the lay ICPE community. He is priest and brother—blessed, supported, and strengthened through the edifying life of a community. This protects him from the common isolation often felt by priests. He is not merely a dispenser of sacraments to his community; he is also a part of it—at the altar for them and around the table with them.

One of our most joyful events as a Mission was on April 10, 2010, the day that Father Alliston Fernandes was ordained as the first ICPE missionary priest. The ceremony occurred at Our Lady of the Rosary Cathedral in Mangalore, Father's birthplace. In this port city of India, priestly ordination is both spiritually and culturally rich. Women wearing colourful saris, indigenous music, and the closeness of a powerful sun on a blistering hot day made the occasion perfectly fitting. A brass band led a procession to the majestic colonial-styled cathedral, followed by the Bishop, altar servers, family, friends, and parishioners—all coming to see their native son raised to the altar. Members of our International Council travelled to be present as well. After the ceremony was over, we were treated to a communal feast under a large nearby tent in celebration of our first priest, who opened the way for others to follow.

Eventually, the number of our missionaries who discerned a priestly vocation required us to open a Formation House. The ICPE Mission Seminary was founded in September 2014 in Wellington, New Zealand, then later moved to Malta in the compound of the Archbishop's Seminary in Rabat. In recent years, a new development has been the Fraternity of ICPE Missionary Priests. These are seminarians and priests whose vocation is either born within the ICPE Mission, or other religious and diocesan priests who choose to be members of the Mission through the profession of the covenant commitment or on a more limited basis.

So, in this variety of expressions, the ICPE missionary life has been and continues to be led wherever we are located in the world. Through the uniqueness of our states, all of us seek to live out the charisms we have been given by offering ourselves to God in spiritual worship. With an eagerness to invite others to encounter the joy of the Gospel, we walk forward, letting our lives speak of this joy and using words when necessary.

Finally, another way that we may be "known" is by understanding what we aspire to as a Mission. This aspiration is best captured by the term "Evangelical Catholics," as defined by George Weigel in his book *Evangelical Catholicism: Deep Reform in the 21st Century Church.*

As Weigel says, we do not seek to adapt catechetical practice and worship styles of evangelical Protestantism to the Catholic Church. We are not the future of either a more progressive or traditional vision of the Church nor are we separated from it as a klatch of elites. What we are is a way of being Catholic, born by the action of the Holy Spirit, prompting continuing reform within the Church guided by the twin criteria of *truth* and *mission.*

We are part of a long tradition meant to clarify the understanding of the Church as "a communion of disciples in mission," aligned with the Church's authentic heritage while addressing the unique challenges of modern culture. We want to be a more dynamic and renewed expression of Catholicism, seeking to live out the vocation of our baptismal covenant with joy and confidence.

Weigel sets out ten distinctive characteristics of Evangelical Catholicism that align with what the ICPE Mission is fundamentally about:

> Evangelical Catholicism is friendship with the Lord Jesus Christ.
> It affirms divine revelation and embraces its authority, which continues through history in the teaching authority of the Church.
> It celebrates the seven sacraments as divinely given means of sanctifying life.
> It is a call to constant conversion of life, which involves both the rejection of evil and active participation in the works of service and charity.
> It is a liturgically centred form of Catholic life that embraces both the ancient traditions of Catholic worship and the authentic renewal of the liturgy according to the teaching of the Second Vatican Council.
> It is a biblically centred form of Catholic life that reads the Bible as the Word of God for the salvation of souls.
> It is a hierarchically ordered Catholicism in which a variety of vocations are respected.
> It is both culture-forming and countercultural.
> It enters the public square with the voice of reason, grounded in gospel conviction.
> It awaits with eager anticipation the coming of the Lord Jesus in glory and until that time,
> Evangelical Catholicism is ordered to Mission—to the proclamation of the Gospel for the world's salvation.

These are the signs by which we would be known. They are the marks that distinguish us. We commit ourselves to be true to them, as we have been the beneficiaries of a grace that came brightly, like tongues of flame—boldly, like the rush of wind—and gently, like a thousand rose petals, falling in an eternal red cascade of love.

After the Evangelisation Course in Malta, a small community was formed in 1980, eventually giving birth to the ICPE Mission.

"The spheres aligned . . . "! Mario and I were married in January 1983.

17 January 1985 – The first ICPE School of Evangelisation launched in Malta, bringing together twenty participants from eight nations.

The School Outreach took us to the vibrant Piazza San Pietro, Piazza Navona, and the iconic Spanish Steps in Rome, where we shared the story of salvation through the pantomime "He is Alive".

September 1986 – After a memorable dinner with Pope John Paul II at Castel Gandolfo, alongside Fr. Tom Forrest and Mario.

From Malta to Rome, the tables were set for the opening Agape Celebration of the second ICPE School, launched in 1986 – a moment that echoed the call to 'Go to all the world!'

The first ICPE missionary community gathered in rented apartments in Malta in 1987, a foundational time remembered as "The Marsaxlokk Experience."

In 1988, a team of ten ICPE missionaries embarked on an eight-week mission deep in the jungles of Borneo, Malaysia. A five-day journey took them into the heart of the wilderness—navigating muddy roads, with jeeps constantly getting stuck. Among them was Rennie, fondly known as the "jungle doctor."

1988 – The second School in Rome marked a pivotal moment, issuing a renewed call for ICPE Vision Carriers. The outreach of this third ICPE School brought us to the streets and squares of Germany, paving the way for a deeper and lasting impact of the ICPE Mission in the country. In November that year, sixty students and staff from nine countries formed the first ICPE School of Mission at St. Gerard's Monastery, Wellington.

1989 – A season of consolidation: ICPE Vision Carriers go through a nine-month Leadership Training Programme (LTP) in Malta.

Meanwhile, negotiations with the Redemptorist Fathers were underway for the acquisition of St. Gerard's Monastery. In September 1990, the ICPE Mission successfully secured ownership of both the Monastery and Church, marking a significant milestone in its mission.

From rented apartments to a permanent home: In 1990, ICPE missionaries settled into their first Mission Centre in San Martin, Malta.

That same year, the ICPE Mission Centre in Allerheiligen was established, becoming pivotal in shaping the Mission's identity.

Wide-ranging and impactful formation modules were conducted in Mission Centres to train, form and empower lay missionary disciples. Two examples are the Pastoral Care Course and the Creative Communications Ministry.

Concurrently, various outreaches were staged from Mission Centres, such as the "Joshua Team" launched from Allerheiligen, on mission to Romania and Russia in 1991.

During the Great Jubilee 2000, the ICPE Mission launched the *JESUS* film, a cross-cultural evangelisation tool presenting Christ's life in a clear, compelling narrative. The widespread distribution helped make the *JESUS* Film one of the most-watched in history.

On Pentecost 2002, the ICPE Mission was granted pontifical recognition as an International Association of Christ's Faithful with Pontifical Right. The Decree was conferred by Cardinal James F. Stafford, then President of the Pontifical Council for the Laity, at the Council's offices in Palazzo San Calisto, Vatican City.

In 2006, ICPE Mission Philippines, led by Esther, launched their mission of "Empowering the Poor with God's Compassionate Love."

The work by ICPE missionaries with the underprivileged in India takes various forms, including catechism in the vernacular languages.

The community in Medellín, Colombia, supports vulnerable communities through multiple initiatives aimed at breaking the cycle of generational poverty.

HopeXchange, the humanitarian arm of the ICPE Mission, alleviates suffering through education, healthcare, and sustainable development. In Ghana, it established a Medical Centre in Kumasi and a school in Kantinkyiren. In Guatemala, it runs the HopeXchange Medical Centre, providing vital healthcare services.

10 April 2010—a landmark day when Fr. Alliston Fernandes was ordained as the first ICPE missionary priest in his hometown, Mangalore, India.

Today, the Fraternity of ICPE Missionary Priests comprises seminarians, deacons and priests—diocesan and religious—who are members of the ICPE Mission, sharing in its spirituality and charisms.

Covenant Celebration 2025, ICPE Mission Singapore.

Covenant Celebrations are the heartbeat of our spirituality, the expression of our faith and mission. We embrace the privilege and calling to live our Baptism—our covenant with the Lord—to the fullest, walking this journey alongside brothers and sisters who share the same call as ICPE missionary disciples.

Covenant Celebration 2025, ICPE Mission Sydney, Australia.

7 June 2024 – The altar from St. Gerard's Church stood in the middle of the sanctuary during the Mass of Thanksgiving for the reopening of Sacred Heart Cathedral in Wellington.

Photo by Annette Scullion: welcom.org.nz

With Mario in St. Peter's Square in Rome at the start of the Synod in 2023—a call to discern together what the Holy Spirit is saying to the Church today, all for the sake of the Church's evangelising mission.

8

consider the lilies

In the spring of 1905, Canadian hymn writer Civilla Martin and her husband were on holiday in Elmira, New York. There, they became acquainted with an afflicted couple—the wife bedridden for twenty years, the husband paralysed and in a wheelchair. The Martins were bewildered by these two because suffering and pain did not seem to register with them. The Doolittles were lively, beneficent, and involved. They ran their considerable affairs as if they had been given a gift, not a trial. Rather than seeking inspiration and comfort, they were the source of these things in their small Christian community.

One day, Mrs Martin's husband was prompted to enquire about their conduct, which defied reason. After all, didn't they know their situation?

"How do you account for this hopefulness?" he asked. "What's the secret to it?"

Mrs. Doolittle answered from her bed with characteristic simplicity: "His eye is on the sparrow. I know He watches me."

Fired by these words, Civilla Martin wrote the lyrics to a hymn and sent them to her composer, Charles Gabriel, who set them to music. *His Eye is on the Sparrow* became a gold standard in Gospel music, recorded by artists everywhere, and was, in fact, one of Whitney Houston's last singles before her death.

I sing because I'm happy. I sing because I'm free. His eye is on the Sparrow, and I know He watches me.

The words are straightforward; they might be dismissed in our cynical age as ringing with too much sentiment and too little realism. We live in a time that is "above" such expressions of naïve trust, just as we live in one that debits contentment, happiness, and joy themselves. Persons who possess them cannot be thought serious or, for that matter, intelligent. And such an attitude is taken as much by those of faith as it is by those without it. We are embarrassed by a lack of sophistication. We are shamed by a faith that confides and surrenders. Such things are for children.

Of course, that is precisely how we were told we should believe—as children do.

The cultivation of providential trust in the life of the ICPE Mission is best explained by our presence in New Zealand—how we came to be there and how we came to develop such a long-lasting ministry in a place so far from our beginnings. It is not an exaggeration to say we ourselves are still amazed by it. Telling the story is also a means by which we can witness how Providence works, as we often recognise its power in hindsight just as much as in the signs and wonders of the present day. Providence is understood both by reflection on the past and by discernment about the present.

I have already related the story of the four Catholic couples who invited the ICPE Mission to Wellington in the late eighties following their exposure to the Catholic Charismatic Renewal and Youth With a Mission. This led to the first ICPE School of Mission conducted in New Zealand at the historic St. Gerard's Monastery. But what transpired in the staging of that School is the witness to Providence that this story provides. Since, as preposterous as it sounded to us that the Kiwis had heard of the ICPE Mission through a former participant at one of our Schools, it was even more preposterous that a chance to establish a permanent presence in Wellington showed signs of becoming a reality.

As it turned out, the Redemptorist Fathers, who had built St. Gerard's after the turn of the twentieth century, were in the process of relocating to Auckland. Through their prayers and hard work, the Catholic couples in Wellington secured the Redemptorist Fathers' loan of the monastery for our School with the blessing of Fr. Humphrey O'Leary, Superior of the congregation. The School was a resounding success and produced much fruit. Some of the couples and other locals were even asked to stay on at the monastery as caretakers while the Redemptorists considered their options about the place. Then, unlooked for and unplanned, an idea was born: we could purchase St. Gerard's and secure a foothold for the ICPE Mission in Oceania and the South Pacific.

Of course, alongside this bold idea were the inevitable doubts about its eventuality. After all, the monastery was worth millions, a price that the Redemptorists could not discount if they had hopes of establishing a home in Auckland and proceeding with their plans.

After all, the ICPE Mission did not have anything close to a budget that could accommodate the purchase.

After all, raising money for a mission so far away from our home base while conducting ongoing Schools and outreaches required manpower that would strain us to the limit.

Then again, somehow, the four couples had heard of the ICPE Mission, brought us to New Zealand, and managed to pull off an incredibly fruitful School there that gave birth to numerous other ministries and a spring of renewed faith. That is the thing about providence: it makes you see another side to things despite evidence that might grossly outweigh it.

So, notwithstanding the obstacles and bolstered by what God had accomplished already in Wellington, all of us—the ICPE Mission and our collaborators in New Zealand—asked for God's guidance, prayed, and fasted. We did this collectively and in small groups, and because a rising tide raises all boats, we asked for reports of any sense as to what the Lord was asking of us. God does not simply promise; He answers, and the testimony of His faithfulness strengthens and emboldens our faith.

What we gleaned from these exchanges was a general conviction that God desired St. Gerard's to remain as it had always been—a "lamp on a hill"—a beacon of faith for that part of the world. Long before, it was consecrated by the Archbishop of Wellington *"to the glory of God"*; if we could transform it into an ICPE Mission Centre, it could continue to glorify Him. So we decided to redouble our prayers for the purchase of the monastery, approach the Redemptorists with our intentions, and set about fundraising to bring it to pass.

In 1988, Mario confidently visited Redemptorist Father Bruce McGill, explaining what we felt God was calling us to do. Father McGill was the only Redemptorist left living in the monastery on that cold, windy day, and he was supportive of our efforts, as was Father Humphrey. The two of them wanted St. Gerard's to remain in Catholic hands. But they had a superseding obligation to the institution's needs. They restated these complex realities of the situation, which Mario appreciated. He remained undeterred.

Events in life often ping-pong about, a tautology people learn to live with; up one day and down the next, good news following bad following good. Fundraising had begun in earnest through word of mouth, supplemented by donations from our own number. We were astounded by a gift from an elderly woman of no great means who gave us $30,000 for our endeavour. As Mother Teresa counselled, this woman had given to the point that it hurt, much like the New Testament widow whose gift from poverty was the Lord's own model for charity.

But even as our work gained traction, the Redemptorist Fathers informed us they'd signed an initial contract to sell the monastery. A real estate developer would purchase the property and convert it into luxury apartments.

That was hard news. It could have defeated us. But as there was still time, and the sale had not been finalised, the ICPE leaders and our New Zealand collaborators kept at their efforts to find the money. There was no doubt about what we believed God's direction for us was, regardless of the impending deal; it became a test of faith.

The four couples who had brought the ICPE Mission to New Zealand launched a major fundraising campaign to raise $150,000 for the purchase. They did this even though the Redemptorists, however sympathetic to the cause, stressed that such a sum was nowhere near the price they would need.

Still, we were praying, we were fasting, we were fundraising—like St. Paul making his tents while at the same time preaching the Word and living the faith. We were buoyed by the news that the apartment deal had fallen through. There was no clear path to success, but we were at least moving in the right direction.

Then, by way of a publicly announced piece of news, we learned that the Fathers had agreed to sell the monastery to a new buyer. This time, it was to be a Wellington-based physiotherapist. The man's plan was to convert the buildings at St. Gerard's into a back treatment clinic. Wealthy tourists from around the world would come to the newly converted spa to be treated and recuperate while overlooking Oriental Bay and Wellington Harbour.

It looked like we had been soundly defeated. Once again, our hopes sank.

But it was not long before they rose once more, phoenix-like. A few months later, the deal with the back pain specialist also collapsed. That amounted to not one, but two transactions—each with buyers with more than enough financial heft to close the sale—that had come to frustration.

On another occasion, the Neighbours' Council near St. Gerard's objected to a group of proposed developers. As it turned out, the golden-tongued champion for the development group who was to make a presentation could not attend for an unexpected reason; as a result, his replacement did a poor job in the delivery. The Neighbours Council turned it down flat.

So many things like this were happening that New Zealand's Cardinal Thomas Williams—who was cheering for our success—told Father O'Leary that all these collapsing deals might be a sign that St. Gerard's was to go to the ICPE Mission. Still, the matter of money stood in the way, and we remained far short.

What followed next was what we now see as one of the deepest testimonies of God's providence in these matters—and there were many.

While seeking God's guidance in prayer, the Lord enlightened Gordon, one of the men in our New Zealand cohort, and revealed the answer. An idea occurred to him that the payment to the Redemptorists could be increased if the single title for St. Gerard's was split into three. The Fathers could sell the Church and Monastery to us together with the lawns as far as the first hedge. They could then sell the land around the top of the cliffs to another potential buyer, and then the land in front of the Church to a third. That meant that the sale price for St. Gerard's proper—the Church and monastery—could be reduced to half a million dollars if we could come up with it.

Mario was in Rome when he got the call. It was the summer of 1990, and he was attending an International Conference for *Evangelisation 2000* at Domus Mariae. He was told that the Redemptorists had agreed to a "tri-parcel" sale of the property, and we could obtain St. Gerard's Monastery for $540,000 New Zealand dollars.

There was only one drawback: he had to raise the money in one week.

Father Tom Forrest, who always seemed to feature in the defining moments of God's unfolding story of our Mission, was also at the conference in Rome. Together with Mario, just before he had to catch a flight home, he approached a top Executive of a Dutch Catholic Foundation who was also participating in the conference. Father Tom asked him, point blank, to help finance the sale so that the ICPE Mission could establish a Mission Centre in New Zealand to train Catholics in evangelisation.

It was agreed that the Foundation would reply to our request by the following Wednesday.

The difficult part of trust in Providence is patience, the hardest virtue to cultivate in almost every context. If we believed in what we discerned to be God's will, we had to have the fortitude to endure the time until the answer came. We had practice in this, however, as the effort to gain the monastery had been both long, arduous, and full of conflicting events—the good cancelling the bad; the bad cancelling the good. To obtain the patience we needed, we had to cultivate a level of detachment—something I will speak of at length further on—a separation of our preference from any one set of circumstances, a trust that did not depend on any one scheme or plan. Wednesday would come, and we would know, and God would be there in any event.

Wednesday did come. The sky opened, and down came the grace we'd hoped for. The Foundation agreed to give us 50% as a grant and 50% as a soft loan. In a flurry of activity, Mario phoned Gordon, and the legal documents were drafted as the two of them and Father Humphrey exchanged long, multi-page faxes.

The ICPE Mission took possession of St. Gerard's on September 1, 1990, almost two years after our first School of Mission commenced in November of 1988. From then on, the ministry flourished throughout the region. In the 1990s alone, the ICPE Mission Centre New Zealand came to be, as did Schools of Missions launched there every year, parish outreaches across the South and the North Island, the start of Youth Alpha, the Wellington Prison Ministry, and the inauguration of St. Gerard's Women's Ministry, among others.

This account of our Mission's history in the South Pacific is a testament to the improbable—at many times, practically impossible—becoming the actualised. There was no ostensible reason for why it should have happened as it did. To review, we were located in the heart of Europe,18,500 kilometres (11,500 miles) from New

Zealand. We had no contacts in that hemisphere to speak of and certainly none with any kind of resources. And yet, approximately two years after Mario's first visit there, we were the owners of a monastery at the very soul of New Zealand Catholicism. From that place, we have conducted 30 years of our ministry to Oceania and Southeast Asia. This is all to say that what we could not have dared dream would come to be—and come to be so soon after we had begun our work—was in God's providential plan. The Mission's mandate was clear: to take the Good News to the four corners of the world. God's strategy to bring that about—where, when, and how—was always His; our part was to trust in it.

The Spirit can come—as it did on Pentecost—in a bright explosion of newness. It is red with life, warm with passion, loud with bliss. He does not leave us after He comes; He abides.

But the days do—as we learn through experience—eventually cool; they darken. We are beings who live in this world, and as such events rush upon us from every direction, sometimes with a fierce strength and wild fury that feels every bit as strong as any meagre faith we've mustered. To survive it, to prosper in it, we must trust. We must take God at His Word. He will not abandon us. After the transformative moment of conversion has passed, whether it comes like a bright sun or a soft whisper, we are not left to fumble about, sustaining ourselves with stale platitudes—surrounded by a graveyard and whistling in the dark. God's love manifested in His providential care to us is real. Trusting this love is hard for finite beings who are prone to forgetfulness and disposed to dread. But He speaks of Himself as our "Rock"—as the Ship upon which we weather all storms.

Trust is born from the friendship into which God invites us—a deepening bond grounded in the unmistakable evidence of who He is: a God of relentless love, mercy, and grace. From the Cross, He extends His hand to us; when we take it, we discover an enduring, unrelenting truth: He will never let us go.

The entire narrative of Scripture is woven with countless examples of God's providential action.

One such account is Mark 8:1-10, in which Jesus feeds the 5,000. Just as in the Old Testament, when God provided for the Israelites in the desert—manna from the heavens, water from a rock—in the New Testament, He assures us of His compassion and ability to provide. While clearly carrying a spiritual significance, the two stories also highlight an important material aspect. God knows we are creatures who need bread for the journey—and not in a purely figurative sense; He is not indifferent and is able to supply in abundance.

Of course, there is a wrong way to understand these things. Trust cannot be confused with spiritual torpor, laziness, or presumption—asking for what we want, but with little or no desire to grow in knowing the Giver of "all good and perfect gift" (James 1:17). God is no genie. He cannot be coerced. To perceive His providence rightly, we must not stop short of what "the Lord shall provide" (Genesis 22:14) really means. While "our daily bread"(Matthew 6:11) in the sense of work, family, health, and friendship is a significant part of His provision—acknowledged in the manna, the water, the loaves and the fish—there is more.

In Matthew, chapter 6, He says:

> Do not be anxious about your life, what you will eat or what you will drink, nor about your body, what you will put on . . . Look at the birds of the air: they neither sow nor reap nor gather into barns, and yet your heavenly Father feeds them. Are you not of more value than they? Consider the lilies of the field and how they grow: they neither toil nor spin, yet I tell you, even Solomon, in all his glory, was not arrayed like one of these.

Jesus defines His saving mission as a service whose highest expression will be the sacrifice of his life for humankind. He came not to be served but to serve, to ransom us from death—now and eternally (Philippians 2:6-7; Mark 10:45). We are rescued from the death of our isolation from God—from an endless "dying"—a falling away that never ceases, a bottom that is never reached. God's provision of His Son as ransom is the highest possible form of giving. What He did not demand of Abraham, He did not forego Himself. God gives not something but His all; God gives his ransom not once but always. All we must do is accept our ransom, or more precisely, accept that we *are* ransomed. Only by accepting God's gift of Himself can we enter a life of friendship with Him (John 3:16). The material dimension of Providence reveals the depth of its salvific significance. In Romans, Paul uses the rhetorical device known as *a fortiori* ("all the more so"):

> He who did not withhold his own son, but gave him up for all of us, will he not with him also give us everything else?"
>
> (Romans 8:22).

If God is willing to go to such sacrificial lengths to restore us to friendship with Him, will He not go just as far to provide for our other concerns to the degree they are consistent with His plan for our flourishing?

Another aspect of Providence is recognising that it calls us out of vice and weakness. We are timid creatures, taking security behind walls, surrounded by treasures and comforts of endless variety. If we have these things, we feel we cannot be hurt—or at least we can postpone what we subconsciously know is bound to happen.

In C.S. Lewis' novella, *The Great Divorce,* residents of a limbo world live in a "grey atmosphere" constantly beset by rain; it soaks everything, pouring into houses without roofs. The shadow people sense something terrible is coming but will not speak of it; they deliberately turn away from signs of impending doom. Even though beckoned by beneficent forces—given the means to flee this dissolving world—they cling to that in which they have always taken refuge, although those things themselves are inundated and decaying. If they would undertake the radical trust Jesus challenges them to have in Him—if they would have the stout hearts to believe that He provides a means to transcend a world that will only fail them—they could be saved.

Such men are like the rich young ruler in Matthew 19. He truly seeks Christ out, pursuing that deeper sense of purpose in Him. The young man has done everything the law commands of him but knows there is something more he still lacks. Jesus, in compassion, offers to provide it: "Sell everything you own and follow me." It is the same invitation made to the twelve—the same invitation he makes for all time, to everyone.

But like the shadow people of Lewis' "grey world," he cannot do it. He turns sorrowfully away, knowing that he has failed and that his failure is one of courage. He slips off to the safety of his material security, too afraid to venture out and trust in the fullness that God created him to enjoy. It is not that Jesus would love the young ruler more if he were to abandon all, but that in failing to abandon all, the young ruler chooses to remain in the chains of a lie; of his own volition, he will not be free.

John Paul II spoke of how modern society is much like the rich young ruler:

> The man of consumer societies is enslaved by possession and immediate gratification, with no other horizon than the multiplication or continuous replacement of the things he already possesses with more perfect ones. We all experience firsthand the sad effects of this blind submission: a radical dissatisfaction— the more one possesses, the more one craves—while the deepest aspirations remain unfulfilled and perhaps even stifled. (*Sollicitudo rei socialis* 28).

We, like the rich young ruler, are invited to leave behind all the things that enslave us. We are called to be freed from an incessant race to have and to horde that which will only waste and fail us. But many more chains can enslave us throughout our lives. This happens when our desires become disordered—out of order and off balance.

St. Ignatius speaks of "disordered attachments" that bind us to them, pulling us away from God and our spiritual growth. Attachments to things, people, or desires are considered "disordered" when they dominate our hearts—when they are excessive, misguided, or placed above God's will. These include the obvious distortions: obsessions with material luxury, power, control, comfort, and all forms of addiction—a healthy desire for financial security can grow into consuming greed, and a longing for love can be perverted into uncontrolled lust. Yet other barriers exist to our true freedom that are equally unhealthy—as in the case of the pursuit of one's career at the expense of integrity or work-life balance, or prioritising a relationship to the extent of isolating ourselves from others and neglecting personal responsibilities. The challenge is to recognise the subtle fetters that restrain our feet from advancing in the way of freedom and peace that could be ours in exchange for detaching from what has misguided our footsteps. Detachment is not renouncing what we hold dear, but reclaiming our hearts, ensuring nothing rules over us but God Himself. This opens the way to live unshackled, drawing fully on His boundless providence and grace.

As His redeemed children, we are encouraged to seek God's guidance for both our earthly and spiritual concerns, freed from the shadows that would keep us from His lighted path. There is great benefit in looking out for signs of God's providential care already present in our lives—in being on the "watch" for it; it strengthens our faith and deepens our trust. When we are attuned to God's loving plan for humankind and for each of us, we can catch a glimpse of what the triumphs and tragedies all mean—the progress and the setbacks that have made up the calendar of our lives. We are encouraged to seek the light of God's hand in the authorship of our story, thereby making sense of even chaos and pain.

Prayer and regular exchanges with those who are wise in the ways of God can help us discern the nearness of God in the different seasons of our lives. Even in moments of uncertainty regarding His will, prayer opens our hearts to the Holy Spirit, who reveals to us that God is present in the details. He can show how His love is intricately woven into our story even when we struggle to see it — when, in truth, we see not the assurance of design but the ambiguity of chaos.

But chaos should not frighten us, as contradictory as such a thing may sound. In 1963, while studying weather patterns, meteorologist Edward Lorenz found that small changes in the initial conditions of a weather model led to drastically different outcomes. This illustrates how chaotic systems exhibit patterns over time. Similarly, mathematician Benoît Mandelbrot found that many natural phenomena, like the apparent randomness of tree branching, cloud shaping, and coastline formation, actually follow mathematical rules that give them structure and regularity. Finally, what is known as the "logistic map" is a mathematical model showing that chaotic systems in biology, such as population dynamics, follow predictable rules and can be measured.

Even within apparent randomness, nature has a measurable order; the same is true for our lives.

If we judge solely by the looks of things, a situation may seem arbitrary and causeless, making us fear that the effects may be terrifyingly unpredictable. Yet, a deeper understanding reveals a clear sense of order and consistency that our limited perspective often misses. God is in the chaos, shaping it into purpose.

In a way, the recklessness that the secular world mistakenly attributes to history's unfolding is something that we, as ICPE missionaries, heartily endorse when it comes to abandoning ourselves to God's providence. We do so confidently assured of His abiding care for us in the good times and in the bad, seeking to nurture our trust in Him for all our needs.

With old stories, even those we believe, it is easy to lose sight of what surrender signifies in reality. The disciples gave up their work, their families, their homes—everything to follow Jesus. That alone is an awesome and sobering thing. But such complete surrender was part of their becoming spiritually free. It was not a freedom amounting to callousness towards the good and the beautiful; we are not asked to despise God's created world. Instead, it was a freedom that is "indifferent," as St. Ignatius counselled, towards any one thing or way of life. Preference is to be given only to that which best serves God. This is the First Principle and Foundation of the Ignatian Exercises.

And it was this upon which we drew during the long, often deflating events in the purchase of St. Gerard's. We had to practice a detachment from the success of the project. We could not fall into the trap of insisting that there was "no other way"—that it "had to be *this* way"—praying a hole in the sky with hands clenched in prayer and eyes squeezed tightly shut against any other possibility. Such behaviour is a subtle temptation that lacks both trust in God's plan and that—like disordered attachments—places a barrier between us and the Lord. It is also an inflation of our own will in disguise when we insist on what we must have and what God must do only because we cannot see other possibilities or fathom raw disappointments.

Reflecting on St. John of the Cross's teaching on detachment, Christof Betschart says the saint encourages us to let go of secondary things so that we can focus on what has lasting, eternal value—Christ Himself. St. Teresa of Avila speaks of exploring the soul as an interior castle where we can move freely despite all limitations, even physical ones. This is the ironic opposite of the walled isolation of those who seek security in earthly resources. Teresa's soul-castle is infinite, protecting her from the vicissitudes of life. Psychiatrist Viktor Frankl spoke of the inner strength people like Teresa possess while in concentration camps. Those with this inward resolve can endure the worst of oppression, while those with merely physical strength easily succumb to it.

Relying on God's providence is a profound journey of trust—a lifelong adventure that shapes the soul. It calls us to embrace challenges as steps toward genuine freedom. Though the path may be undeniably difficult, each trial strengthens our faith, guiding us toward a life of purpose and deep, unshakable peace and joy.

In our own experience, there are many accounts of everyday grace and provision that have seen us through. The commonplace mercies supply us with news of God's nearness and build up our trust in Him.

When our community began in Malta at Villa Lauri in 1981, we set about refurbishing a small house for guest speakers. There was little money for it, so progress could only go so fast. At one point, we came across a water heater that we needed, but we had to make the purchase by the following day. A young member of the group went out, sold her bicycle—which she needed and valued—and presented us with the funds from the sale with a smile of utter satisfaction on her face. Her entire countenance disclosed a perspective otherworldly in nature: she was a free being, unencumbered by distractions, fully aware of the paradox that she was both the giver and the recipient of grace in this one act.

A small gesture? An ordinary kindness? Can any act of kindness and generosity, which restores and heals and builds, ever be small? Indeed, would that every day be exactly as that one was?

The creative, generative dimension of Providence is also illustrated by a young couple who had left everything to join our community. A relative of this couple vehemently opposed their choice. He was an agnostic and never lost the opportunity to hurl insults their way. The relative was, in fact, unwell, and doctors had prescribed a rest abroad for him and a young son he was raising alone. As an answer to prayer, the young couple who had suffered his abuse, received a gift meant to provide them with funds for their first holiday. Instead, they gave the money to the relative who had turned enemy—the sum covered expenses both for the man and his son.

I can only testify that the young couple did not "suffer nobly" with "brave faces" in this act; they were beside themselves with fulfillment. They had worked without rest for three years in a row, but their gift redounded upon them, lifting their spirits to new heights. Their relative with his son returned home a different man. Having encountered Christians on his trip and, in turn, the love of Christ in a profound way, the man completely changed his life.

We know parents who struggled to clothe their young children or send them to a safe school, sons who needed to visit ill and dying fathers, and ministries that had to be financed to remote places. Repairs had to be made; food had to be found; medicines and supplies had to be bought. In each case, someone came through—either by way of one of our missionaries, by way of sympathetic, supportive neighbours, or on too many occasions to count, by way of anonymous patrons who left bundles of food and bags of clothes or stepped in to pay bills that were due.

It might be claimed that these people are not "red martyrs." Their sacrifices are quaint, but they suffered no scourging or exile. All I can answer is that they were the instruments of providence for someone else, the free givers of what they had freely received (Mt. 18:8). They were ready to do whatever God called for, be it leaving the plough or taking it up. And through this life of trust, they became that much more the kind of people that their Master would have them be.

For the secular world, all of this might be put down to mere coincidence. And to put faith in coincidence, for such a world, is to indulge in wishful thinking and base superstition. Christians see things differently.

St. Thomas Aquinas argued that Divine Providence is in the general and the specific details of life. In his *Summa Theologica*, he says that as God governs creation, He guides all towards its ultimate purpose while at the same time respecting human freedom. He honours our choices and lets us shape our lives in contribution to His divine plan. His nearness and care manifest in the small details of life that provide opportunities, direction, and provision. Part of our trust in Him is growing as discerning disciples—developing an awareness of events and what they mean in the light of God's will. In that way, we are mindful of what He desires from us and can know what to choose so that our will conforms with His.

We rely on God, trusting Him to give us what we need emotionally—as we are humans, prone to weakness; spiritually—as we have souls, prone to loss; physically—as we have bodies, prone to decay; and materially—as we have needs, prone to waste. We ask for these things but also ask to be detached from an inordinate desire for them; as such, we ask for them only insofar as they will help sustain us in our call to give our lives to others. This is the spirit of "generous living," a golden thread woven through our ICPE Mission spirituality: a detached reliance upon God's providence leading to a life poured out for the good of the world.

The poor widow in the New Testament is the icon of such living, the pattern of how it manifests in action. She gave joyfully—drawing Jesus' blessing; humbly—without show or praise; sacrificially—out of her want, "all that she had"; charitably—born from a love of her neighbour; and freely—by a deed of her uncoerced choice. Whether it be time, talent, or treasure, as ICPE missionaries, we seek to replicate the poor widow—whose name is ironically but appropriately lost to history—in the abundance of her charity.

It may well be the case—and often is—that the testimony of biblical sources, saintly reflections, and personal anecdotes can only go so far in persuading an audience, even one of believers, that God's providential care is working in their lives.

After all, they may say, I feel lost most of the time. I am confused and fearful despite my pleas for help.

After all, they may say, I have prayed for provision—I have needed things desperately that I was certain were God's will—but nothing came; nothing was sent.

After all, I don't deserve His help, being what I am.

After all, at some point, despite that old song—the grass, for all its glory, is cast into the oven; at some point, the sparrow falls.

Another Saint spoke to the inner resolve that comes with trusting in God's way—a resolve that can withstand the worst of assaults. St. John Henry Newman wrote:

> God has created me to do Him some definite service. He has committed some work to me, which He has not committed to another. I have my mission. I may never know it in this life, but I shall be told it in the next. I am a link in a chain, a bond of connection between persons. He has not created me for naught. I shall do good; I shall do His work. I shall be an angel of peace, a preacher of truth in my own place, while not intending it if I do but keep His commandments.
>
> Therefore, I will trust Him, whatever I am, I can never be thrown away. If I am in sickness, my sickness may serve Him, in perplexity, my perplexity may serve Him. If I am in sorrow, my sorrow may serve Him. He does nothing in vain.

> He knows what He is about. He may take away my friends. He may throw me among strangers. He may make me feel desolate, make my spirits sink, hide my future from me. Still, He knows what He is about.

We must believe that God is there, too—in the times when the sparrow falls.

He watches. Even then. After all.

9

wounded healers

For years, poinsettias haunted me.

Lovely as they are—Bethlehem's heavenly red fire signaling the birth of the Christ child dressed in the colour of His passion and death—still, I could not tolerate them. Well-meaning friends who sent gifts of poinsettias in the spirit of Christmas unwittingly filled me with acute anguish. I could not have them in the house.

But it wasn't always so. There was a time when they meant only what they were intended to mean. There was a time when they were a regal part of my Christmas pageantry just as they are for everyone else. Something changed all that.

I am the youngest of six children in what was a warm, loving Maltese family. The grace of that caring home I value among my most significant blessings. So when I became an adult and got married, one of my fervent dreams was to have a family like the one that raised me. Wanting to belong and to have something to belong to is a fundamental, instinctual desire, a primordial part of human nature. The family unit is a counterpart to and replica of the eternal belonging that is the Trinity itself. So there was no question of its importance to me; I had never conceived of a life without children being part of it.

We finally discovered that I was to have a child, four years after our marriage. To receive the good news that you have longed for is one of life's great delights, a happiness intensified by the anticipation that precedes it. It was 1987, and the news of the pregnancy added to the joy in our lives as we were then living within the folds of our first ICPE community in Marsaxlokk. The number of family and friends that shared in our blessing was an added gift. The mission was flourishing and bearing fruit, and now our personal lives were also doing so in this marvellous way.

To add another dimension to the grace-filled nature of those days, I was pregnant at the same time as one of my sisters, one of my sisters-in-law, and two other women in our local community. The air was electric around us as we prepared, planned, and anticipated the coming months. Bonds of shared gratefulness are powerful things, especially among women about to bear children. They are radiant in the pleasure of their gift and recognise its mirror in those who share its beauty—Mary facing Elisabeth, Elisabeth facing Mary—each an ark bearing the mystery and miracle of life, awash in the effulgent glory of God's favour. They say that women glow at such a time; it is no wonder that they do.

Mine was an uneventful pregnancy. There were no complications, and when I went into labour the first week of December, the procedure was as normal and natural as I could have hoped. My relief and consequent joy were also just as I thought they would be. No surprises. Holding my child for the first time was the rarest of all desires come to pass.

It had finally begun—a whole life that I had made plans about for my whole life.

I was a mother. I had a son. His name was David.

The time immediately following his birth was normal, too, as expected and customary as one could imagine. The night and day were no doubt made up of deep rest after physical exertion, of bouquets of flowers and well-wishing cards arriving with cheerful visitors. The nurses brought my baby to me throughout the night for feeding, and I'm sure at some point I began to prepare for the second day.

That would be another beginning since Mario was to come back to the hospital and collect us. We would get in the car and drive home—not just two people who loved each other anymore, but three: a family on the verge of an unknowable future, together in a world brimming with bright possibilities—a world so much larger in scope for the very fact that our son was now in it.

When morning finally came, I awoke, anxious to rise, ready to commence our new lives. Mario was on his way. The nursery had been prepared at home and all was in place. There would be a lot to do, of course, as I'd not only have the baby, but it was also nearly Christmas. I would have plenty of help, though, surrounded by family and friends who had done this countless times before. It was nearly time to go.

The door opened, and the nurse came in to bring me David. She laid him in my arms, then left us to start our lives together, mother and son.

I was supposed to cradle him, feed him, comfort him. The nurse was supposed to return after a while and help us prepare to leave. The hospital was supposed to discharge us and send us on our way. That was what I had planned.

But when I looked down at David, he was not the hungry, lively baby that he should have been; instead, he was lethargic, unresponsive. He would not—could not—feed. A sleepy indolence lay over him, a dull pall from which I could not rouse him.

I flushed, afraid, then tried again. Then again. Then again.

All at once, I knew. I knew everything that was supposed to be—everything I had planned—had gone terribly wrong.

I jumped up, wrapped David in a blanket, and ran out into the hall. I remember a cleaning woman mercilessly scolding me for trampling over her glassy, newly polished floor. But I had to rush on, clutching my child, desperate for help.

When I finally found the station, everyone was busy. Finally, I managed to flag down one of the nurses and call her over. I was sobbing uncontrollably by that time, barely able to explain what was happening, trying to make her comprehend that a doctor had to come right then, immediately.

But the woman put it all down to the hysteria of a first-time mother. She said there was no need for this level of panic. She would take the baby, and the doctor would come by in time. I was to go back to my room, she said. I was to wait, she said.

Unnerved, I only bewildered Mario when he arrived, breaking the news of what had just happened. He had come to bring the two of us—wife and child—home with him, but he was instead met with the shock to learn that his newborn son would have to stay.

Then, on the heels of that blow, he and I were dealt another. The doctor had seen David and was transferring him to the intensive care unit.

There was more shuffling about—more mystery as to what was causing this inexplicable turn, this merciless threat from out of nowhere. The torment of such times is in not knowing and in a creeping fear that—worse still—no one else knew either.

At some point, someone sent us home. Again, we were told to wait.

There was heavy rainfall that night, and a thunderstorm flooded the streets. We slept off and on, overwhelmed with fear and confusion. The hours were filled with prayers. Then, as dawn broke, I recall the sharp sound of the phone ringing at 6:30 the next morning. The Director of Paediatrics at the hospital wanted to see us as soon as possible.

We gathered ourselves together, hearts thrashing, and along with my eldest sister and trained nurse, Rita, headed for the ICU.

I remember Mario knocking on the door to the unit and identifying himself. He was told to stay outside as the doctor was on his way. We had not met the Director of Paediatrics before, so we did not know who we were expecting.

Still, maybe there was a development; maybe the doctor had an idea of what was happening to David and had come up with a strategy to cure him. The three of us were the only people in the hall that morning; all was strangely quiet at that time of day.

Then, suddenly, a doctor came out to us. For some reason, he was already speaking as he approached.

"The baby is not going to live," he was saying. "But don't tell the mother. Not yet. She's just given birth."

He stopped—noticed me.

Perhaps from what he'd been told, he thought there was only a male member of the family—the father—outside the ICU door, waiting to receive the news. But as our eyes locked, he knew right then who I was; he softened as he heard me speak.

"I am the mother," I said. "I am."

Those were the only words I could find. After what I'd heard, I was robbed of any others.

My mind was a chaos of refusal, denial, disorder.

There must be a mistake, I thought. The doctor must have misspoken—or I must have heard him wrong. It was impossible.

My baby? David?

For a time, there was no such thing as air.

The conversation went on around me, and at some point, I found myself being gently pulled towards the side of the hallway. Mario had his arm about my shoulder, leading us towards a long, narrow window. After the storm, the sun was peeking through the clouds; it was the only bright place in that dark, cold corridor.

It was a weekday, and down below us, in a courtyard, a group of schoolchildren were playing just before classes—tag, hopscotch—laughing, running—waiting for a bell to ring to begin their day—a day like the many, many other days they would know—all the days that—for them—were yet to be.

I collapsed against Mario.

David. None of this—laughing, playing, learning, growing—would ever be his. None of it would ever be ours. I was his mother. Mario was his father. But we would never hear him call us so.

In time, the doctor told us that our son had fallen into a coma, though they could not then identify the cause.

What followed were three excruciating days and nights that are still painful to recall. They sent me home with my parents, though, of course, it made no difference where I was; my anguish was as strong in one place as it would be in another. As C.S. Lewis said, loss is the sky. It follows us everywhere.

Mario went through his own agony, camped out in the corridor next to the window in the ICU. There he could watch our son through the ice-cold glass, lying in an incubator, fighting for the little life that he had left.

Five days after one of the happiest events in my life, the doorbell rang. I was with a family friend, Father Joe, who had brought me communion. The two of us were sitting on the sofa, meditating over the Book of Wisdom:

> …the souls of the righteous are in the hands of God,
> and no torment will ever touch them….

Someone answered the door, and Mario, accompanied by my parents, walked into the room. His gaze found mine.

"Għandna qaddis," he said to me, softly, in Maltese. "We have a saint."

As though I was hearing someone else speak, I found myself repeating softly what he'd said.

"Għandna qaddis."

My father, stricken and overcome, collapsed and had to be helped from the room. Mario and I, beyond even the possibility of words, could only hold each other. The room fell silent.

Five days. The journey from the pinnacle of joy to the pit of grief had taken but five days.

We left my parents' house some days later and returned to our apartment. Our friends in the community had quietly dismantled the nursery we had so painstakingly prepared for our son. They wanted to spare us that.

But as it was nearly Christmas, they thought it best to leave the poinsettias sitting about, for whatever good they might do.

I opened the door upon the sight, and knew then that my walk through this, the darkest of all the shadowed valleys, had only just begun.

This is the story of the ICPE Mission—the explanation of its charism told through its history. So, the purpose of this narrative should not be confused by any one person's experience. But I believe it is important to show that the personal lives of ICPE missionaries and the life of the ICPE Mission as a whole have been no different than that of any other individual or organisation, secular or religious.

None are spared pain, loss, conflict, or disillusionment. The rain falls on whom it will; we can expect no less. Christians, like any other, ask "Why?" at such times. They are just as shaken by unspeakable tragedy, inexplicable randomness, grave injustice.

But for all that, Christians can walk through their suffering with a difference. Theirs is not just another means of "coping" with adversity—yet another option among the "self-help" missives at the bookstore. It does not offer anaesthesia for pain in an attempt to mask or distract; it does not deny suffering's reality.

Instead, Christians look to the Crucified One. His Cross does not insulate us from suffering but unlocks and informs every mystery of it. Through the enigma of a God-love so strong that it enters into our suffering, our own passions create a communion with His. The intimacy between we who suffer now, and our Saviour who suffers with us, is realised through the power and mission of His Cross. Hope survives yet, unbowed, albeit cruciform. Christians believe that their goal is still winnable and unchanged, even if sought with half of one's heart missing; even when lamed by the merciless blows of circumstance.

Christians on the way of the Cross know they can be transformed into something new, if only for the fact that they endure without changing their minds. Their faith is not belief in a mere set of facts about Christ but something much more. They stake their lives on following Him wherever He leads—to Galilee, to Tabor, and even to Calvary. Their Saviour is still their Saviour, not aloof from their pain, but the One who suffers with them, the One who mounted the Cross.

The Cross is, in fact, the affirmation of life in all its conditions and situations. As St. John Henry Newman explains in his sermon *"The Cross of Christ: The Measure of the World,"* the Cross is the ultimate standard by which we understand the world, our values, and our relationship with God.

"Behold my servant Job," God said to Satan, not only at the beginning of Job's trial, but also—and with a difference—at its zenith—when he was devastated by injury and sat among the ashes. We behold in Job the marvel of his rock-like faith, a badge larger because of its survival. We also see his trust in God's wisdom and care and a genuine yearning for Him despite his torment. What we behold in Job of the Old Testament, we hear echoed in Paul of the New, when he speaks of a strength gained through weakness—of a resilience born from the trials through which Christ's power brings him (2 Corinthians 11:24-27; 12:9-10).

We do not seek out suffering—indeed, we need not seek it out as it comes to all of us eventually, in one way or another. And we never see it as a type of payment remitted in exchange for blessings to come. Such is a perverse masochism that caricatures the faith.

Yet, when we mount the Cross with Christ, we find God showing Himself to us in a way we have not previously known. Christ, the Wounded Healer, heals and restores us, then sends us into the world to share with others what we have received in abundance—mercy and grace—so that *we* become wounded healers ourselves. Like the resurrected Christ—the God who "bears scars," as Edward Shillito calls Him—we are summoned to reveal our woundedness and serve the world through our scars.

As ICPE missionaries, we rise to bear up those in our number and within our various communities who are stooped from carrying their countless, heavy burdens. I speak not only as someone who seeks to do this for others, but as one who has been the recipient of just such provision herself.

Two months after David died, in February of 1988, we were as busy as we had ever been. We'd just formalised the unity of different ICPE and local communities, and afterwards, had flown to Rome to run our third School of Mission there. We only had time to fly back to Malta for some family wedding before we set off for Wellington, New Zealand. That trip was for our first School of Mission there. On top of all that, we had prepared and sent our mission team on the signature expedition into the jungles of Paitan.

In addition to this flurry of events, on a personal level, the doctors had found that David's cause of death was due to a rare metabolic disorder. As it was often inherited, Mario and I were sent for genetic testing to discover if we carried gene mutations of the type responsible for our loss.

So consciously and subconsciously, physically and emotionally, I was taxed to the limit. It had almost been a year since David's passing when, while out for a jog with Mario on a winding path in Wellington, I suddenly felt dizzy and fainted. I lost all colour and am told I took on the pallor of one quickly slipping away. At the hospital we learned that had Mario not performed CPR and gotten an ambulance to take me there, I would have died. There, the doctors diagnosed me with an abnormal heart rhythm that had to be monitored lest it reoccur.

The fainting episode acted as a trigger that re-awakened the underlying trauma. I fell into an acute level of post-traumatic stress, with its consequent anxiety attacks, bouts of depression, and other problems. Worse, such things were not always understood or acknowledged—even among Christian communities—in those days.

At long length, and with professional help as well as that of our family and friends, I was able to regain my mental and physical strength. Those people were the Cross upon which I leaned, and they never let me fall.

But suffering is not limited to the individual. Groups and organisations go through their own sets of trials, and their transformational journey is much like those undergone at the personal level. Over our forty years as a Mission, we were faced with financial woes, displaced from familiar environments, forced to close vital ministries due to resource shortages, and lost young missionaries to illness. We also had our share of internal conflicts and twice went through especially dark periods.

In 1995, we were a relatively young organisation built on friendship and family connections. All of that had been our strength, an intimacy that sustained us. But it caused ironic complications when we began to expand at a rapid pace. Clear lines of authority and accountability, as well as a formalised structure, had to be established.

Growing pains are part of any thriving enterprise. They are often unpleasant and can even seem counter to core principles. Things have to get done, and what was always a casual and heartfelt association of close friends can seem to have lost its way when new lines of authority must be adopted and respected.

As our mission went through that process, years-long friendships devoted to serving the Lord by pulling in the same direction started to pull apart in different ones. Small groups of conflicting ideas became satellites unto themselves, impoverishing the whole. The pain of this breakdown in old relationships was agonising, and some of the groups eventually found it best to pursue their own separate ministries. Things got worse before they got better, but they only got better—however haltingly—through encountering each other with the common objective of reconciliation. Changing minds was not the goal, but rather a return to Christian unity. In time, it came, achieved through a sincere dedication to peace.

In our experience, conflicts within an organisation can arise on four levels: philosophical, as to what the mission is; practical, as to how it should achieve its goals; administrative, as to who should do what; and interpersonal, based on human nature and the inevitable clashes that arise from it. At any of these points, fractures can occur. Sometimes they are too wide and complete to overcome.

In 2002, we enjoyed the unforgettable events surrounding the Pontifical Decree's consignment in Rome. But even in the midst of that celebration, an unanticipated storm was quietly brewing. We found ourselves thrust into a prolonged, intense confrontation at the ICPE Mission's leadership level soon after the pontifical right grant. The conflict dragged on for over two years. None of the attempts at reconciliation—neither through external mediation nor internal outreach—could ever heal the breach. In the end, it was clear that the only thing to do was for the two individuals to part ways with the ICPE Mission. The rift remained. It was a bruising failure that is sore to the touch even now.

In the *Spiritual Exercises*, St. Ignatius of Loyola warns that after periods of spiritual consolation—such as the pontifical recognition—when elated in a state of closeness to God, states of spiritual desolation are prone to follow. What were hope-filled times struck through with charity and goodwill can give way to their opposite—times ridden with abrupt challenges that lead to feelings of dejection and abandonment by God. He cautioned that although this ebb and flow was natural to the spiritual life, at the individual and communal level, we are to remain on our guard.

The hard fact is that leaders of any organisation, spiritual or secular, must be committed to building teams, strengthening cohesion, and enhancing impact. If they perceive a threat to those good things, which they unavoidably will, they must address them. This calls for both courage that does not invite conflict, and humility that exercises authority with the meekness that Christ counselled. Over the years, those of us in leadership positions have strived to adopt this approach. Yet, despite our best efforts, we haven't always seen the result we'd hoped for. As ICPE missionaries, our personal and communal struggles expose our fragility and brokenness. These painful experiences strip us to the core, revealing us as mere "jars of clay" holding an imperishable treasure (2 Corinthians 4:7).

Yet, even in our weakness, we are called to the hardest of the New Testament charges, "Love your enemies"(Matthew 5:44). There is no way around the fact that it is an unconditional command. We are to love our enemies despite their being unlovable—loving *despite* what we see and experience, not *because of* what we see and experience. Beauty, intelligence, wit, loyalty—such things inevitably attract us. But loving that which repels us out of its hostility or injustice is the discomforting Christian mandate.

It is natural, and all too common, that our enemies become less than human to us. Because of their opposition, we can no longer see their faces—can no longer recognise them as children of God. That is because their antagonism towards us stands in the way; it masks who they are. To love them means to rip away that mask and to restore their faces—so that we once again see our brothers and sisters (Hebrews 2:11) for whom Christ died (1 Corinthians 8:11). And in finding a way to love our enemies—to forgive them—we liberate ourselves from endless cycles of hostility that hold us hostage.

Undoubtedly, this can be an enormous task, especially when the damage inflicted is grave and long-lasting. Even the very idea of forgiveness can trigger an instinctive sense of repulsion. Therefore, it is crucial to honestly acknowledge the magnitude of the challenge. Otherwise, offering such advice runs the risk of fuelling resentment—people may respond by accusing you of recommending something you could never do yourself if you truly understood the depth of the pain—or of suggesting that hurt can be fixed easily by simply adopting the right "attitude".

The truth is that forgiveness—like love—is a verb. It's a practice, a habit that must be cultivated. It's a choice, and it is not always convenient. The same could be said for reconciliation.

ICPE missionaries quickly learn that Christian community is a network of human relationships whose nature is fragile, imperfect, and potentially wounding. Gathering where Christ's presence is among us is our goal but so is seeking true reconciliation with one another. We teach that Jesus comes not to abolish or deny enmity, but to conquer it through love. We can and should detest wrongdoing; we cannot and must not hate the person who exhibits it. Reconciliation refers to the mutual effort and ability to work through the conflict with certain spiritual tools being indispensable in the process: a great degree of patience, the energy to be resilient, and the wisdom to work through the necessary conversations, confessions, listening and explanations that go into reconciliation. However, in recognition of the challenges in negotiating peace, it's important to cultivate a realistic understanding of the limits and boundaries of what can be achieved in a given situation.

By way of example, my own father's response to a professional injustice proved a model of Christian conduct for me. It was not an injustice perpetrated by the person who benefitted from the act, but one perpetrated by a system that did not value him as it should.

My father was a foreman in the government Water Works Department, and he, along with other colleagues, was due for a promotion. There were eight people in our family and he was the sole breadwinner, so recognition of his outstanding service would have been both a deserved honour and a much-needed change of fortune.

However, promotions in the Maltese civil service are a very political affair; party alignment at any given time mostly decides such things, not merit. So, much to my father's disappointment, when the promotions were announced, only one individual—known for openly supporting the ruling party back then and with inner connections—was chosen. It wasn't that this man was undeserving, but that many others were equally so.

But rather than being bitter about the matter, my father congratulated his new superior, who happened to be an old friend. They both recognised the unfairness of the situation yet did not let it drive a wedge between their friendship. They met often, even after my father transferred to another department. They regularly visited each other at Christmastime and kept a standing date for tea and cake at Caffe Cordina, a popular coffee place in Valletta, when they retired. They lived as true friends until their ripe old age.

Faceless injustices—those that are the result of systemic unfairness—are customarily the hardest with which to cope. They make us angrier because they are born of circumstances that can seem irremediable. But my father said that visceral reactions such as resentment and hurt, normal as they may be, could chain us to our suffering. If indulged, they breed and poison. Freedom comes from detachment—forgiveness; we do not have to deny injustice or excuse it, but we can choose not to be bound by it. My father was a free man.

This episode often reminds me of Fyodor Dostoevsky's novel *The Idiot*, a story about kindness and innocence in a world of cynicism and moral decay. He references the suffering we endure in relationships as something that can lead to compassion, humility, and connection with others—a way to transcend ego and foster empathy:

> There is nothing nobler, nothing greater than the spirit of deep and genuine Christianity, which calls for total self-sacrifice, for complete abandonment of our own personal pride, and for love of one's neighbour, and is the root of all faith. Suffering is essential to widen our horizons, to enlarge our vision, to understand our fellow man.

And as the old saying goes, those who forgive don't have as much to remember. They are shed of the burdensome ledger sheets and inventories of curated grudges amassed over the years. They travel through life lighter, existing in the present, free to see and experience things afresh rather than through the clouded lens of bitter resentment.

This also points to the Paschal Mystery, which reveals suffering as an integral part of salvation history—but it doesn't end there. As we "live and move and have our being" in the resurrected Lord (Acts 17:28)—as our lives are hidden within God in Christ (Colossians 3:3)—we see that our lives follow the cycle of His suffering, dying, and rising again. We may be born into a world of suffering and dying, but we are not its progeny.

It does not have the final word over the children of Light.

In 1991, three years after the mental and physical anguish resulting from David's death, Mario and I decided to consider having another child. The doctors could not identify the specific metabolic disorder that had taken our son's life, and we were told that the only way to know whether all our children would carry the same medical condition, would be to conceive again. We weighed all our options, prayed, and decided to take the risk.

We had just launched the Mission Centres in Malta and Allerheiligen when I got pregnant. We were cautious, of course, but hopeful. Some metabolic disorders are linked to the X chromosome, and females may have milder forms of the disease than males. They may even be asymptomatic carriers only. So we prayed for a girl.

There were no complications in my pregnancy, just as there were none before. Our spirits rose with the days and months, just as they had before. We were surrounded with friends that were a family of constancy and strength, like always. Plans for the future were made.

Naomi was born in a university hospital that specialises in metabolic disorders, thankfully and providentially only an hour and a half from Allerheiligen.

Her birth was without incident, just as David's had been.

And I held her just as I had him—in a holy bond, a transfigured moment outside time and circumstance.

A liver biopsy revealed that Naomi had been born with Carbamoyl Phosphate Synthetase 1 (CPS 1) deficiency. CPS 1 deficiency is an extremely rare metabolic disorder with very poor survival rates. The estimated incidence is fewer than 1 in 1,300,000 live births, making that approximately one case every 300 years in Malta.

Our two children, David and Naomi, were only the fourteenth and fifteenth recorded cases of CPS 1 deficiency in medical history.

Though known as an anchoress now, the medieval mystic Julian of Norwich spent most of her life in the world. She lived through the great plague, and several commentators suspect that she likely lost her own family to it. All that is known for sure is that at some point she entered the cloistered life. And during one of her communications with God, she was graced with revelations as to the vastness of His care, experiencing it so profoundly that her reflections still resonate fourteen centuries later.

Despite what she was allowed to see, Julian was perplexed by something—perhaps by the very size of the love she beheld: if God is love and loves us so deeply, then why do evil and suffering exist?

So she posed the question to God, and she received two responses. First, she learned that God would perform a deed on the last day of the world to "make all things well." She wrote that God uttered the phrase "All shall be well, and all shall be well, and all manner of things shall be well," because He wanted his children to be enclosed "in rest and in peace."

But God's other response to Julian's question resonates with me even more deeply, now, after the loss of my children. It tells of God's nature and how He relates to my suffering by way of Christ's agony on the Cross. God, Julian wrote, "is our clothing, who wraps and enfolds us for love, embraces us and shelters us, surrounds us for His life, which is so tender that He may never desert us." It is a love so great that He refused to stand aloof from our suffering, watching it dispassionately from a distance. Instead, God became human and suffered, and in so doing, "He saw and he sorrowed for every [person's] sorrow, desolation and anguish."

When we grasp that God shares in our suffering, truly understanding what it means to endure pain, our anger transforms into love. Our suffering is re-dimensioned, mysteriously becoming a path to transformation.

The medical staff at the hospital did a brilliant job throughout the eleven months of Naomi's short life. They provided all the medical assistance necessary to keep her happy for as long as she was with us. And one month after her birth, we took Naomi home to Allerheiligen.

We were equipped with all the instructions for her special diet, as well as a list of medicines that she needed at different times of the day and night. It was a harried existence for her and us. Twenty-one times we had to rush her to the hospital. All told, she fell into five comas and underwent several hemodialysis surgeries, feeding tube insertions, and countless medical interventions.

But nothing broke her spirit. Caring for her was not difficult because of that fact. She brought us, and all around her, an unfailing delight.

Mornings, she would come to the edge of her cot and make her presence known to us as if to say, "Wake up! Let's enjoy another day together!"

And I, with half-opened eyes, looking at her cute, chubby face, would softly whisper to God, "Please be with me if You'll be calling her Home today."

Evenings, when the lights were out, I would cradle her and sing her lullabies. I could feel and listen to my child breathing and softly whisper gratitude to God for one more day.

Mornings and Evenings. They are the way God expressed His creation of the universe, the cycle of dawns and dusks with which we are so familiar. They echo the light and dark of our lives and are always within His plan. The first day, the second day, the third—morning and evening, evening and morning—He breathed life into His children, and when finished, looked upon it and saw that it was good. Then He rested.

Julian of Norwich, troubled by suffering and loss, was assured by God that all would be good—well—in the end; despite everything—dark and light, light and dark, He comforted her with news that His children should rest in that peace.

One evening, I sang Naomi her last lullaby. And she rested in peace. And it was good.

The Allerheiligen community accompanied us throughout this challenging chapter of our lives. Their emotional and practical support buoyed us above the overwhelming waves that threatened to swallow us. The prayers that they, our families, and so many others around the world offered for us were heartfelt, fervent, and unceasing.

Celebration is at the heart of our life together as the ICPE Mission. So we gathered for a Thanksgiving Mass and a feast to honour Naomi's entry into Heaven—where her evening had become an eternal morning. We were surrounded by friends, family members who travelled from Malta, her doctors and nurses who drove all the way from the hospital in Freiburg, and her Allerheiligen family who had showered her with love and affection throughout her fragile, short life.

As her pure white casket was lowered into the earth of the Garden of Resurrection—the name I've come to give the cemetery in Oppenau—I realised that with her, I was also burying our dream of ever having a biological family.

Many things in the modern world tell us that we can soldier on through grief and other losses—health, security, or lifelong hopes—by deciding to "get over it." We are told to seek "closure" through strengthening our will, indulging in distractions, or pouring ourselves into new pursuits.

But the profound impact of loss involves recognising just how deep such personal matters cut, as parts of our very selves are tied to that lost relationship or hope.

My own grief was like a Tsunami. I was giving up a narrative—a life story that I'd believed from my childhood had been written for me. And the process of mourning involved reshaping the tale of my life into something different. I was travelling into an undiscovered country where I had never meant to go.

Several passages from literature help convey what I mean.

In a famous essay, "Welcome to Holland," Emily Perl Kingsley expressed the change in her life story when she gave birth to a Down's Syndrome son. She says that a mother of a disabled child is like someone who has planned her entire life for a trip to Italy. She buys all the guidebooks and learns some of the language, packs her bags and gets on the plane, only to land and have the flight attendant welcome her to Holland.

At first, she is shocked. This is not what she has wanted—it is not where all her life she has dreamed of going.

But there is no changing the fact of where she is; here she must stay.

In time, she comes to understand the beauty of the place—more subtle, less dramatic—different, yet a wonderful land where she can be. She grows accustomed to her new life.

Still, she says, everyone she knows is always coming and going from Italy, carrying on and on about how extraordinary it is:

> And for the rest of your life, you will say, "Yes, that's where I was supposed to go. That's what I had planned."
> And the pain of that will never, ever, ever, ever go away... because the loss of that dream is a very, very significant loss.

But, she says, if one spends all of her life mourning Italy, she will never come to understand the loveliness of Holland.

In my case, I had to learn the new landscape of my life, to find my way about in it. And in time, I grew in my capacity to find joy and hope.

Moreover, as a Christian, I am mindful of something more—greater—yet to come. I am mindful that, as the theologian Peter Kreeft says, death seems unreal to us because we know that love is too strong for it. Love, in the end, will make death a lie.

The great American editorialist William Allen White wrote of his remarkable sixteen-year-old daughter, lost in a tragic horse-riding accident. In his eulogy, "Mary White," he spoke of a life too outsized, too incredible, to be confined by a limit.

> A rift in the clouds in a gray day threw a shaft of sunlight upon her coffin as her nervous, energetic little body sank to its last sleep. But the soul of her, the glowing, gorgeous, fervent soul of her, surely was flaming in eager joy upon some other dawn.

Although we are told in Scripture that our eternal life transcends the relational bonds we have known here on earth, we are not told that they are refuted or denied. Those we love, those who love us—all who have been friends in this life—will grow in an ever-expanding, ever-deepening ring of belonging—with each other, with those we have not met here, and with the triune God, Whom we will spend an infinity coming to know.

We will not be resurrected amnesiacs, cut off from and shorn of the holy love we have been fortunate enough to have, a love that lives and defies any shroud or tomb. Our capacity to love will grow infinitely, and encompass those of all time, but it will lose none of its capacity to love what it has always loved.

I am David and Naomi's mother. Mario is their father. They are our children. That is a reality yet to be experienced in its fullness. It shall be—in some other dawn.

Until then.

10

the kumasi girl

The wind speeds of a typhoon can be clocked at up to 300 kilometers, or 186 miles, per hour. The waves they generate can exceed 10 metres—roughly the size of a three-story building. As water weighs approximately 1,008 kilograms per cubic meter, tides driven by hyper-charged gales have the impact force equivalent to a wall of barreling freight trains when they crash ashore.

Given these facts, the ruination caused by such fury is as broad and deep as it is lasting. Buildings, homes, and infrastructure are laid waste, economies are disrupted, and whole ecosystems can be damaged or lost through changes in ocean temperatures and salinity levels. Deforestation, mudslides, and soil erosion ensue, as can the spread of invasive species transported by the storm. Outbreaks of disease from contaminated water are common. Of course, the loss of life is the most significant devastation; in 1970, a Bangladeshi typhoon killed an estimated half a million people. Deaths in the thousands are customary.

All of southeast Asia is extremely vulnerable to typhoons, but the Philippines is the country most frequently hit. The archipelago of over 7,500 islands is situated in such a way that its coastlines miss few of the many violent weather events that form in the region.

We established the ICPE Mission Philippines in 1997, settling first in the capital city of Manila. Nine years later, we moved to Tagaytay, just south of Manila. There, new leadership undertook a ministry consistent with the Church's preferential option for the poor, meaning that as the People of God, we are called to prioritise the needs of the poor and vulnerable, and ensure their dignity is upheld in society. The community was directed by a new Mission Statement: "Empowering the Poor with God's Compassionate Love." As high levels of persistent poverty had traditionally plagued the country, there was much to do. But the challenges of a ministry in a place like the Philippines are exacerbated by the fact that obstacles are not only a matter of economic disparities and societal indifference. They are also a matter of nature itself, which shows indiscriminate hostility there with the regularity of the seasons.

Our missionaries found it nearly impossible to "prepare" for the unpredictability of violent weather. They stockpiled food, used every available container to store fresh water, and did what they could to patch the roof on their old, poorly constructed housing to stave off the inevitable cataracts of water pouring through the ceiling at weak spots. When the cyclonic storms came, prayers for protection were constantly offered as it was not a question of whether destruction would follow, but to what degree.

Our mission's first exposure to the power of typhoons in Tagaytay came soon after we moved there in 2006, when howling winds, flying car parts, tree branches, and horizontal sheets of rain scourged our community house. The missionaries lost electricity and water, but unlike so many others who were less fortunate, they did not lose the roof over their heads. In 2010 and 2011, even more violent typhoons hit our house. Flooding reached calf deep in the rooms; again, crippled by a typical loss of fresh water and electricity, the missionaries were faced with the overwhelming plight of anyone who cannot escape the ferocity of natural disasters—backbreaking work just to clean up, dry out, and salvage what had somehow escaped the wrath of the storm. The aftermath reduced them to living in refugee camp conditions; repairs to make things livable again had to wait until the rains finally stopped—and the rain could go on for days. Paper records were lost to dampness and mould, and what furniture and possessions could be saved had to be dried out in the sun. The pattern of such an existence repeated with woeful regularity each year in the rainy season.

It was not just the force of the typhoons themselves and the environmental havoc they wrought that impacted the Mission. Disruptions of their ministries increased their burden as well. Poverty-stricken families had become dependent upon them. That they were able to complete any of their outreaches to the poor of the area—even their tradition of Reverse Carolling, a custom of visiting the poverty-stricken with hampers of food at Christmastime—is a great testament to their commitment.

But the fact that even in their own distress they did not forget their neighbours, whose troubles mirrored theirs, is emblematic of the spirituality the ICPE Mission has meant to bring to the region. They did not leave; they stayed. They did not turn inward due to their plight, but their plight became an opportunity to find and help those who shared in it.

The religious grounding of our presence in Southeast Asia is based on one clear, undeniable fact: the poor cannot flee from their predicament; they have no choice but to remain and face it, as there are no resources or options with which they can take refuge against it. They are never outside the whirlwind—neither the literal torrents of wind and rain brought by the annual typhoons, nor the unyielding scourge of hunger and poverty that greets them each morning and lingers with them through the night.

Therefore, our goal as a Mission is not so much to reach down and help the poor up, but to stand alongside—shoulder to shoulder—provide what we can, and assist them in facing whatever life brings. They are not objects of our charity, but brothers and sisters in distress. The importance of this stance—the crucial posture of this orientation—is key to understanding what our ministries mean in regions beset by an intractable level of poverty. It has many scriptural and theological foundations.

We seek solidarity with the poor and the underprivileged because Christ identifies with them and stands in their place. In Matthew 25: 31-36, Jesus expresses righteousness in terms of acts rendered to Him as one of their number:

> Come, you who are blessed by my Father; take your inheritance, the kingdom prepared for you since the creation of the world. For I was hungry, and you gave me something to eat, I was thirsty and you gave me something to drink, I was a stranger and you invited me in, I needed clothes and you clothed me, I was sick and you looked after me, I was in prison and you came to visit me.

What Jesus describes is not sympathy for the downtrodden, but empathy with them—an empathy that results in *active* compassion—clothing, feeding, visiting—not a passive pity that provides a substitute or alternative to identifying with the poor. Of course, alms-giving—offering monetary resources to relieve suffering—is a good thing. Sometimes, and for various reasons, alms are all that can be given. Yet what we seek as a Mission is not to posit ourselves in a vertical relationship: the giver above a beneficiary who receives—but in a horizontal one: the sharer beside a brother or sister, who needs.

Why this orientation is important is because it allows the missionary to share the space of the poor—to live within it. The distance of a theoretical appreciation of another's suffering is eliminated when we take on a practical, experiential fellowship with those who suffer. It enables us to see with our own eyes, hear with our own ears, experience under our own skin, the struggles of the poor, and thereby truly *recognise* their suffering.

A boardroom explanation of graphs, charts, and data can only go so far; even a public relations campaign of moving videos and heart-rending pictures keeps the audience at a distance. But actually seeking our own "Calcutta," as Mother Teresa put it—venturing into those spaces around us where suffering and need cry out—brings the harsh reality of distress close. It ceases to be a mere idea and becomes a real encounter. As a result, the chasm of separation that fosters indifference is bridged, and the one who was once merely an abstraction is now recognised as a child of God—*like* us, a reflection of ourselves—whose needs call for the same care and urgency with which we tend to our own.

This reflects the spirit of Pope Francis' encyclical *Evangelii Gaudium* (The Joy of the Gospel), where he urges a compassion for the poor to replace global indifference. It also echoes his institution of a World Day of the Poor to encourage the global Catholic Church to recognise and address their needs. Moreover, this approach mirrors that of Father Gustavo Gutiérrez, Catholic theologian and founder of *Liberation Theology*, when he preached that if the Church were to participate meaningfully in the world, it had to respond to the harsh realities faced by a majority of the earth's inhabitants.

What is more, Jesus says that in this expression of love—when we love those whom He loves—those who have nothing in this world to recommend that we love them—we are loving Him. Like they, He became a thing-"most reviled"—scorned by men—despised, stricken, afflicted. As theologian Megan McKenna profoundly observes, "To ignore the poor, is to ignore Christ Himself".

For us, this means that we champion the rights of the poor when we can, challenging the modern inclination—even the emphasis—of consumerism, excess, and instant gratification. Preserving and conserving is our answer to the waste of a disposable culture. We foster simplicity in living—though never in opposition to beauty; we seek to live below our means so that we can have more to share; we find ways to sustain and repurpose our resources rather than upgrade them or cast them out. We adopt a disposition towards our possessions in keeping with that counselled by St. Ambrose of Milan, who said, "The bread in your cupboard belongs to the hungry; the coat hanging unused in your closet belongs to the one who needs it; the shoes rotting in your closet belong to the one who has no shoes."

This positioning is reinforced by ancient concepts, both classical and spiritual. "Economy" comes from Greek and translates as the "managing of the household"—good stewardship of what one has so that it lasts as long as it can and produces familial flourishing to the maximum degree. This is the tenet of "generous living" that we foster in our missionary formation—the spirit that filled the poor widow when she "shared her mite" with those who "shared her plight." Jesus recognised the value in her contribution because it was active compassion for those she recognised in the way that she knew herself, a gift that far exceeded the monetarily larger, but spiritually indifferent—and therefore negligible—contributions of the rich. The revelation given to the widow was that other people were like her, and she, like them. In serving them, she created a world that was a home, one that tends to and cares for all beneath its roof. Theologian and advocate Mary Jo Leddy says this kind of epiphany makes us co-creators of a more humane existence.

Conversely, when we fail to recognise our brother, we pass him by on the road, as the priest and Levite passed by the man beset by thieves (Luke 10:30-37); we step over him, as the rich man stepped over Lazarus at his doorstep (Luke 16:19-31); we do not feed him, clothe him, or visit him, as the goats accused at the judgment had not done for those in want (Matthew 25:31-46). Only when we first recognise those in need can we choose how—or even whether—we will respond. The crisis of conscience that precedes an act of generosity can only arise when our eyes are truly opened; it is the threshold moment, the catalyst for everything that follows. In that instant, the suffering of others does more than confront us; it convicts us. We not only *see*, but recognise all the times that we have *failed* to see.

In Shakespeare's greatest tragedy, *King Lear,* the foolish sovereign is said to have but "slenderly known himself." This was the greatest of errors to the classical mind, as the Greek philosophical maxim warned each individual "*Gnōthi Sauton*": "Know Thyself."

Self-reflection was understood as the key to authentic humanity, and in Lear, the bard draws the portrait of a man who squanders his kingdom by failing to recognise himself in his fellow human being. Amidst the typhoon-like tempest that besets him on the wild heath, the half-mad Lear has a moment of lucidity when he is confronted with the banished Edgar, pretending to be a deranged beggar. Lear marvels at what he beholds—an unclothed, drenched, shivering creature exposed to a rampage of the elements:

> Thou art the thing itself; unaccommodated man
> is no more but such a poor, bare,
> forked animal as thou art....
> Poor naked wretches, wheresoe'er you are,
> That bide the pelting of this pitiless storm,
> How shall your houseless heads and unfed sides,
> Your looped and windowed raggedness defend you
> From seasons such as these? O, I have ta'en
> Too little care of this...

Lear's crisis is like that described by C.S. Lewis in *The Problem of Pain*—a means by which a confrontation with the wretchedness of our fellow human beings is a gift of grace: "God whispers to us in our pleasures, speaks in our conscience, but shouts in our pains: it is His megaphone to rouse a deaf world."

What strikes me most about our missionaries is not just how they respond to God's call—hearing Him shout, seeing and recognising the pain of His world—but the indomitable spirit with which they undertake their service. It is a vigorous spirit that does not shrink or flee from the storm but rises to meet it. Theirs is no naïve hope, but one grounded in faith, empowered by the vision of God's Kingdom advancing subtly through the message of the Gospel and the demonstration of Christ's love wherever they serve. This hope makes them over, inside and out, quickening their souls; they are fleet of foot, strong of arm, not only respecting the dignity of those they serve, but restoring it when it has been lost, then maintaining it after it is restored. They rekindle, then feed the flame. And they never walk away; rather, they work to make it spread—to catch fire beyond the reaches of that to which mere humans may aspire, knowing that God's breath bellows life into what they do.

The service to the poor in the Philippines has been extraordinary, all the more so considering how profoundly destitute the conditions prove to be. The poverty-stricken there live like squatters wherever they can find—at a dump site, along creek sides, in flimsy, make-shift cardboard structures. Many are relocated by the government outside the cities; they often live in cemeteries and fall victim to crime. Sanitation is impossible. The poor work when they can, but never consistently, so the only food they get—when they get it—is rice or vegetables. They scavenge everywhere. Malnourished, disease overtakes them easily, and when they fall ill, their recovery rates are poor for the obvious reason that they cannot afford medical attention. Their whole existence is preoccupied only with subsistence—enough food to live and stay as well as possible. They do not have the luxury of any other hopes.

The ministries in the Philippines have reached out to women, children, and youth, strengthening the faith and providing tutorial skills whenever possible. But among the many ways the ICPE missionaries recognise and respond to the poor is to make personal encounters with them. They have walked miles through rice fields and forests—gone into the slums and the cemeteries—with hampers of food and clothing, yes, but also with guitars and the Gospel, to provide not only material needs, but spiritual sustenance and hope as well. The poor are impoverished in more ways than we ever know; their lack of physical needs destroys their psyche too; how could it not? But when the missionaries arrive, if only to provide a temporary reprieve from hunger and loneliness, an epiphany occurs. Hope returns as they find that they are not below someone's notice; they are not too low for Christ to find them. These visits are especially transformative when they occur at Christmastime, by way of a custom known as "Reverse Carolling." This custom was instituted by ICPE missionaries and has served hundreds of families.

Traditional carolling in the Philippines requires that those who are visited support the carollers with a donation of some sort. Of course, as the poor cannot pay anything, they are not visited; or, in the event they are, the carollers are turned away.

But the ICPE missionaries have taken this tradition and converted the dynamics; they are the hosts and make the provisions. The poor are their guests. Food and fellowship are exchanged among equals, candles are lit, the Gospel is read, and the guests are asked what prayers the carollers can offer on their behalf.

Our missionaries have related many stories about these visits that testify to their life-changing effects. One man in a remote locale reached only by the longest and most arduous journey was so amazed that anyone would come to see him, that he said the angels of God must have brought them. He was so moved that he climbed a coconut tree to get coconuts for all—to share what he had with those who had shared with him—his gift for theirs—and they rejoiced in the joy of the Christ Child, a gift for all.

Another trip was to a family in a 4 x 4 metre (12 x 12 feet) house. The door hung by its hinges; the window was paneless. But the couple had a new baby, who was being cradled inside a basket hanging from the ceiling. The story of the Lord born in a stable, swaddled in a manger, was read aloud. The place and time and people there were blessed in its holy reflection.

Then there was a family with many children, living in a makeshift home by a refuse dump, who made their living by reselling plastic bags they found and washed. When asked for their prayer intentions, they looked about their place, at their children, and said that they had everything they needed. God had been good to them, they said. Such a statement wrung out the hearts of those who heard it—to witness such contentment was a grace they had never expected.

God's providence has been abundant in the Philippines too. Following typhoon damage in 2009, the missionaries stepped out in hope and faith to provide groceries, medication, and sleeping mats to affected families. Their prayers for help from abroad were answered to such a degree that they were able to use the money to address their immediate needs as well as those related to future storms. The missionaries sought God's help in obtaining a motorcycle for a working man who needed transportation to help care for a daughter suffering frequent seizures; in securing a new van for their work, by way of a missionary sister who exchanged all of her birthday gifts in order to match the necessary sum; and by the provision of a parish in the Czech Republic, who staged a ball each year in order to raise funds for the youth ministry. When the Mission has called, He has answered.

The effect of the ICPE Mission in India is no less remarkable than that of the Philippines. We established our presence there in Bangalore in 1999 and set up a new community house in Mysore in 2016.

In Bangalore, the ICPE missionaries serve families in slum areas consisting of one-room huts. These families work long hours at low-paying jobs, usually as construction workers and housemaids, and barely scrape by. Under such conditions, with so little time of their own, the need for the faith to "come to them" is even more pronounced. Visits from the missionaries bring the Gospel to where they are, in the time that they have, and provide the kind of dignity that is the fruit of being seen, recognised, and blessed that someone ventured to come—not as an act of *noblesse oblige*, but as a friend.

The trips also help the missionaries understand what the community needs. Often, expectedly, it is food or help with medical expenses; sometimes it is more. The ICPE Mission Bangalore has partnered with other charitable organisations in the region to support a number of children with their educational costs. Alleviating some of that burden takes the pressure off families in other respects, which is always the case.

ICPE Mission Bangalore has established eight prayer groups across the city's vernacular languages, reaching around 500 people each week. Their impact is widespread and compelling. One woman, prophetically named Esther, began her faith journey with the Mission. She has since become such an enthusiastic evangeliser that she has introduced somewhere around 40 people to Christ and to embrace the Catholic faith. Esther is an example of how the change in one life can ignite a spiritual outpouring in others; a missionary never knows what a world of difference a small prompting here or there might make—what one more visit, one more call, one more prayer can mean to spark a ripple effect of faith.

Two special ministries in Bangalore provide for the Gerizim Home (Gerizim Rehabilitation Trust), an institution founded in 1989 in service to disabled children, and the Jerome Home, founded in 1937 to serve destitute elderly women.

The Gerizim Home is completely dependent upon donations for the forty-some-odd children in the house. The children are mostly orphans who have lost both parents, sometimes to murders that they have witnessed, and they customarily fall victim to mob violence. This phenomenon is acute in certain areas where ethnic conflicts are strong. The ICPE missionaries provide financial support, make regular visits, supply care needs for infants, and make sure that each child receives a personalised Christmas gift.

The Jerome Home is run by religious sisters who also depend upon donations to help elderly women who have been abandoned by their families. The poignancy of these women's state, cut off from everything familiar and everyone that they have known, deserted by those who should have been their source of comfort and care in their old age, is overwhelming. Supplying the home with financial support is part of the project, but equally important is the ICPE missionary's visits. The provision of presence—simply presence—to an aged person means as much to that individual as anything. Holding hands, listening to stories, exchanging the news of life—all of these things are the gentle way in which the elderly are told that they matter, that they are as valuable in the eyes of God as they ever were.

We are no less a miracle of God's grace when we have outlived our ability to contribute to society than we were at our strongest and most productive. No life, not that of the disabled child nor that of the enfeebled elderly, should be required to make an argument for its right to be. The missionaries have testified that in the crying child, in the lonely and destitute old woman, they see more clearly the brokenness of humanity and the depth of evil. But they also recognise the face of the suffering Christ to whom they minister.

In Mysore, the approach is the same: house visitation to those living in poorly ventilated dwellings, some next to open drains full of refuse. The ICPE missionaries provide help with groceries, predominantly to widows, as well as medications and educational support for children. Through their visits, the missionaries assisted a widow who did not have the money to provide for one of her daughters who needed brain surgery. Her trust in God's providence brought her through the crisis, as the money was raised, the procedure performed, and her daughter fully recovered. As is often the case, the people served by the ICPE missionaries in turn became inspirations to the missionaries themselves. While they seek to instill conviction and trust in the Lord, the missionaries witness these qualities being embraced and lived out with such genuine fervour that it leaves them both humbled and awed.

The Mysore community also has a mission to the central prison in the city. They reach out to inmates who are open to their invitation—never imposing themselves upon them but extending an opportunity for moral engagement and spiritual counsel. In collaboration with the Prison Ministry India, they reach out to those of different faiths or none and cautiously maintain a presence there. The thirst and openness to the Gospel are tangible, which motivates them to continue their trips to bring the faith to those with whom Christ identifies in his parable of the sheep and the goats.

In sum, the ICPE Missions in the Philippines and India are emblematic of a practical, lived Christian experience meant to bring hope to those in need. This is an active, transformative hope—not a hope of mere aspirations and wishful thinking. It seeks to realise its purpose through spurring Spirit-driven change. It confronts the material, meets it at the crossroads of faith and action, and actively participates in building there the Kingdom of God.

She was holding her knees to her chest, crouching with her back against the wall, rocking to and fro as though to brace herself for whatever spasms were about to hit.

She could not have been more than ten years old, a lonely barefoot beggar, dressed in the drab, dusty clothes of so many poor people in the Ghanaian city of Kumasi. She had probably come to the yard outside the Pastoral Center where Mario was staying to find help, but whatever need she had for herself or her family—food, medicine, clothing—was overshadowed by what appeared to be a searing, intense pain. It was as if the composite of griefs in her life had manifested into one concentrated anguish, attacking and paralysing her where she sat.

She had no one but herself. She had nothing but her pain.

It was October of 1997, and Mario had come to Kumasi, Ghana—joined by a team of fellow ICPE missionaries from Europe—to help form lay catechists for the diocese, a function we had provided to the Archdiocese for some time. We were also forming an ICPE community there and periodically speaking at seminars. But that night, a trip meant to help the Church advance its spiritual objectives—something that Mario had seen as his and the Mission's basic calling—became the beginning of a new ministry, indeed an entirely new stress and focus, all from the sight of that young girl in torment.

He stopped, amazed that no one was paying attention to her—perhaps because in such a place, pain and want are so conventional that they have become banal. It is a sad fact that we can become accustomed to what we see, even things that in another place or time would make us recoil. If familiarity breeds contempt, as they say it does, it can also harden and desensitise. It is a great struggle to remain empathetic towards that which is close by—towards things that "have always been that way" and therefore do not attract our notice because they are so routine.

But Mario—not only a visitor in Kumasi, but also one unable to speak the language—had no way to help that girl. He had no idea how to get a doctor for her, which is precisely what she needed right then. At that time, the ratio of doctor-to-patient in the Kumasi region was about 1 per 31,100. Powerless, he could only walk away—just as all the others around her were doing. True, it was not out of indifference to her suffering; he left her because he was fundamentally unable to answer her need. But still, he had to walk away, and the sorrow of such a thing would not let him sleep.

All through the night, he saw her—a girl being consumed by an assault, a veritable storm of pain, becoming smaller and smaller as the world walked away.

He says that at that moment, Matthew 4:23-24 came alive for him. There, Scripture speaks of Jesus both preaching *and* healing diseases. It was not either/or; it was both. God created the whole person—the soul and the body—the spiritual and the material—and desires to heal them equally. That revelation led to another. In James 2:16, the apostle is clear as to the fitting Christian response to the needy:

> If one of you says to them, "Go in peace; keep warm and well fed," but does nothing about their physical needs, what good is it?

And the scales fell from his eyes.

Up until then, he'd seen evangelisation as separate and distinct from acts of charity. They were not integrated things—dimensions of a whole—but were instead discrete activities to be pursued exclusive of one another. In fact, he admits that prior to his Ghanaian visit in October of 1997, he'd regarded practical efforts, the works of mercy, as a somewhat lesser spiritual calling. Preaching the Word and transforming souls therefore was the main thing; the rest was thought to follow as a matter of consequence.

A girl in pain—a girl he could not find again the next morning—who had disappeared as the world walked away—changed all that. Our ministry from that point on would no longer be divided from the works of charity. We would both proclaim the Gospel throughout the world as we had first set out to do, but we would minister to its physical needs as well: body and soul—one unified being with two inseparable dimensions.

The following morning, Mario explained this sense of a new calling to Eugene and Ania, who were not only regular, hard-core ICPE missionaries to Africa, but also among the pioneers of our work in Ghana. They decided that given Mario's conviction about the sureness of the plan, a visit to the then Bishop of Kumasi, Peter Dwasi Sarpong, was in order. They arranged a meeting during which the idea was set out in forthright terms: Would the Diocese consider giving the ICPE Mission a piece of land so that we could build a hospital?

Bishop Sarpong responded with quiet thanksgiving: "This is the best thing you could do for my people," he said.

Let me be clear about this. In all his life, Mario had never built so much as a birdhouse, let alone a hospital. He had wanted to be a doctor in his youth, but his life had obviously taken a far different direction. In fact, none of us in the ICPE Mission leadership had any background in the medical field—none whatsoever. We also had no earthly idea where the money would be found to do such a thing.

But not ones to let a lack of knowledge, training, resources, or time stand in the way of a big idea (in fact, I wonder if those deficiencies haven't become the very conditions we're drawn to about a project), into the breach we rushed.

As usual, Providence worked the wonders necessary to cover our lacks. The Ghanaian Ministry of Health and other medical groups helped us identify the kind of hospital that the people needed. We were then able to make plans for a more expansive design than we'd first thought, one accommodating additional departments and specialising in certain key areas: Paediatrics, Imaging and Diagnostics, Ophthalmology, Orthopaedics, General Surgery, Gynaecology and Obstetrics, Craniofacial Malformations, and Acute Diseases.

Then, to really put the wind at our backs, Pope John Paul II selected the proposed Ghanaian Hospital as one of the 100 humanitarian projects for the Jubilee Year 2000. Through the Ghana Mission Foundation we established in Malta, all the funds for the first phase of building construction came from the people of Malta themselves. It is hard to raise money for abstract, "impersonal" things like buildings and infrastructure; people are much more willing to give money for treatments or procedures. But without those who contributed to raising the former, the latter would never have come to be. We were, and still are, particularly grateful for those first believers in our vision.

In 2001, the diocese of Kumasi donated 6.5 acres of land in Kumasi upon which to build the hospital. The next year, a well-established building contractor was engaged in construction. Exactly five years after Mario had seen the girl who inspired this new mission, Silvana, of our leadership team, who was an integral part of so many of our ministries in Ghana, represented us in a sod-cutting ceremony to commence the work on the project. The event was attended by a group of dignitaries and blessed by the then Archbishop Sarpong.

It took years of work—construction and fundraising—but we were all present when the President of the country, John Kufuor, and Archbishop Kumasi Mensah joined us in dedicating the hospital to the glory of God and the needy in 2008. In 2016, the first surgeries were conducted in what would come to be known as the *HopeXchange Medical Centre - Ghana.* An official opening followed two years later, inaugurated by Mario as the President of HopeXchange, together with Cardinal Peter Turkson, the then Prefect of the Dicastery for Promoting Integral Human Development.

No longer would the healthcare of the Ghanaian people be dependent upon castoff medical equipment and nearly expired medications donated by Western organisations. The *HopeXchange Medical Centre - Ghana* began providing excellent medical services, as well as employment for the community—close to 450 full-time employees at the time of writing. It also built a culture of holistic patient care based on compassion, dignity, and the sanctity of human life.

The Medical Centre is now constantly expanding its services. Besides the main, 120-bed hospital, a three-story annex has been built to house an industrial kitchen for patients and staff, administrative offices, and a hostel for visiting doctors and ICPE missionary teams. We are currently building a "Mother and Child" hospital in the same compound to address the exceptionally high mortality rates in Ghana associated with child-bearing women and children under five years of age. It will have 60 beds, an operating theatre, and departments dedicated to obstetrics, gynaecology, paediatrics, and anti-natal and post-natal care.

Many of those occupying key positions in the hospital are members of the ICPE community who have changed jobs and sought training and qualifications to occupy roles required for service there. Other missionaries and volunteers assist in fund-raising for the

Ghanaian projects. It has been an immense undertaking, but the *HopeXchange Medical Centre* has become the flagship for the mercy work of the ICPE Mission.

The philanthropic efforts in Ghana have not stopped at the medical field, however. Dominic, a Ghanaian ICPE missionary and the current manager of the *HopeXchange Medical Centre*, determined that a village some distance from the hospital was in serious need of a school. Children in the community were having to walk along a busy highway, undertaking long journeys to get to and from school and risking serious injury in the process. The villagers there relied solely on subsistence farming with no commercial occupations available, so the need for a school was serious.

So, in 2012, Dominic, along with the ICPE community he had founded in Kumasi, set out to establish a school in Kantinkyiren, a village in the Ashanti Region of Ghana. A traditional leader in the native community donated 5.04 acres of land, and a prominent Ghanaian family funded the construction of the building, named *Cosmas Osei Forson Basic School*. Eighteen teachers currently educate more than 500 students at the primary and junior high level, as well as in a crèche for early education. Plans are underway to expand the school in stages. The comprehensive vision of infrastructural development for the school includes a kitchen, playgrounds, a high-tech library, a school bus, and the ongoing provision of uniforms for the students, among other needs. The final phase of the plan is to establish a HopeXchange Youth Development Centre to provide career guidance and skill acquisition for young people in the district. This would help curb youth delinquency, which is a major concern in the area.

Clearly, a focus on children—first inspired by the "Kumasi Girl"—and always among the most vulnerable in developing countries, has been a fundamental priority of *HopeXchange*. The soon-to-be-opened "Mother and Child" Hospital, the Kantinkyiren school, the planned Youth Development Centre, and our Medical Centre's departments in paediatrics, obstetrics, and pre/post-natal care are evidence of that commitment. They are complemented by yet another initiative, begun in 2006: the *HopeXchange* Long Distance Adoption Programme. Interested parties can support a child from an underprivileged area by providing basic needs such as food, medicine, and schooling. This care helps that child overcome the daunting challenges posed by a poverty that threatens his or her future. Since its inception, the programme has happily produced many successes who are now pursuing university studies or have job opportunities that would never have been available to them before.

Best of all, the flourishing that has come from *HopeXchange*, the arm of the ICPE Mission reaching out to alleviate suffering in underprivileged areas around the world, is not limited to Africa. In 2006, Father Joseph Camilleri founded a hospital in the impoverished Jalpatagua region in southeastern Guatemala, near the border of El Salvador. Known as the "San Juan Bautista Hospital," Father Camilleri's charitable enterprise was the only medical care available for a population of over 150,000 people.

When he was reaching retirement age, Father began looking for some group with a strong Christian ethos to take over his work. His sister who assisted him in his charitable work, had just listened to a radio interview in which Mario spoke about our *HopeXchange Medical Centre - Ghana*. This seemed like the answer to her brother's prayers. Father Camilleri contacted us, got to know us, and decided to transfer the hospital to *HopeXchange*.

Mario and Paul Boitmann—our CEO for the NGO we set up in Guatemala, "HopeXchange Central America"—visited the hospital regularly. They finalised the contract in September of 2019, making what is still locally know as San Juan Bautista Hospital into our *HopeXchange Medical Centre - Guatemala*. Our efforts to bring Christ's compassionate love to the suffering had extended to the Americas.

HopeXchange Medical Centre - Guatemala employs 50 people and provides a full complement of medical services to the area, including surgery, paediatrics, gynaecology and obstetrics, and internal medicine. It also provides external services in cardiology, oncology, nutrition, psychology, physiotherapy, and speech therapy. Furthermore, San Juan Bautista has a world-class Community Health Worker Programme developed by Yale University. That programme aligns the surrounding villages with the hospital through communication initiatives. Like its counterpart in Ghana, the Medical Centre in Guatemala observes a Christian mission dedicated to providing high-quality, holistic medical care to those in most need of it.

The "X" of the *HopeXchange* logo is in the form of the Cross of Jesus Christ, where the exchange of all that is desolate, despondent and doomed ultimately took place—where the God-made-man took on all suffering, transformed it, and won our deliverance from sin, death, and despair.

There is no stopping the assaults of human existence, be they natural, in the form of the typhoons of Southeast Asia—or material, in the form of needs—food, clothing, shelter, medicine, companionship, love.

These things are all poverties, and the Lord said that the poor would always be with us. But if that is so—if the naked, the sick, and the dying are always there—if the Kumasi Girl is always alone and in pain—then we must in turn be always with them.

Always. At the intersection of the Cross, where hope is reborn, and lives are transformed.

11

from hilltop to marketplace

> To everything there is a season, and a time to every purpose under heaven. (Ecclesiastes 3:1)

Altars are heavy things. Old altars are all the heavier, typically made of marble as they are. Intense labour goes into their construction, and though their appearances may belie the fact, they can be comprised of many parts. Once installed, they are meant to stay in place—barring some great change in the world.

But the world—particularly the modern world—is made up of great changes; there is perhaps nothing more characteristic of it. While builders plan for the present and for what they can reasonably foresee of the future, the future has a way of unfolding in ways that could never have been fathomed. Sometimes, stock must be taken and new decisions made. Sometimes, altars must be moved.

To move such a structure like the one at St. Gerard's Monastery in Wellington, plans must be carefully laid. Floors have to be reinforced, and routes planned to allow for the weights' ponderous transference as efficiently as possible. The top slab of the altar alone weighs somewhere close to a metric ton.

Skilled masons have to chisel into the joints to separate the pieces—mensa, columns, throne, steps—all carved out of green marble from Galway and Devonshire, white marble from Carrara—and a frontispiece inlaid with Italian mosaics of the Annunciation.

The masons have to disjoin the body of a whole structure that has stood in one grand monumental unity for over a hundred years at the front of the church. If care is not taken, the sheer mass of pieces that have stood in tension against each other for so long—holding each other in place—can collapse and shatter through the sudden relaxation of that very tension.

A whole geometry of pulleys, wires, scaffolding, and tow straps must be engaged to lift the liberated parts—each marked carefully for the day when they will be recollected—recalled—to one another and stand as they were meant to stand. Each part must also be stored in its own wooden ark, and each ark brought through the church in a solemn cortege to a place where the individual loads are lifted into the air, dangling improbably beneath the hoist of a crane, and placed onto the back of the transport, as though upon ships bound across great waters.

The monastery of St. Gerard in Wellington, which always served as one of the foundational Mission Centres for the ICPE Mission, was designed by the renowned architect John Swan for the Redemptorist Fathers at the turn of the twentieth century. Among the many aspects of the church that Swan designed was that beautiful altar. Over a hundred years of Masses were celebrated at St. Gerard's, the bread and wine transformed into the body and blood of our Lord, offered for the world's redemption.

That offering of the Divine Self is the central tenet of the Christian faith, the infinite inundating the finite—in it, within it, among it, amidst it—a litany of expressions to express an existence reclaimed and restored—the altar upon which all is altered, forever.

For thirty years, the ICPE Mission was graced to enjoy St. Gerard's as a sphere from which so much of its work could be accomplished. We conducted eighteen Schools of Mission there and a multitude of ministries already recounted in earlier chapters.

But New Zealand is earthquake prone. The old structures of St. Gerard's, perched beautifully though precariously upon a hillside, have always been compromised by tectonic upheavals. So the required strengthening of the complex for safety's sake entails major engineering feats that have, predictably, major attendant costs.

Following the Covid pandemic of 2020-21, during which programmes all over the world had to go online, we entered a period of discernment. It wasn't just that life itself had changed so dramatically for over two years. In some ways, that change was only a confirmation of what we already knew. For some time, the world had been becoming—and now was—a different place to be in. There is a season for everything, as the Scriptures teach, and we must be aware of and attune ourselves to the changes of these seasons.

Since the beginning of our evangelisation efforts, the Mission Centre was the model from and around which we organised our work. Missionaries lived in a community, based in one place, and came and went as called. In many ways, the season of the Mission Centre was as necessary as it was natural. We gained and established our identity in this model—coalesced around our charism—and put our calling into action by way of various outreaches and ministries.

A degree of institutional cohesion is required at the beginning of an Institute—and for a long time after—as it takes root, grows, and flourishes. So a particular locus, and in our case, a number of them throughout the world, gave our missionaries a place to which they belonged, were formed, and could grow in their evangelistic endeavours. Without the "brick-and-mortar" season of an enterprise, stability and belonging would suffer.

But around 2008, we gradually started to sense a different call. Our foundation was secure and our purpose—though always open to the Spirit's guidance—was on a clear path. We had received the Church's recognition through the conferring of Pontifical Right in 2002, and we knew what we were about. So we were in a stable position from which to assess new directional paths.

One thing that prompted the new path was a culture that had become a wholly different place as the twenty-first century neared the mark of its first quarter. It was far different from when we began in that church meeting hall back in the 1980s. It was a world of the internet and telecommunications that would in a few short years lead to Ipads, digital formatting, and Zoom calls. It was becoming a universe of lateral moves, podcasts, mergers, consolidations, disbursements, and reconfigurations. In short, it was a world that was both a vastly smaller place—a thousand miles separation transversed by a Wi-Fi connection—and a vastly larger one—overwhelming people with floods of information, obligations, and diversions that pulled at and isolated them in a chaos of hyper-speed noise. The human soul yearned for what it always had yearned but reaching it in this new era would take a different kind of evangelisation—one as fluid, nimble, and agile as the times.

Other signs that we needed to discern a new path were the spiritual climate around the world and the dwindling numbers who were applying for our schools and programmes. For a variety of reasons with complex causes, our efforts to reach people in this ever-changing world needed to be rethought. Facts had to be faced. We were compelled to close one Mission Centre after another, each for pressing reasons, and only after much prayer and consultation.

Therefore, after a great deal of reflection over some years and a period of prayerful discernment, we came to a clear realisation. The Mission Centre model had served us well in its time, but that time had now passed. A new season had begun. We would no longer have centres from which our missionaries would come and go *about* the globe. Instead, they would be everywhere *throughout* the globe. No longer descending from the hilltop to the marketplace to carry out our mission, we would live and labour in the marketplace ourselves, to seek there the seeds of the Gospel we could nurture and help bloom.

Once the decision was made to close St. Gerard's and sell the property, plans for donating the altar to the nearby Cathedral of the Sacred Heart were put in place. But though that great change was perhaps the most metaphoric in our mission's assumption of a new way of life, the packing up of the adjacent monastery was no less transformative. It is best expressed by speaking of the reorientation of lives that were once centred around it.

There was a library to disburse—the painstaking task of triaging books—some to donate, some to give away, some to keep and pack. There were many things left over from the years when the Redemptorists lived there—missals, icons, altar stones, and even relics of saints. Blueprints of the original building plan turned up and parts of an important crucifix that had once stood atop the shrine of Our Lady. And then the years' worth of furniture, supplies, and miscellaneous objects that have been accumulated must be dealt with in a similar manner. Our community members had to come up with their own organisational and engineering schemes, sometimes involving their own sets of scaffolds and "fire brigades" to hand off large cupboards and cabinets and boxes.

The thought process of a move like that is intricate. Where should it all go? Who would want to take this or that—either out of need or sentiment—and who compiles the complicated inventories to keep track of where, when, and which items went to what group? Scheduling the disengagement from a place —the disassembling of a lifetime—is in many ways much harder than beginning to live in one. Perhaps that is the defining difference between consolidation and separation; there is one direction towards which all the former is directed; there are so many directions in which the latter can be aimed.

There were also many visitors who came by during the process of leaving St. Gerard's. People from the community of course, but also the Redemptorists to whom the buildings and grounds meant so much. Then there were museum curators, photographers, and news people. St. Gerard's being such an integral part of the Wellington landscape, a change in its future generated a natural public interest.

But the greatest impact was on those of us who had spent so much time there over the years. So many of our Schools had been conducted at St. Gerard's, making it a place of transformative encounters. Some of the community members' children had grown up there, and so their formative memories were entirely associated with the place. Others recalled the feast days and celebrations in which the Catholics of Wellington congregated and deepened their faith—in particular, the "Worship Nights" that became for many a formative example of what it meant to praise and adore God. And the staging of the many ministries and outreaches from Wellington were ever-present to all. The recollection of these memories, evoked through the process of detaching from St. Gerard's, brought the community together in a way that only a common objective can do.

The renewed closeness gave us strength as we turned to live out our new model for the mission and the tasks that lay ahead for it.

The closing of St. Gerard's and our consequent integration into the community was in some ways made easier because we had sensed this trajectory for some time. It was prefigured in the circumstances that resulted in the closure of our other great foundational Mission Centre at Allerheiligen.

For around fifteen years, from 1990-2005, Allerheilgen was a thriving place. Our programmes and activities were filled to capacity and at one point we even sought overflow accommodations in the surrounding neighbourhood. Planning to fulfill the logistical needs themselves was a major task, as we were happily troubled by the growing fruitfulness of our missionary endeavours.

But the change that was slowly creeping over the world—the one that we'd sensed long before the global pandemic hit in 2020—and of which it was in many regards symbolic—began around 2007. That was when a global financial crisis hit with a force unparalleled since the Wall Street Crash of 1929, followed by the Great Depression. Such an economic disaster had a profound effect on our ability to fund projects and meet our expenses. It had an effect even more grave upon the wherewithal of others to participate in our ministries. Reaching a breakeven point became harder and harder for event after event.

We also detected a distinct shift in the spiritual climate throughout Europe and the World, one occurring in tandem with the economic crisis. While church attendance and religious affiliation had been in decline for some time, the problem became both more acute and sweeping.

It is natural to think such things are temporary in the beginning. There is no need to overreact at the first, or even second, signs of a downturn. Besides, change is unpleasant and comes with its own costs. These lead to what modern social commentators speak of as "investment bias"—the idea that people are loathe to face, or admit, that something is no longer working due to the fact that they have put so much into an enterprise. It "has to work" because it has worked for so long.

But little by little, much like the virus that gripped the world in 2020, a malaise had crept into the Allerheiligen community. It affected the group's vision, cohesion, and spiritual growth.

Mario and I had lived in Rome for ten years when the problems manifested most profoundly, but we travelled back to Germany often during that time. So we were aware of what was happening and the ICPE Mission's leadership took action to right the ship. We even brought in professionals from outside the community to identify the causes and to suggest solutions. But despite many meetings comprised of these professionals, the leadership team, and the community members, the answer to the situation was not to be found in following the old model.

Allerheiligen had been a type of the "mountaintop ministry," from which we invited others to come to us. As I've said, for years there was no reason to question this mode of operation. But as we had sensed—and as the facts on the ground revealed—that was no longer the case. A changing economic and financial landscape, as well as a new spiritual distance and religious anomie, had beset the world. These things worked in tandem to make our old model obsolete. A new season was upon us, and we had to be not only aware of it but also willing to respond to it. And we had to respond to what we saw with the trust that Providence would provide, as always.

It was time for Allerheiligen to close. And as members of the ICPE International Council, it was our job to make this final decision and help those in the community, both locally and abroad, to embrace it. The loss was in some small way lessened by the fact that the closure happened concurrently with the 2009 opening of the more modest "ICPE Mission Deutschland" community house in Mannheim.

Understandably, as Allerheiligen had been a "motherhouse" to our Mission for two decades, this change came with its own set of particular griefs. But most everyone who at some point served or lived in that community, in time came to understand that it was the right thing to do. Prized as that location was, it had been entrusted to us for its season and now it was time to part with it. The call was taking us in a new direction, one that we expected would revitalise our evangelistic efforts, being more responsive to the times. We have to be clear-eyed and unsentimental about things when an entrusted asset—as Allerheiligen undoubtedly was—has served its purpose. God had given it to us for a time; it was His and to Him it was returned. So in 2011, new deeds were signed, transferring the compound of Allerheiligen to its new owners, just over two decades after the Archdiocese of Freiburg, Germany, had welcomed us into its fold.

Allerheiligen is a permanent part of our history, the place where the spirituality of the ICPE Mission was intensely lived. If it were not for those years—the spring and summer of our lives—there would not be a harvest to pass on to the generations that followed. The spirit born of that place is in the hearts of all who now carry the light of Christ to the four corners of the world, in the seasons that are now coming to be.

The closing of these two foundational Centres—St. Gerard's and Allerheiligen—were the largest and most emblematic of our transition to a new mode of operation—away from the "Mission Centre" model, from which we "came and went," and toward the "marketplace" model, with our missionaries living in their respective homes and united with their respective communities in their localities. But the closing of our other Mission Centres, occurring apace over a decade—Poland in 2012; the Philippines in 2018; and India in 2023—were each uniquely difficult but necessary.

Transitioning to a new way of life—from full-time missionaries who gave up regular jobs to full-time missionaries who maintained them—was a challenge for everyone. There were housing and job concerns, of course, but also the difficulties of disconnecting from what had always been a cultural base—one through which long relationships had been formed. Every change involves loss, some more than others.

In communicating this change in living out our charism to our missionary community, Mario and I found guidance in the Old Testament. What we said to the Mission at the closing of St. Gerard's applied equally to each of the other closures:

> We are at a place where a pillar from the Old Testament—Abraham—was, when God called him to sacrifice his only son.

> Abraham must have wrestled with God in his heart and suffered profoundly walking up the mountain all prepared to slay Isaac, in obedience to God. The same God who had promised to make Abraham the father of all nations was now asking him to sacrifice the son of His promise. Just like Abraham, we do not have all the answers to the many questions, but what we do know is that today, after a long, serious, and broad communal discernment, the right thing to do is to let go of St. Gerard's Monastery and Church.
>
> Abraham kept walking up the mountain, taking one step after another. He built the altar, arranged the wood for the fire, then bound his son to the wood on the altar. All this, while still believing in the promise of God…
>
> So we, too, dear friends, will take these steps of obedience, trusting that the Lord—who is calling us to surrender back to Him the unique gift that St. Gerard's has been—will be faithful to His promises for us. He will be faithful to provide new gifts and new avenues for us to make Him known in the world today.

The God who entrusted us with lay missionary communities and enabled us to serve Him from Mission Centers was the same God to whom we now returned them. He had opened every door, provided every missionary, and supplied all we needed to bring together a people who would be formed as His disciples, His missionaries—even when we could not fathom how to meet incalculable needs.

Like Haggai, the Lord was saying to us all:

> Be strong, sisters and brothers, take courage all you peoples of the land and work, for I, the Lord, am with you.

This was the same God we had to trust—and that we must continue to trust—in the years to come.

He makes all things new.

By 2012, the ICPE International Council had laid a strong foundation in Rome for the Mission and its future administration. The office there could manage efficiently without the President actually residing in the Vatican neighbourhood. That being the case, it was decided that while Rome would remain the key reference point for the enterprise, we had reached a stage where we could broaden our future main leadership opportunities without restricting them to those residing in the Eternal City itself. As a lay mission, this would allow us to have an even more "outward" looking face, one turned towards the world where we are sent.

And there was no getting around the fact that technological capabilities were so transforming the world, that it was possible to be effectively "present" in a place though not actually so. As a result, the leaders of the Mission agreed that Mario and I could relocate to Malta in the Spring of 2013, while regularly visiting our Rome office as need be. Time has proved that administrative model to be an effective one and has brought Mario and me back to the place where everything began.

In the post-Mission Centre season of the ICPE Mission, our lifestyle is now like the way of life other brothers and sisters in Local Communities have been living for several years. Following this development, on July 28, 2023, during an international gathering in Kuala Lumpur, Malaysia, all the Local Communities within the global network, formally became part of the Institute for World Evangelisation – ICPE Mission, recognised as a private international association of the faithful of pontifical right since 2002. This incorporation reflects their shared spiritual unity, rooted in the charisms of Worship and Evangelisation, and a common Covenant with members who previously lived in Mission Centres or as ICPE Communities of Companions. In response to Pope Francis' call to be *missionary disciples*, all the members embraced a unified identity as "ICPE missionary disciples," as part of "ICPE missionary communities", emphasising their shared mission and calling in their daily lives.

Wherever our missionaries are, they meet in each other's homes in small groups or in halls as a larger community. They are involved in parishes and ministries around the diocese and beyond, and carry out their own particular projects to share the joy of the Gospel with the people among whom they live, work, and socialise—extending their reach further still.

After all, as the laity are, by definition, engaged in the world of jobs, schools, families, and civic concerns, a lay mission reaches its fullest expression when it is integrated into that very world. We work within society to sanctify it—to align it more closely with God's purpose—a role entrusted to us by Vatican II. However, as Donna Orsuto insightfully highlights in her work *Holiness*, any sanctification we are called to bring is ultimately God's work, where "*in the mix of divine initiative and human cooperation, the water of grace is blended with the cement of committed discipleship.*" This divine-human partnership is what shapes our mission in society, as Orsuto further emphasises:

> We are called, chosen by the architect himself, to be so much more than simply cosy cottages lining quiet rural streets in a quaint village. We are living stones and we are being built into a grand edifice where the Triune God desires to dwell in full communion with his people in the thick and thin of tumbling reality.

Christians are 'sent' into the public square—the marketplace—in a form that is fluid and adaptable to its needs. Their ability to see and hear with greater clarity, to act and respond swiftly as part of its fabric, represents the missionary life in its fullest expression. Like Paul, the apostle *and* tentmaker, the missionary disciple works and prays in a seamless life.

Of course, many of our missionaries also contribute their time and talents at the international level of the ICPE Mission. They serve on different teams that focus on the common, foundational aspects of our life and mission as a global community. Work at the local level does not preclude participation in the larger field, nor vice versa.

Karl Rahner and Henri De Lubac are two theologians who were present during Vatican II. They both contributed significantly to the theological understanding of the "secular" role the laity play in the Church and the world.

Rahner, a German Jesuit theologian, portrayed the adult Christian as someone who lives in a "grace-filled mystery" where God is present in the everyday realities of life. His concept of the "everyday mystic" highlights the idea that adult Christians are called to experience and respond to God in the ordinary moments of their daily existence. A mature Christian, according to Rahner, is someone deeply attuned to the presence of God in all things. Thus, the Christian lives out his or her faith in a way that integrates the sacred and the secular, embodying a hopeful and active engagement with the world.

The French theologian Henri de Lubac's theological insight was that the natural and supernatural are not separate, nor are they parallel orders. For de Lubac, the natural world is directed towards the supernatural fulfillment of God's plan:

> Nature, precisely as nature, has no complete meaning except in reference to the supernatural call that brings it to its final fulfillment.

This is a vision of hope and integration, where human life is seen as fundamentally oriented toward divine communion and where the Gospel is actively transforming the world from within.

The Biblical foundation for this approach is found in chapter five of Matthew's Gospel. There, Jesus addresses his disciples in the metaphors of "salt" and "light."

> You are the salt of the earth. But if the salt loses its saltiness, how can it be made salty again? It is no longer good for anything, except to be thrown out and trampled underfoot.
>
> You are the light of the world. A town built on a hill cannot be hidden. Neither do people light a lamp and put it under a bowl. Instead, they put it on its stand, and it gives light to everyone in the house. In the same way, let your light shine before others, that they may see your good deeds and glorify your Father in heaven.

He provides a profile for the Christian witness, the role that His missionary disciples must take. Like salt, they bring out flavour and depth by seasoning what is there, blending into the substance to which they are added. Salt, essential to perfection, does its work by dissolving into what it is added. So too for missionaries in the marketplace. Integrated into society, missionary disciples are less visible, though every bit as present and active, partnering in Christ's mission to "make all things new", where faith is not passive but an active force for good.

Christ also describes his community as the "light of the world," placed on a lampstand so that its glow can reach those in the shadows, in the dark. This shining "before others" is not synonymous with an arrogant desire to elevate oneself above others or to boast a pretended superiority. Instead, it involves the necessary visibility of "a city set on a hill," which "cannot be hidden." This light that the missionary disciples carry merely reflects another Light—the Light of God, which shone in Christ.

The paradox of the "salt" that disappears and the "light" that shines, together express a mysterious fruitfulness: the necessity of giving, of being, and existing not for oneself but for others, for all, for humanity. This openness and expansiveness take on the dimensions of universality, as suggested by the crescendo of terms: earth (v.13), world (v.14), all (v. 5), humanity (v.16).

So to be both "salt and light" is to let one's works shine though actions that bring wisdom, flavour, and illumination, so that others may find meaning and enlightenment. As Peter's letter also reminds us: "Conduct yourselves honourably... so that, when they see your good deeds, they may glorify God" (1 Peter 2:12).

"God uses the ordinary to achieve the extraordinary"

This phrase is something that those in the ICPE Mission say all the time. Small things can have great effects, an idea deeply rooted in Scripture: Moses' staff that God used to part the Red Sea and bring water from a rock (Exodus 4,14), a young shepherd and his simple sling with five smooth stones who defeated the giant Goliath (1 Samuel 17), the widow's small jar of oil that paid off her debts and sustained her family (2 Kings 4), a boy's lunch of fish and loaves that fed thousands with leftovers remaining (John 6), Peter's shadow that healed the sick (Acts 5), the touch of Jesus' garment by the woman with a bleeding disorder for twelve years resulting in her healing (Mark 5), and the ground wheat and crushed grapes that become the glorified, risen body of Christ—to name a few. More recently, despite her short life and hidden existence in a Carmelite convent, we have seen the principle of "small things" exemplified in the life and writings of St. Thérèse of Lisieux. It is a truth built on trust and humility that God can use anything, however small—whether individuals, objects, or actions—as instruments to achieve everything within His will. The phrase is so central to our day that it is included in the ICPE prayer. We petition God to "*Use the ordinary, use our lives, to accomplish the extraordinary deeds of your love in the world today.*"

In our integrated approach to living as missionary disciples, this is how we perceive the work that lies before us. It is in the ordinary spaces of our lives that the extraordinary unfolds, where God's love and glory are made manifest. Therefore we seek to be ordinary people, living ordinary lives while trusting God to accomplish the extraordinary. At the wedding in Cana, simple stone jars and plain water became the vessels for a miracle, as God transformed what is common into something exceptional. This is our purpose too—to offer the ordinary to Him and trust that He will work through it for His greater glory.

There are several models for this life in the New Testament, and Joseph of Arimathea is one of the best. We live in a time in which complete strangers with huge platforms jockey for the power to influence the lives of others, to make them their followers, and to profit from the consequent prestige. Entire careers are constructed around gaining some aura of "expertise," even if it is absolutely baseless. People follow other people only because those are the people that everyone follows. The French social philosopher René Girard posited the concept of 'mimetic desire' as the greatest human motivator. Rather than being attracted to things based on their inherent worth or value through rational thought, we desire things simply because others desire them. In other words, we mimic others' appetites, seeking what is sought, whether we truly want it or not—even convincing ourselves that it is desirable and that we indeed want it. Thus, deception builds upon deception in a vicious circle of vacuity.

In contrast, Joseph of Arimathea shows us that small acts of faithfulness can lead to astounding influence and have a great impact when we stand up for what is right. Joseph was a businessman and a secret follower of Jesus. After Jesus' death, something shifted in Joseph—he identified with Jesus and bravely took it upon himself, at great personal risk, to seek Jesus' body and to secure its burial. He even gave up his own tomb for that purpose.

In one way, such "last things" are small, even unpleasant, but necessary duties. They are the ordinary jobs of everyday life. But Joseph was faithful to the mission—to accomplish a grim and in this instance, despised task—burying one whom the state deemed a criminal. Joseph did this because he knew who he was—a man of integrity, a man with courage enough to see to necessary things. And from that tomb—Joseph of Arimathea's tomb—where the ordinary work of burying the dead was fulfilled—the event that changed the world took place. Joseph was an ordinary man called to extraordinary things.

Joseph of Arimathea is a powerful, relevant, and compelling example for the working Christian of how to live as an authentic missionary disciple—with trust, humility, and integrity—in an increasingly hostile culture. Our modern view of the workplace—with its toil and strife—is not entirely unwarranted. The work environment can test a person's faith by its unfairness, ambiguities, stress, and unethical practices. It can also be self-serving, pulling us away from other duties, particularly personal ones, that conflict with it.

But the God of the universe is also present in our workzone where we can hone our virtues and mature our faith. This can only happen when we remain open to what we can learn of ourselves and of human nature as we labour alongside others. Furthermore, it can be deeply transformative to recognise that work is a sacred activity, helping us to fulfill our God-given potential if we employ it in a way consistent with God's will for human flourishing. The most secular of places can be a proving ground for our souls.

For the ICPE missionary, it has always been the case—whether on the hilltop or in the marketplace—that the posture we take towards God is one of being a respondent. Like the young woman from Nazareth, whose *fiat* opened the door for Jesus Christ, the Saviour, to enter the world, we give our 'yes' to His will, according to His Word. Accordingly, the Marian feast of the ICPE Mission is the Annunciation. Just as Mary welcomed the Divine in an existential act of hospitality, so do we seek to honour and receive the mystery of God in the course of our lives. As a discerning disciple, Mary was open, receptive, and sensitive to the movement of the Spirit in her.

This makes her the blueprint for how to live as a missionary disciple in the public square. As a woman filled by the Spirit and led by the Spirit, she acted boldly, loved deeply, and served God humbly yet courageously in her earthly life. But she is not merely a distant form, an abstraction to which we pattern our lives; she is also a sister who walks the path with us and a mother whose intercession nurtures, inspires, and sustains us.

So as missionary disciples in the marketplace, we bring our faith with us to inform our engagement with every dimension of life there. We listen for God's guidance on how to respond to all aspects of society where there is a lack—injustice, deprivation, waste, exploitation—and how He would have us influence these trends as active members of the community. That may be through medicine, education, science, the arts, or whatever other talents we may be called upon to employ. We are not merely present; we are sent.

In the new season of the ICPE Mission's life, the one that began with transitioning from the Mission Centre model to the marketplace model, we have followed a path much like the altar at St. Gerard's. We moved slowly, but purposefully, from our place on the hill to our place within the public square.

On 21 July, 2023, the altar—disassembled and placed within a collection of wooden arks for the journey—was placed upon the transport truck for the long descent down Mount Victoria. All of Wellington and its harbour lay below as the engine started, the wheels engaged, and the massive load inched its way through the steep streets toward Kent Terrace. That busy thoroughfare, at the base of Mount Victoria, led past the iconic Embassy Theater and other city landmarks towards Cambridge Terrace. It then entered the bustling heart of downtown Wellington.

From there, the route carried on close to the waterfront, the skyline reflected in the bay, and past civic monuments like the Michael Fowler Centre and Te Papa Museum. The truck then took a turn onto the final stretch, from Molesworth Street, and through the Thorndon neighbourhood. The roads widen slightly at that point, and the surroundings take on a mix of residential charm and institutional buildings, giving over to the foot of Hill Street. The spire of Sacred Heart Cathedral came into view, and the transport bearing the altar began its gentle ascent.

It only took fifteen to twenty minutes, start to finish, for the journey to be completed—an ironically short time considering the more than a hundred years the altar had served in one place. But now, here it was, beginning its service in another.

Sacred Heart Cathedral in Wellington, also known as the Metropolitan Cathedral, was reopened after extensive renovations with a weekend of celebrations from June 7–9, 2024. The reopening marked the completion of a six-year restoration and earthquake strengthening project that began in 2020 after the cathedral was closed in 2018 due to safety concerns. The Archdiocesan Mass of Thanksgiving included the return of the bishop's chair (the cathedra) to its rightful place in the cathedral and the formal reopening of its doors.

And in the middle of the sanctuary was the altar from St. Gerard's—all of his parts reassembled—all together once more. Candles were lit upon its table and it was formally vested and blessed.

The procession to the altar is a prayer in motion, a visible reminder of the unity of God's people and the shared journey of faith. There, the priest leads the faithful in the great praise and thanksgiving of the doxology: "Through Him, with Him, in Him, in the unity of the Holy Spirit, all glory and honour is yours, Almighty Father, forever and ever"—a proclamation of Christ's presence in the Eucharistic sacrifice and the unity of the Trinity.

And we, as ICPE missionary disciples, join Christ in the offering of ourselves in His service—through, with, and in Him—who is with us wherever we go, who is always, already there.

12

the view from here

5.45 a.m.
A Friday in December, the first week of Advent.

A storm blew in from the Mediterranean last night, bringing a rain that washed and cleansed the old limestone village where we live. I heard it fall throughout the evening, but as I rise, the clouds have mostly cleared. All the rough weather has passed now. We've had a very dry winter thus far, so the rain was more than welcome.

I slide open the doors that lead onto the terrace. The cool morning air drifts inside. It's both fresh and earthy—that loveliest of smells they call "petrichor," when a shower falls upon dry ground and releases its rich, loamy fragrance. It's as if, in its relief, the parched earth is offering back thanks through imparting the present of such a scent.

From our top floor terrace, we look out upon fields that lead to nearby villages far in the distance. The sky is still soft with dawn, the sun peeking through the clouds as it rises in its slow march. It begins to free a slow gift of honey-coloured light, casting it down in a growing arc of effulgence.

Sparrows greet me. They perch on the terrace railing and dance around the flowerpots to drink the rainwater. A dawn chorus rings from the nearby trees as birds swoop and flit and glide—as though rejoicing in what God has made them to be—as though relishing in the delight of the pleasure He takes in what they are.

Gerard Manley Hopkins once spoke of such a sight in his sonnet "The Windover"—of a common kestrel— "brute beauty"—dancing upon the high currents, resplendently indulging in the wondrous nature with which the Creator endowed it.

Still glistening from the storm, the world looks new and crisp from the terrace.

It will be a warm day, I can tell; it will be a bright day.

As is our custom, Mario and I prepare a cup of coffee to savour during our prayer time—mine in an armchair tucked into the corner of our small home office, his as he sits at one end of the living room couch. We learned this from Christ, who often left his disciples to find a deserted place to be alone with the Father. He demonstrated how a greater intimacy with God is impossible without silence, without creating stillness around us for a hushed interlude with Him. In fact, many spiritual authors speak of silence as *God's language*. St. John of the Cross expressed this most profoundly:

> The heavenly Father has spoken one Word: It was His Son. And He speaks it eternally in an eternal silence. And it is in silence that it can be heard by the soul.

Soon enough we will begin our routine of checking and responding to emails, sent from near and far. Missionaries in a cavalcade of time zones—some rising, just as we are, and others now readying for bed—need to discuss their agendas and coordinate their meetings. Later, the house will have to be straightened and the lunch prepared to get a head start on things. We will spend the morning administering affairs with Coordinators and making plans for travel. There is a visit to Asia coming up, and various details to arrange. After so many years, travel is as customary to us as home itself—the road out and the road in, one life with two directions.

But all of that can wait.

Prayer must start the hours. It must lie alongside the light as it lengthens the morning the way a lyric lies along a tune.

Though still a bit tired on this Advent dawn—at the end of another full year of our work—I remember that even when we feel too weary to look for the light, it was the Light who had first come looking for us. And the Light had taken the form of a child in Bethlehem these two millennia past. That is the season now upon us.

The soul stirs at such a thought; it rushes to seek out and welcome the Lord who had deigned to lower himself into a cradle, who had outrageously come to us and for us, a people who did not even know we were lost.

In this divine embrace, we grow as missionary disciples—not through mere action, but through an intimate journey of communion with the Lord, mirrored by the beloved disciple who placed his head on Jesus' chest (John 13:23). That communion is forged in prayer. As we draw nearer to Christ, we begin to see His loving plan unfolding—not just in our own lives, but in the world around us. We come to understand our role in His mission to restore creation to its original glory. Prayer doesn't just shape us—it transforms us into bold, authentic disciples, empowered to live out our faith as missionaries, bringing hope and light to a world in need. Just as Jesus's mission led Him to lay down His life for His friends, we, too, are called—echoing the words of Pedro Arrupe, the visionary Spanish Jesuit—to be "men and women for others," working alongside Him to heal, save, and restore the world by responding to its deepest needs and cries.

But the fruit of prayer is directly tied to the diligence with which it is cultivated. Prayer is not an optional discipline for the missionary disciple. Like an athlete who must train, like a musician who must run through her scales, the missionary disciple must pray. We can, however, allow ourselves to fall beyond the voice that beckons us. Then the less we pray, the less we want to pray. Like the mind and body, our soul has a purpose; when neglected or misdirected, it withers and dies.

Conversely, in a sweet irony, the more we pray, the more we want to pray. Prayer does not slake but only intensifies our longing for God. "*My soul waits for the Lord more than watchmen for the morning*" (Psalm 103:6), declared the psalmist. The thirst that God alone can quench grows into a greater, more intense thirst for that which quenches it: "*As a deer longs for flowing streams, so my soul longs for you, O God*" (Psalm 42:1).

Ezekiel boldly declares in the Old Testament that God's Spirit takes our hearts of stone and transforms them into hearts of flesh, igniting within us the power to live as His beloved children, increasingly attuned to His will. This radical transformation begins in each of us at baptism—when we are immersed into the life of the Father, Son, and Holy Spirit. In that moment, we receive not only a new identity but an invitation to enter into a deeply intimate relationship with the Creator of the universe, our Creator.

Jesus perfectly mirrors this communion with the Father, as described in 1 John 1: "The Word (*Logos*) was *with* God". The word "with" reveals the quality of relationship the Word (*Logos*) had with the Father for all eternity. In the original Greek, this phrase also means that the Word was eternally moving *towards* God. Far from being in a static relationship, the Word is constantly pressing closer and closer to the Father, eternally penetrating more deeply into the heart of God and being joined to Him by the pure passion of the Spirit.

In the same way, we are invited to live our lives as a journey *towards* God, pressing always deeper into His heart and His loving plan for us. And in Jesus, we are given the Way that leads *towards* the Father—in Him, through Him, and with Him.

Like our Lord, our humanity—body and soul—will one day be resurrected. And there, the obscurity of faith will give place to the light of vision, where the Light of Glory will shine on the face of God so that we may behold Him face to face, as He truly is. Our joy will be complete, and our desire, longing, and thirst will be met. But as Aquinas affirms, our soul will continue to deepen its understanding of Him eternally, ever growing in contemplating and enjoying the infinite depths and beauty of that knowledge—like sparrows bathing in the dawn of a growing light.

8.30 a.m.

We start our workday at the office located in a small apartment across the landing from where we live.

I usually first connect with Daniela, the remarkable secretary at the International Office in Rome for the past twenty-three years. We chat briefly and then decide together on the priorities for the day.

Mario will be heading to Washington D.C. for the National Prayer Breakfast in February. So Daniela needs to look at flights and accommodation for him. That annual event convenes people from government, business, and different faith communities to promote unity and dialogue. Its objective is to emphasise the role of faith and prayer in public life and act as an example of the same. Then we have to confirm our registration for the annual Meeting of Moderators of Associations of the Faithful, Ecclesial Movements, and New Communities held in Rome by the Dicastery for Laity, Family, and Life.

With those tasks started, I move on to emails. We'll be delivering a seminar to married couples in March, so that has to be arranged, and then we need to register our participation in the next webinar on "Communal Discernment in Organisational Renewal" as alumni of The Discerning Leadership Program.

The email responses are interrupted by calls I have to take on various matters; this morning, one of our leaders in the field updates me on a pastoral situation that requires handling. We make it a priority to stay available to, and as closely involved as possible with our missionaries wherever they are, and in particular, with our leaders.

In a world so vast, we must remain close by any means that help us to do so. Missionary life—whether in the hilltops or in the marketplace—is in many respects just as it has always been: a pioneer or group of pioneers braving some unsettled front for the Lord. But that life needs the sustenance of its supporting community—its "homestead," as it were—and we strive to maintain that for them through regular communication. They are not alone out there, we assure them; we are close.

After another talk with Daniela, I go over the agenda for the following Monday's online meeting with the ICPE Formation and Spirituality Teams to prepare for the ICPE Mission's annual retreat. This common retreat aims to deepen different aspects of our spirituality. This too is an important priority, to maintain the strength of vision and calling of those who have chosen to live this way of life. It is a touchstone for us, constantly maintaining our theological perspective so that our missionaries know fully why and what they are about.

Mario tackles some emails. A priority today is to check with a good friend of ours about his availability on our proposed dates to conduct another workshop on Communal Discernment with our leaders. In 2021-22, we served together with him on the Vatican Commission of Spirituality in preparation for Phase 1 of the Synod on Synodality. Mario then prepares for a series of online meetings for the day. He needs to check in with the management of the HopeXchange Medical Centre in Ghana, conduct a regular meeting with the ICPE priests, and then spend time mentoring a couple of our main leaders in the responsibilities of their respective positions. These one-on-one meetings have become more of a priority now for Mario and me as the Mission transitions to a new top leadership body. There is a great deal to keep an eye on, to make sure that everything is running like clockwork as far as possible. And that is the largest part of our daily tasks: bringing order and maintaining symmetry in the life of the Mission itself.

But it would be wrong to see this bringing of order and symmetry as a mere "dry" administrative task, just as it would be wrong to reduce missionary life to a checklist of "good deeds," laboriously performed. The truth is, the life of a missionary disciple is, at its core, deeply creative. We are called to contribute to the beauty of the world through order and symmetry—the hammer and chisel, the blood, sweat, and tears that shape any true transformation.

At the same time, we must be attuned to the world's beauty in all its variation and texture—the wild dawn chorus of a hundred birds—the riot of sunset hues in a cloud-streaked sky—the "Pied Beauty" of Hopkin's world that applauds God's masterpiece of angles, contrasts, and dimension:

> Glory be to God for dappled things –
> For skies of couple-colour as a brinded cow;
> For rose-moles all in stipple upon trout that swim;
> Fresh-firecoal chestnut-falls; finches' wings;
> Landscape plotted and pieced – fold, fallow, and plough;
> And áll trádes, their gear and tackle and trim.
>
> All things counter, original, spare, strange;
> Whatever is fickle, freckled (who knows how?)
> With swift, slow; sweet, sour; adazzle, dim;
> He fathers-forth whose beauty is past change:
> Praise him.

We live in a world crafted by God, a world He gazed upon and declared "good." Though that world is fallen, it is our sacred duty to recognise and cherish what is beautiful, to cultivate and enhance it, and to restore the beautiful where it has been lost. In this way, we become co-creators with God who—through His Spirit actively at work in the world—is continually "making all things new" and beautiful again like the Garden of Eden—redeeming, restoring, and rebuilding His Kingdom on Earth.

I'll never forget being "surprised by joy," to borrow from C.S. Lewis, as I stood before Botticelli's painting "Primavera" at the Uffizi Gallery in Florence. The allegory of spring's arrival expressed through mythical deities is rendered through a flood of natural imagery. Mercury, Venus, Chloris, Zephyr, the Three Graces—young and serene—are dressed in diaphanous garments moving in a fresh breeze, amidst a verdant landscape burgeoning with blossoms and fruit and all that has returned to life. The whole of the masterpiece is greater than any of its masterful parts, creating a confluent power that moved me deeply. The painting captured me the way happiness and love capture people, all at once telling them in an epiphanic moment what they are made for.

To understand beauty's role in our lives is to understand ourselves. An orientation toward beauty is intrinsic to our nature. Toward the end of his letter to the Philippines, Paul writes:

> Finally, brethren, whatever is true, whatever is honourable, whatever is just, whatever is pure, whatever is lovely, whatever is gracious, if there is any excellence, if there is anything worthy of praise, think about these things.

Therefore, we should attend to the beautiful not only because it is good in and of itself, but because beauty draws a person toward immaterial truth and goodness. Truth, goodness, and beauty are intrinsically equivalent. Beauty makes us *long for* higher things, which motivates us to *pursue* higher things, which leads to our ultimate fulfillment. We recognise beauty as a reflection of God because it transcends ordinary experience and explanation, pointing to something greater than ourselves.

Pope Benedict XVI often spoke of the *via pulchritudinis*—the "way of beauty"—as a profound path to encountering God. He emphasised its significance in modern times, stating that "the deepest meaning [of beauty] must be recovered by men and women today." For him, beauty—whether found in creation, art, or human expression—was not only an aesthetic experience but also a vital means of evangelisation, drawing hearts toward truth, goodness, and ultimately, the divine.

Writer Gregory Wolfe expounded on the power of beauty in his book *Beauty Will Save the World*, remarking on how many artists have seen that quote from Dostoyevsky's novel, *The Idiot*, as profoundly true despite what may seem a hyperbolic expression:

> The late Aleksandr Solzhenitsyn—as stern a moralist as the world is ever likely to witness—came to believe in the wisdom of Dostoyevsky's insight, as he argues in his acceptance address for the Nobel Prize in literature. So, too, another writer who experienced the ravages of totalitarianism in the twentieth century came to testify on behalf of beauty. Czeslaw Milosz, in his poem "One More Day," writes:
>
> *And though the good is weak, beauty is very strong.*
> *Nonbeing sprawls, everywhere it turns into ash whole expanses of being,*
> *It masquerades and shapes and colors that imitate existence*
> *And no one would know it, if they did not know that it was ugly.*
> *And when people ceased to believe that there is good and evil*
> *Only beauty will call to them and save them*
> *So that they still know how to say: this is true and that is false.*

Wolfe argues that civilisation cannot be saved by political rhetoric or religious moralising alone—essential as these may be to the human experience, they are not enough to secure its survival and flourishing. Beauty, however, is universally experienced as transcendent, making it a powerful gateway to the divine. Even those who reject organised religion often find themselves drawn to a mysterious sense of the sacred—a longing stirred not by doctrine, but by the undeniable pull of beauty itself.

As the Church, the People of God, we are not merely stewards of truth but also bearers of beauty. Through who we are, and all we do, we are entrusted with the mission to unveil the beauty that awakens souls to the Divine.

11.30 a.m.

We meet together to prepare our input for the last item on the agenda of the following morning's ICPE International Council and Community Coordinators' meeting. Today, our Coordinators come from a long list of nations around the globe: Malta, Sicily, Poland, Germany, Ghana, Philippines, Korea, India, Singapore, Malaysia, New Zealand, Australia, Colombia, Guatemala, and the United States. They coordinate missions of varying sizes, from as small as the presence of a couple running thriving ICPE ministries in their country and beyond, to a community that exceeds two thousand members across an entire continent.

The leadership structure of the ICPE Mission is designed to maintain regular communication and foster strong relationships within the global network. The International Council convenes online throughout the year with an annual in-person gathering lasting a week. Additionally, the Council meets with the Coordinators of the communities of the various communities through regular online sessions, complemented by in-person meetings every two years. To strengthen ties and offer pastoral care, Council members—or their representatives—conduct periodic visits to the communities across different countries. Then, to enhance connection and support, the Council and Coordinators are organised into smaller cells, which meet online regularly for prayer, mutual encouragement, and shared input.

It is a time of transition for the ICPE International Council as new members take up the torch, stepping beyond the thresholds and frontiers of the past forty years to embrace the opportunities and challenges of this new era. As such, we take great care in crafting a motivational message for the meeting we are to have tomorrow.

We want to say that—as lay people—the entire world is our mission field. The whole stage of daily life is our evangelistic arena. At present, there are approximately 1.39 billion Catholics around the globe—17% of the world's population. So, such a staggering number presents a set of equally staggering challenges:

What if that 17% of the world's population embraced their faith with intentionality and radical commitment?

What if their deepest aspiration was to become great saints—not simply through prayer and devotion, but by excelling as great parents, educators, healthcare professionals, athletes, entrepreneurs, lawyers, public servants, writers, artists, and environmental stewards?

What if through seeking to live holy lives, they could transform their societies in every aspect, bringing the light of Christ into every corner of the world?

In the Book of Acts, we find a profound example that offers a fresh perspective on navigating the overwhelming feelings of hopelessness that plague modern culture. Paul arrives in Athens and sees a city consumed by idolatry. His initial reaction is raw and honest: "His whole soul was revolted at the sight of a city given over to idolatry" (Acts 17:16). This visceral moment is often overlooked in favour of his later address before the council of the Areopagus, when he teaches those present about their "Unknown God."

However, this early response serves as a striking contrast to Paul's approach in his famous speech. Instead of remaining fixated on his initial revulsion, Paul discerned the positive signs and spiritual hunger beneath the Athenians' idolatry. He acknowledged their longing for truth and meaning and then engaged them with a tone of hope and connection rather than condemnation. They would not have built an altar to that which they did not know unless they were humble enough to know their knowledge was incomplete.

This example serves as a guiding principle for ICPE missionary disciples. Like Paul, they are encouraged to adopt this posture of discernment, to look beyond the surface of cultural challenges and to recognise the authentic desires hidden within. By identifying these signs of spiritual yearning, missionaries can engage constructively, fostering transformation and hope where others might see only despair. This approach transforms what may initially appear bleak into an opportunity for deeper connection and expectation.

That is the message with which we hope to motivate our gathering of leaders in the ICPE Mission, in this present time and place. But I venture it is a message for all Christian leaders, everywhere and in all times, as they face the day that brightens before them.

1:00 p.m.

We leave the office and walk back to our apartment for lunch. Afterwards, we maintain our little luxury of a cup of expresso, a habit born of living fifteen years in Italy. The news is on T.V., so we catch up on world affairs, then take time to talk with family and friends.

We're blessed by the small but cosy apartment we call home—with its terrace that looks upon fields, that is visited in the morning by sparrows, that glows with a palate of soft light reflected from the faces of old stone. It allows us a comfortable familiarity within which we can cultivate our fundamental humanity.

Yet homes are not meant to be simply shelters in which we carry on the basic, crudest needs of existence. A home is a sacred space where we express the essential simplicity and beauty of our faith. Throughout the philosophical tradition, order has been considered a fundamental feature of the beautiful, and this principle can transform our approach to homemaking.

To live beautifully is to embrace both what we are given and what we can create, channeling our creativity into our homes. It is about bringing beauty into the everyday—not through grand gestures, but in the quiet, intentional moments that shape our lives—the way we organise the living space where the family gathers together, the way we set the dinner table, or the way we create a play area or reading corner for our children.

In their book, *Theology of Home*, authors Gress, Mering, and Schreiber capture this vision: "Even menial tasks like laundry and dishes can take on an ease when understood in the context of a larger effort to create beauty in the everyday." They remind us that these seemingly tedious chores are not just parts of a banal routine; rather, they contribute to the larger project of homemaking, giving meaning and purpose to the ordinary. Homemaking is more than a task—it is an art, a reflection of our values, and an invitation to bring order, simplicity, and beauty into the centre of daily life.

There is hardly a heart that beats among those who are fortunate enough to have had a good home that does not relate its strongest emotions to memories that surround it. Indeed, at this time of year, Christmas, we are drawn closest to the hearth. Most would admit that their norms and standards of happiness were formed in their homes—that when they seek to create an environment of sanctuary in their lives, they reach back to get it from some storehouse of sights, sounds, and scents. Those things have an atavistic power, one even strong enough to make us "sick" with longing from time to time.

We are indeed "exiles" on this earth, looking for our way back to our true land. But we have a foreshadowing of it when graced with the experience of home. That, too, is part of our missionary task, to foster the comforts of refuge, belonging, and solace wherever we can in what is often a hard and alienating world.

2:30 p.m.

Back to the office. We prepare to record a short Christmas video message for the global community, to wish them the tidings of peace and joy. Advent, though the final liturgical season of the Church's calendar year, nevertheless celebrates the beginning of our salvation history. This gentlest of all seasons, though often overshadowed by hectic distractions, calls for attentive devotion to the wonder of the Incarnation.

Christmas newsletters are coming in from different communities, each reporting the highlights of the year. There is one from the ICPE Mission Philippines, with photos of the Reverse Carolling event that reached out to 120 families this year. The team was comprised of ICPE missionaries as well as members of the Balikatan ministry, which is a programme of the ICPE Mission Philippines. The newsletter tells of the joy they shared, the strength with which they were blessed, and the splendid weather that made possible a mission that is as rewarding to them as it is an eagerly anticipated tradition for those they visit.

While Christmas newsletters are a unique gift to us and the global community during the Advent season, we regularly receive short video clips and updates shared by the different communities and ministries throughout the year on our common chat group and social media. Technology has allowed us to provide witness to each other of how God is working through our different missions, and that in turn keeps us aware of all that we are doing as a whole. It's important that each feature and aspect of our mission knows about the larger design in which they play a role. The work of one is the work of each—one bread, one body, one call.

6:00 p.m.
When we've finished with the Christmas video, we return home to get ready for an afternoon tea at the ICPE Priests' Household in Rabat. There we'll catch up with our two transitional deacons to hear news of their involvement in the parishes and of their progress on dissertations written in pursuit of licentiate degrees in Pastoral Theology.

We leave Rabat to drive to the parish Church in Balluta for a Mass of Thanksgiving on the 40th wedding anniversary of a couple who are our long-time friends. Afterwards, there's a reception where we meet up with friends we haven't seen for many years. So we invite them over for dinner next week to reconnect and exchange updates.

They are no longer practicing Catholics. It is a fate I likely would have shared with them had it not been for that experience long ago—sitting on a rock in Marsaxlokk Harbour, yearning for God. He sought and found me (Matthew 18:12) through someone who approached with a simple request to mind a group of children during an Evangelisation Seminar. I could never have imagined then all that would come to follow—just as Mario could not have dreamed of what ducking into a building to stay warm on a blustery day in Scotland would come to mean.

It is common for some of our friends in Malta to ask what many Catholics today are asking: Why should anyone become or remain Catholic? Growing up, during Catechism class, we are taught to respond to the question "Why did God make you?" by: "God made us to know Him, to love Him, and to serve Him in this world, and to be happy with Him forever in the next."

This realisation of God's will in human life often happens gradually—as it did in Mario's and in my life—rather than instantaneously. Each person is on a unique spiritual journey; as such, each has a different pace of growth.

As missionaries, we are called to meet people where they are—to help them progress step by step toward a fuller relationship with God and the Church. This approach is not a compromise on truth or moral principles but instead underscores God's patience and mercy. It avoids harsh judgments of those who have not yet fully embraced or understood certain aspects of faith. As Ignatius of Antioch—Church Father, Bishop, and Martyr—asserted: "Christianity is not a matter of persuading people of particular ideas, but of inviting them to share in the greatness of Christ."

As that is the case, we must always be mindful that to God belong both the way for each person to find Him, and the time—however long it takes to do so.

10:00 p.m.

Home again.

We prepare a cup of hot herbal tea and check messages and emails that require prompt attention. Mario's final phone call for the day is with our American office to discuss some administrative work. Once we're satisfied that everything is sorted—at least for the time being—we can begin to shut down the house.

Lights off. Another full day.

Serving God and His people brings us joy, purpose, and fulfillment. Honestly, it can sometimes overwhelm, crush, and exhaust us too. But that is the reality of every call from God. He calls us to die to ourselves, to live for Him and for others. Love calls us out of our solitary lives and to make a gift of those lives to all we meet.

The call of the Christian life is not to retreat timidly from what might be challenging and even daunting circumstances. We can always choose the small, safe life. But only when we boldly face risks and darkness with confidence and purpose, only when we step out of the boat, do we experience the miracle of walking on water.

"*Do not be afraid*," Jesus told his followers. And so they left all behind and followed him.

But that was not a call just to them, in that time and place. He calls *us* too. Now. And we too can follow. And we will continue with every dawn and every dusk, by His grace and mercy, until the end. This was our prayer on July 30, 2023, during the International ICPE Community Conference in Kuala Lumpur, Malaysia. On that day, having been married for forty years, we consecrated our lives to the Lord through private promises witnessed by the community, renewing our commitment to serve the Church through and in the ICPE Mission for as many years as He grants us.

No, we do not always know where He will lead, so I often remind myself of Clement of Alexandria's words, "Faith is the union of certainty and hope, reason and mystery. We see as through a glass darkly, and yet we walk confidently."

Soon, Mario and I will leave the Mission in others' hands. I cannot know or see where the Lord will take it. But I know what we hope, and have faith, will come to pass.

Our greatest assets and blessings as an ICPE Mission have not been our properties or programmes. They have been our people—the missionary disciples themselves. Throughout these forty years we can testify our ICPE family has been blessed with great saints. They are people in love with God and with those on whom Jesus lavished His mercy: the modern-day tax collectors, Samaritans, lepers, and prostitutes—the poor and the marginalised, the possessed and the blind, the lame and the disabled, the uneducated and the unremarkable. We dream of the Mission persisting in its call to be a crucible of holiness, of friends of God, and Christlike men and women, in the ranks of the Church spoken of by Chesterton—one that will not "move with the world," but will "move the world."

We trust that the Mission will continue as a source of influence in the Church and the greater society. For as long as it has existed, the Mission has exerted influence not necessarily because of the size of our communities or the number of our programmes, but because of our relevance to the People of God. Influence stems not from quantity but from the quality of vision, the method of its execution, and an unwavering commitment to its success. Borrowing a term from historian and philosopher Arnold Toynbee, the ICPE Mission seems to have emerged as a "creative minority"—a subgroup in the Church that—because of its driving passion and vision exercises influence beyond its numbers.

We trust that the Mission will continue to be characterised by partnerships that leverage resources, expertise, and networks to fulfill its work and that of the Church, more effectively. This is where we believe God is working today—through relationships in which both parties share responsibilities, risks, and benefits; the two groups have a deep level of commitment and shared investment, decision-making, and accountability for the outcomes. Our history is rife with such partnerships, such as YWAM, The Jesus Film Project, CHARIS, the different projects in various dioceses worldwide and with different ecclesial movements, and those who have helped realise *HopeXchange,* namely, Yale University School of Medicine, Innsbruck Medical University, and Agostino Gemelli Medical University, among others.

We aspire to remain a prophetic people, called to live and speak in ways that challenge the *status quo* and reflect the values of the Kingdom of God. Being prophetic means interpreting the signs of the times through the guidance of the Holy Spirit. It means recognising and responding to the challenges and needs of the present moment. It is a courageous stand, and in many ways even an uncomfortable one. It often requires countercultural action. It demands choices that embody Kingdom values and the bold proclamation of the Gospel message of justice, love, and salvation that confronts sin, injustice, or societal norms. This is a path that requires unwavering faith, courage, and a willingness to join God's transformative work in the world.

Soon, we will step into a new year; in a short time, we will even face another decade.

And as we do, we pray that God pours out a fresh anointing upon us as the ICPE family, so that we may embrace whatever He is calling us to do, wherever He is asking us to go.

It is dark outside.

The doors I had opened in the morning—upon the cast of a sun rising on a landscape fresh with rain, sung to by a choir of birds at rest and in flight—are closed shut now upon a world going to sleep.

But on this Advent night, it feels like a sleep of the hopeful—the sleep of the free and redeemed. It is a sleep that awaits a new dawn, one to be followed by an eternity of dawns, and a light that will never again fall below a horizon.

The Incarnation is the astonishing mystery of the infinite God choosing the confines of the fragile human form. It is the breathtaking reality of divine majesty wrapped in humility, a love so profound that it enters the smallest, most vulnerable spaces of life. In the quiet of a manger, heaven's glory became earthly smallness—not as a display of power, but as an intimate gesture of love, drawing near to redeem and restore.

My mind wanders back to that child long ago, the infant brought to our missionaries in the jungles of Paitan. His parents bore him through a darkness that seemed impenetrable. He was wracked with pain and sores that seemed incurable.

And all we could give him was our faithfulness. We bathed his wounds, dressed them, prayed over them, and offered him up to his Saviour. The light we worked in seemed too weak for the scale of his need.

And yet, somehow, it was strong enough. It cast itself down with unseen power to cleanse and make him whole.

What a light, that it can—that it would—do such a thing.

What a grace it is to bear it, so that others may see and know.

That is our mission—will forever be our mission.

To bring the Good News of Zion—a light for the cities and the towns, a light for the jungle and the mountain tops.

To shout with the power of the prophet, even as the growing arc of His glory unfolds:

Fear Not. Behold. Here is your God.

index

Author Index